W9-ALK-301

Valuing Common Stock

Valuing Common Stock

The power of prudence

George Lasry

amacom
A Division of American Management Associations

Library of Congress Cataloging in Publication Data

Lasry, George.
Valuing common stock.

Includes bibliographical references and index.
1. Corporations—Valuation. I. Title.
HG4028.V3L35 332.6'3223 78-24023
ISBN 0-8144-5491-7

Published by AMACOM, a division of American Management Associations, New York.

First Printing

To Dr. F. Palmer Weber

Acknowledgments

I would like to take this opportunity to thank all those people who were helpful to me in writing this book.

Reed Rubin, of Tucker Anthony, R. L. Day, Inc., gave me a great deal of practical advice, especially in the formulation of the concept of capital value.

Dr. Pierre Sprey was particularly helpful in clarifying the mathematical concepts I have used. His detailed corrections of much of the manuscript give credence to the epigram that a man is the wiser for the friends he keeps.

Abraham Serfaty, economist with the Savings Bank Association of New York State, was very helpful in clarifying certain economic concepts.

James L. Van Alen was very helpful with general advice on the presentation of themes.

I would also like to thank Lewis Siegal of Thomson, McKennon Securities, Inc., and Richard Brignolli for his help in understanding certain aspects of the efficient market theory.

My father, Elias Lasry, who has always exemplified the reasonable businessman for me, gave me many valuable critical comments.

I owe a debt of gratitude to Professor Arie E. David, Temple University Law School, for his continual advice and support and clarification of many of the legal aspects of this book.

Dr. F. Palmer Weber, to whom I have dedicated the book, is a "renaissance man" from whom I, as well as many others, have been privileged to learn the business of our securities market. More than anyone else, he is responsible for instilling in me the respect for American liberty, for sound judgment, and for the love of business.

In closing, I would also like to thank Lillian Garambone for reading an all but illegible manuscript and Eric Valentine, of AMACOM, for continually expressing his confidence in this enterprise.

This book was written while I pursued my normal investment activities. I hope the reader will enjoy reading it as much as I enjoyed writing it.

George Lasry

Contents

1 Introduction

The purpose of this book is to give the shareholder, whether he is an individual investor or a fiduciary, a complete perspective of the valuation of industrial common stock. He will not only be able to understand how to determine when an equity is over- or underpriced, but—what is just as important—he will be able to arrive at a clear understanding of all the concepts and theories underlying his judgment.

Understanding how to price common stock is complicated, for it involves understanding what a share of stock is, what it represents, what its rights are, and even its duties. Valuing equities is not like valuing a piece of machinery, a building, or even a commodity. As difficult as it may be to value these, they are easy to define; at least it is not difficult to understand what they are and what they can be used for. However, valuing common stock presents the difficulty that even if we know how to define it, we may still not understand the consequences of our definition. It presents the same kind of difficulty normally associated with money. What is a dollar bill? What does it represent? Has its definition been subject to historical change? How are we to value it: in terms of purchasing power? Gold? Other currencies? Interest rates?

The first question raised in this book concerns the definition of a share of common stock. This is not as obvious as the popular guides to investing make it out to be. A share of common stock does not represent a share in the ownership of the assets of a business. It represents a claim on the income derived from these assets by the people entrusted with their management. Therefore, no attempt at valuation can ever be undertaken without first understanding the relation between common stock and the corporation.

All the books written on valuation within the past thirty years avoid this issue. They all assume a certain definition and understanding of common stock and then proceed to discuss how it can be valued. I have avoided the fallacy and facility of this approach. We must remember that the question of valuation is first and foremost a question concerning the valuation of property. If we do not understand the nature or substance of this property, we cannot possibly develop an adequate and relevant procedure for valuing it. Once we understand what kind of property common stock is, so much of the confusion and irrelevance about how to value it can be removed.

Valuation is a very subjective affair, not only because it depends so much on the personal requirements and expectations of the individual doing the valuing, but also because it involves a determination of value for the benefit of only one interest. In this book we are primarily concerned with understanding value from the perspective of the shareholder, whether an individual or a trust. All too often no difference is made between the value of shares for the shareholder, for the corporation itself, or for management.

It is my hope that once a shareholder understands all the complexities involved in the process of valuation, he will arrive at a new insight into what he has been doing for years, perhaps even successfully. This book is not written as a convenient guide for making a million quickly. Fortunes are made through care, diligence, discretion, and, ultimately, providence. However, the book will give the reader a thorough understanding of all the theory and the legal and economic principles underlying the process of valuation. Every attempt is made to confront each issue head on. Every legal and economic concept used is explained and interpreted.

Most books that try to tell the investor how to value stock present him with a series of formulas and procedures derived from the author's experience, implying that the author's successful experience can be gainfully transmitted. This is a dangerous implication, for experience can rarely, if ever, be transmitted. The very implementation of an investment policy is itself dependent upon the requirements and expectations born of experience. They must be applied with prudence, or practical wisdom, and will always have to be reexamined and interpreted by each individual. Rather than offer ready-made procedures based on experience, I hope to raise all the pertinent questions and issues without which an inquiry into the valuation of equities would be futile. The investor will therefore be able to arrive at a more thorough and practical use of his experience than he could arrive at by not questioning his assumptions.

Contrary to what some authors claim, there are no secrets to successful investing. Successful investing involves discipline in thought as well as practice. This book will give the reader a standard against which he can develop and measure his own discipline in both these areas.

Some Misconceptions

There are many popular misconceptions about the nature of valuing common stocks of which the reader should be fully aware. Here is a list of the more important ones, contrasted with the correct view.

Misconception 1: A share of common stock represents a share in the ownership of a business.

Correction: A share of common stock represents a claim against future earnings and a residual claim against retained earnings.

Misconception 2: Common stock is property that is essentially no different from other forms of property.

Correction: Common stock, unlike other forms of property, has no use value but only exchange value.

Misconception 3: How we measure and anticipate future earnings determines the success or failure of our judgment.

Correction: Future earnings projections are useless in forming a judgment of value. Earnings reports are useful *only* when they are analyzed in conjunction with the net assets used to produce them.

Misconception 4: The price-earnings ratio is useful in forming a judgment of value.

Correction: The principal ratio for making a useful judgment of value is the return-on-stockholders'-equity ratio.

Misconception 5: Book value is useless in a judgment of value.

Correction: Book value is indispensable in providing a prudent judgment of value, but only when it is used in conjunction with the return-on-equity ratio.

Misconception 6: Expected values are indispensable in forming judgments of equity values, by discounting the present value either of future dividends or of earnings.

Correction: Expected values are, by and large, useless in judging the value of common stock. Since the shareholder, unlike the bondholder, holds no contractual right to be paid from future earnings, he can never make a judgment of value by calculating the future.

Misconception 7: Common stock has no intrinsic value different from its market price.

Correction: The value of common stock is a function of its exchange value, not its market price. Market price merely provides us with an indication of what others are willing to pay for a limited amount of stock.

Misconception 8: A shareholder cannot form a fair, reasonable, and equitable judgment of value independently of its market price.

Correction: Fair, reasonable, and equitable judgment of value does not depend upon market price. It depends upon the relationship of stock's book value (*BV*) to its return-on-equity (*ROE*) ratio in consideration of the shareholder's opportunity cost (*OC*). I call this the expectancy value (*EV*); it is conveniently expressed by the formula $EV = BV(ROE/OC)$. This value provides a legitimate and reasonable basis on which a shareholder can estimate the benefits he will derive from owning common stock.

Misconception 9: A shareholder is like a rentier. His activity is passive. He can only wait and hope.

Correction: A shareholder, if he is to act prudently, must continuously interpret, monitor, and judge all information made available to him by management. The degree of his activity depends upon the extent to which he attempts to reach an understanding of this information. Without such an active effort at interpretation, disclosed information can be deceptive and misleading.

Misconception 10: Management and shareholders have identical interests and concepts of value.

Correction: There is an essential and intrinsic conflict between the value concepts of management and of shareholders. The prudent shareholder must accept this fact in interpreting information for the purpose of forming value judgments.

Misconception 11: Probability theory and statistics are useful in forming judgments about equity values.

Correction: Probability theory and statistics are useless in the formation of value judgments because shareholder expectations about the future are intrinsically uncalculable and because the past behavior of stock prices is largely irrelevant in the process of valuation.

Misconception 12: Stock prices reflect all knowable information instantaneously.

Correction: Stock prices reflect only the price paid for the quantity of shares traded. Thus prices reflect information as it is interpreted by the buyer on the one hand and the seller on the other.

Misconception 13: Disclosed information can be the object of rigorous statistical study.

Correction: Information is disclosed in a climate of real and not probabilistic uncertainty. It is meaningless outside the context of real communication between parties with different interests.

Misconception 14: Risk is exclusively a function of probability theory.

Correction: Risk is a consequence of real, not mathematical, uncertainty.

Misconception 15: Since the future is uncertain and since the stockholder has so little power over the future of his investment, judgments of value are of no consequence.

Correction: An investor is able to cope with future uncertainty by the prudence with which he formulates his expectations.

Misconception 16: It is impossible to consistently and rationally discover under- and overpriced equities.

Correction: The purpose of valuation is to be able to distinguish between over- and underpriced equities according to some rational and consistent scheme.

Misconception 17: Academic business economists, using advanced mathematics, have made important contributions to understanding the valuation of common stock these past thirty years.

Correction: Most of the mathematical theories on the valuation of common stock are irrelevant to practical equity valuation.

The Rationale for Valuation

The question must be raised as to why anybody should invest so much of his time not only in the demanding activity of trying to judge the value of individual equities for himself, but also in trying to understand the significance of the premises and attitudes underlying these judgments. The answer to this question is not only economic, for it may be that circumstances, wisdom, or providence will not bestow upon the individual investor a measure of profit so far in excess of his minimum expectations that he feels his time was well spent. The answer is above all moral; it depends upon how much an investor values his liberty to buy and sell, transact business, and negotiate with others a price he himself accepts as reasonable.

Without a concern for value and without the ability to make personal judgments that can serve as a basis for real transactions, there can be no liberty. This concern with liberty is inextricably related to the concern for life and for property. In some parts of this world, business is at best a tolerable form of human behavior; in the United States, it is a constitutional right that can be enjoyed and abused by anybody.

Therefore, I have undertaken to write this book from a certain sense of moral inquiet about the business of our securities market.

Common belief has it that the basic problems of the securities market are of a procedural nature. How should we proceed toward a national securities market? How should brokerage firms function? How much should the investor pay for services supplied to him? What new forms and procedural complications will government agencies impose upon business? There is no denying the importance of these problems. Yet, as I see it, the most crucial issues are not procedural but substantive, and substantive issues are always issues about values.

The 1950s and 1960s were terrible times for the securities markets, in spite of the enormous profits few were privileged to make, because they were almost entirely bereft of any legitimate concern for reasonable values. New issues were sold to the public irrespective of any concern with the reasonableness of the prices at which they were issued. Fiduciaries who should have known better invested the public's money in "growth stocks" and other conceptual machinations at prices that bore no relation to the values involved. Fortunes were spent and charged for research reports that analyzed everything but the value the investor received for the price he paid. Just to top things off nicely, a new investment theory was developed, subsidized to some extent by Wall Street, which extolled the virtues of choosing stocks by throwing darts at pages of *The Wall Street Journal* and denigrated the superfluous and "unscientific" preoccupation with valuation.

In good part, the procedural problems originating in the back offices of Wall Street firms may have been initiated by a great disrespect for the reasonableness and sound judgment without which no businessman or enterprise can persist. Fortunately, the last half of this decade presents a brighter perspective for the securities industry, whose expectations, having been drastically reduced, are now more reasonable. It is to take advantage of this new and auspicious climate that I have written this book.

I hope it will be understood that the concept of fair and equitable value is as important to the preservation of liberty as it is to good business. In our economic system the reasonableness of the pricing structure depends upon the degree to which informed and dissenting businessmen can negotiate. Although business can exist in a context of manipulative or oligopolistic pricing, it is doubtful how long the securities market can persist within this climate. What is at stake is not a luxury but the possibility of investing one's savings with confidence in fairly and equitably priced capital instruments. The effect of coercive, unreasonable, and unfair price is not as crucial for consumer goods as it is for those goods no person can do without—and certainly the Constitution and Congress, through the enactment of ERISA, have given adequate credence to the belief that savings are essential to survival.

As an economic and political person, an individual can express a choice in one of two ways: he can either buy or sell, or he can vote. The peculiarity of common stock is that it involves both of these alternatives. The enormous complexity underlying the valuation of common stock is largely due to the inextricable interrelation of these two aspects. If only a judgment about buying were involved, an investor's duties would not differ from those of a bondholder. If all one had to do to acquire was vote, all acquisitions would be political, and there would be no individual wealth. Common stock involves the curious combination of both, with the consequence that the price paid affects not only the magnitude of the right to vote, but also the extent to which common stock can be considered property.

Until now the right to vote, and its derivative appraisal and equitable rights, have been largely ignored by the individual and institutional investor. I suspect that the pension plan revolution initiated by Congress through ERISA will change this drastically, and that the essential activity of valuation will receive the attention it deserves.

2

Incorporation

In this chapter we shall be concerned with incorporation as a principle governing the valuation of financial capital, specifically common stock. To appreciate the importance of this principle, we will have to understand the extraordinary influence of the corporate form of business on our concept of capital. Today a corporation is formed with great ease and little money. Hardly any kind of business activity is conducted through any other legal vehicle, and it is almost impossible to raise capital for any other form of business. Indeed, we have come to expect that any business organization is a corporation; if it is not—say, if it is a partnership—we immediately ask what convenience or tax advantage this offers the businessman that the common corporation does not.

The History of the Corporation

Many people take the modern business corporation for granted as an institution that has existed, more or less in its present form, since men have been free to do business. But the modern business corporation is not a natural phenomenon; it is a relatively recent contrivance owing its origin to certain unique American legal innovations. Specifically, our judiciary developed the concept that people are free to associate for the purpose of business and, furthermore, that the result of this association, the corporation, is itself subject to the same laws of contract governing the right to liberty and property that all persons, under our Constitution, are entitled to. The modern business corporation, in other words, is a peculiarly American phenomenon. To ignore its uniqueness or to take it for granted is to ignore the notions of property, claims, and expectations that it encompasses.

On the other hand, incorporation as such is an ancient concept. Even the idea of limited liability to investors can be traced back at least 2,000 years to a noncorporate form of limited liability partnership used by the Hebrews. The specific institution of incorporation was an invention of Roman law; its purpose was the creation of a person endowed with immortality, or perpetual succession as it came to be called. No field of English law owes so much to the legacy of Rome as corporate law.

Originally a corporation was formed not for business but to ensure the perpetuity of power invested in nonbusiness activities. The university, for example, was established as an incorporation of its various colleges of learning. The church owed the practical perpetuity of its spiritual power to the incorporation of its various ecclesiastical bodies. Even the king owed the constitutional legality of the perpetuity of his power to the fact that he was indeed a corporation and, hence, "invisible" and "immortal." An important consequence of the power of kingship invested in his corporate, not human, person was his ability to grant the privilege of incorporation to those subjects in whom he chose to invest this power.

The power to delegate power became a prerogative of the crown, which authorized charters regulating new and acceptable forms of corporate activity. Similarly, government, through the power of its sovereignty, was uniquely authorized to grant the corporate right, limit the corporate activity, control the corporation's membership, and limit the right of dissolution. The corporation was indeed a form of government granted by government. This is evidenced by the fact that to this day, corporations are governed by voting, which is, in effect, a political rather than an economic right.

The earliest corporations were nonprofit organizations. It was only with the development of foreign trade in England that the crown granted the right to form joint-stock companies, a particular form of corporation, to certain businessmen who applied for the monopoly of conducting a particular form of trade. Probably the earliest business corporation dates to the end of the fourteenth century in England. The seventeenth century saw the emergence of the East India Company and Hudson's Bay Company in England and the Dutch East India Company in Holland.

There were very few similarities between these and the modern American business corporation. These companies were all monopolies not only empowered by government, but backed by the full force of the state. The number of shareholders was very limited, and authorization for the exchange or sale of shares was hard to come by.

Government authorization was needed to increase the number of shares outstanding in order to raise additional capital. In other words, the business activities of these companies were severely curtailed by the government granting their monopoly power.

It is interesting to note that the development of the options market on the shares of the Dutch East India Company in Amsterdam arose as a consequence of the need to provide an adequate vehicle for speculation. Since bearer shares were illegal and buyer and seller had to meet at appointed times at the company offices in order to transfer ownership, it became expeditious for those who only wanted to speculate to trade in options rather than the shares themselves.[1]

It would not be much of an oversimplification to say that in most of the Western world, incorporation is a convenient legal instrument for the exercise of power, whether political, ecclesiastical, educational, or economic. Yet it is precisely in the way this power is defined that the modern American business corporation differs most from its Old-World counterpart. In the United States the development of corporate law has emphasized the distinction between special privilege and business utility. Today a big business corporation is powerful, not because of the special privilege of monopoly power bestowed upon it by the federal government or the state legislatures, but because of its independent ability to perpetuate profits from its capital resources.

The main consequence of this is that there is a complete separation between the exercise of power by the corporation's management and the provision of the financial capital, or capital claims, allowing for this exercise of power. In the United States the government does not provide or control the capital resources (socialism), nor does it have the right to limit the management of a company to those people, or that class of people, upon whom it has bestowed its special privilege (oligarchy created by monarchy). As Adolf A. Berle, Jr., put it, the modern business corporation has given rise to the notion of "power without property" and, conversely, property without power.[2]

Much of this can probably be observed in the modern European corporation as well. Yet what makes this a particularly American phenomenon is the extent to which the notion of the modern business corporation is a consequence of the courts' interpretation of the Constitution and, in particular, of the Fourteenth Amendment. Let us see why Nicolas Murray Butler said that the limited-liability corporation is "the single greatest discovery of modern times . . . even steam and electricity are far less important . . . and they would be reduced to comparative impotence without it," and why Charles W. Eliot referred to it as the "most effective legal invention . . . made in the nineteenth century."[3]

The Corporation in the United States

In 1819 Judge Marshall wrote the majority opinion for the *Dartmouth College* v. *Woodward* case. Adhering to seventeenth- and eighteenth-century notions of British law, he described the corporation in now famous words as "an artificial being, invisible, intangible, and existing only in contemplation of the law. Being the mere creature of law, it possesses only those properties which the charter of its creation confers upon it, either expressly, or as incidental to its very existence. . . ."[4] The state of New Hampshire had tried to unilaterally alter the charter of incorporation of Dartmouth College in its desire to impair the college's right to contract and property. Judge Marshall effectively stated that even though New Hampshire had granted, by special privilege, the college's corporate charter, it could not violate its "immortal" and inviolate right to exist, own property, and honor contracts like any citizen. He set the stage for the right of the business corporation to persist as an entity independent of the state that had originally granted it the privilege of its corporate existence.

In 1868 Congress ratified the Fourteenth Amendment to the Constitution, which stated that "no state shall make or enforce any law which shall abridge the privileges or immunities of citizens of the United States; nor shall any state deprive any person of life, liberty or property, without due process of law; nor deny to any person within its jurisdiction the equal protection of the laws." Through two decisions rendered by the Supreme Court in 1886 and 1888, the proposition was accepted, furthermore, that the business corporation definitely was to be considered a person under the Fourteenth Amendment, pursuant to the Dartmouth College case.

In 1890, as James Willard Hurst has pointed out, "the court firmly established the principle that corporations might seek protection of 'liberty'—freedom to transact business—and of 'property'—assets—against unreasonable or discriminating state laws."[5] In the United States, the authority to grant the privilege of incorporation rests not with the federal government but with the states themselves. (Today Ralph Nader feels that this historical practice ought to be changed in the case of the large business corporation.) Until 1890 the states reveled in the exercise of their supreme power of monopoly privilege. It was as if they sought to reinstate the privilege of power from which the Founding Fathers sought so much to flee. It was only toward the end of the nineteenth century that the character of the modern business corporation began to evolve.

Until 1801 only 317 corporations had been formed in the United States.[6] Nowadays, I suppose as many as that file petitions for bankruptcy or dissolution weekly. Since the state legislators felt they were the New-World heirs to the Old World's legacy of sovereign right, they granted few corporate charters, and, more importantly, they thought that it was their sovereign duty to interpret the corporation's public purpose as they saw fit. Since they were empowered to grant monopoly rights, they also thought they were empowered to interpret the exact limitations of the corporation's use of property. The main victims of their interpretation of power over the corporate "person" were the railroads and public utilities. The expense and effort involved in persuading the state legislatures to grant monopoly privileges for the formation of railroads, for example, was often of the same magnitude as the actual capital expense of laying rails.

However, toward the end of the nineteenth century, as a consequence of the Supreme Court's interpretation of the Fourteenth Amendment, the power of the state legislatures to dispense the privilege of monopoly right was severly curtailed. If the states could no longer decide how a corporation should use its property, if they had to treat the corporation as a person with the same economic rights as all American citizens, they could no longer restrict its right to contract. Except in the case of regulated businesses, the states lost their right to control business by limiting the scope of the corporate charter. They had to abandon their historic privilege of defining the social responsibility, as they saw fit, of the business corporation. The concept of state sovereignty in regulating business affairs became subservient to the sovereignty of the law of the republic.

Led by New Jersey and Delaware, the states abandoned their monopoly as legal interpreters of the public good and allowed the corporate charter to degenerate into a mere formality serving the convenience of business and not government. The lawyers and entrepreneurs reaped the rewards of this convenience and newly found privilege. The states themselves became content to merely receive the income from the fees paid for the privilege of filing for incorporation. Virtually any entrepreneur who could pay the expenses for incorporating and was able to come up with a new corporate name was granted incorporation. Like some countries in the Caribbean today, the states vied with each other for the fees provided by this new source of income. Of course, the number of new corporations formed far exceeded what anybody could have anticipated. Since the states were forced to trade a measure of their sovereignty for money, they made the most of it.

This was a momentous and thoroughly unique occurrence whose consequences Europe could not anticipate. In James Willard Hurst's words:

> The new style of corporation statutes in effect judged that corporate status had no social relevance save as a device legitimized by its utility to promote business. The obverse of this judgement was that the regulation of business activity was no longer to be deemed a proper function of the law of corporate organization. The function of corporate law was to enable the businessman to act, not to police [his] action.[7]

A new American was born. Invisible. Immortal. Protected by the laws of contract to a life, liberty, and property of its own. An American owing its power not to any sovereign, nation, or state but to the businessmen who conceived it and made it a going and profitable concern.

As practiced in the United States, incorporation gave rise to a new attitude toward the exercise of economic power. No longer was the power to control property, own land, monopolize trade, and distribute income the privilege of government. It became the privilege of the businessman, the entrepreneur who could create power and dispense it as he saw fit. By means of the modern business corporation, the businessman was able to usurp a good measure of the historic right of government to control the use of property for the public welfare. We are all familiar with the abuses of this newly created source of power and with the consequent actions of the federal government through the Sherman Antitrust Act, the Securities and Exchange Act, the Federal Trade Commission, and so on. Today most businessmen, especially the managers of our large corporations, are fully aware of the social consequences of their exercise of power. Some of them refer to their awareness as "enlightened self-interest."

The emergence of the modern American business corporation introduced a new concept of property. Since the control of economic power now became the right of business and not of government, government abandoned its Old-World right to allocate economic power in exchange for the constitutional right of limiting its abuses. Except in certain instances, government no longer granted the largesse of a right to economic power to a select group of people.[8] Businessmen not only could accumulate whatever assets they chose and incorporate, they also could distribute the shares in these corporations to whoever had the money to pay. The right to receive nominal or bearer shares depended upon the will of the stockholder, not government. The federal government did everything in its power to foster the development of a free securities market that would permit the orderly and intelligent trading of shares. Consequently, business became empowered to define the meaning and value of property.

The creation and exercise of economic power became the monopoly of business in two respects. First, businessmen were able to sell the public a kind of property that was devoid of any of the power, control, and utility normally associated with the ownership of property. This is the notion of property called capital stock, defined as a claim on the corporate income and divisible into shares. Second, businessmen were able to retain control and power over another kind of property, the corporation itself, by controlling the managers responsible for the production of the corporate income.

The New Sovereigns

Entrepreneurs and investment bankers took full advantage of this new and native American. Perhaps the greatest of these was J. Pierpont Morgan. He realized the potential for raising capital provided by the emergent business corporation and proceeded to create a monopoly, the United States Steel Corporation. He understood that capital funds could be raised only from the American middle class in a climate of confidence, and confidence to him meant monopoly. He persuaded Andrew Carnegie to sell his dominant steel company, which had a replacement cost of $75 million, for $300 million in the gold bonds of the newly formed steel corporation.

Carnegie's company gave him the edge he needed to purchase an additional $600 million of steel-producing assets. He then went to the public and raised $1.4 billion in common and preferred shares on the basis of the expected profits this new monopoly would provide its investors.[9] About $676 million of capital assets was involved, but the public paid double this amount for the privilege generated by this new monopoly that J. P. Morgan, not a monarch or a government, had created. The trend was set. Incorporation, with all its attendant privilege, power, and social impact, became the domain of the new sovereigns of Wall Street.

The success of the modern corporation was sparked by two important advantages it offered over other forms of business. First, it afforded management legal protection in the maintenance of its control and authority over the dispostion of corporate assets. Second, it provided a new and relatively easy way to raise capital (in amounts, one might add, in excess of the company's capital assets). Yet the enthusiasm for this new American corporate device was not unanimous. Andrew Carnegie, for one, did not much care for the public corporation because he thought the information he would have to supply his shareholders could limit his exercise of control. At the other end of the spectrum, Bayless Manning and others, realizing the possibility of abuse created by a lack of effective government control over management, have been critical of the public corporation's lack of significant social responsibility.[10] Nevertheless, whatever criticisms may be leveled against corporate irresponsibility, the corporation's unique utility for business remains the basis of the American industrial economy.

The Shareholder and the Modern Corporation

It would be difficult to arrive at a sound basis for estimating the value of a share of common stock without an understanding of the significance that incorporation has had in shaping the exercise of economic power and in defining the concepts of property and capital. Specifically, it would be imprudent to acquire property without knowing the extent to which we also acquire the right to use it.

Popular wisdom has it that ownership of a share of common stock is ownership in a share of the equity of a going business. However popular this assumption may be, it is an unwise one, for it implies that an owner of common stock has a partner's share in the decisions affecting the management of the firm and the disposition of its assets. We are all familiar with the angry shareholder who questions the propriety of management's purchase of a Lear jet with "his" money, or of the university trust fund that has decided that its equity ownership in a corporation bestows upon it the "ethical" right to voice a partner's opinion about the extent to which the policies of the corporation are in the public interest.

In fact, a share of common stock is simply a share in the title to a claim on the income of the corporation. This title encompasses a claim on the residual income, the retained earnings and original capital, and the expected income produced by the net assets of the corporation. Only the corporation itself holds title to all its assets and liabilities. A shareholder only owns a claim on income and not a share in the corporate title to its net property. A thirsty shareholder of a brewery cannot walk into "his" company and demand that a case of beer be charged to his equity account.

Defining the shareholder's claim is not an easy matter. If the corporation were in dissolution, then, after the priority claimants had been paid off, he would be entitled to receive his residual share of the remaining assets. If the corporation continues to function, it is more difficult to understand what a claim on income means. It is not a claim subject to a specific contract, such as a bondholder or even a preferred stockholder might have. It is not a claim that is defined by any contractual definition of performance. The shareholder cannot sue management if it doesn't measure up to his expectations or if it produces losses—as long as he has not been willfully or negligently cheated. Sometimes it would be more reasonable to conceive of a stockholder's claim as a privilege, or perhaps a right to expect largesse on the part of management.

Voting

However ephemeral the shareholder's claim appears to be, it does leave him with certain rights. He has, first of all, the right to vote for a board of directors who are supposed to represent him. His vote is also necessary in all matters required by corporate charter, such as amending the charter or dissolving the corporation. Finally, he has the right to vote in all matters requiring majority shareholder approval. The New York Stock Exchange thinks so much of the right to vote that it will not permit the listing of any nonvoting shares.

The distinction between the theory and practice of this right is a source of confusion. In theory shareholders are entitled to choose and vote for a board of directors who represent them, not management. In practice management selects the directors whom it hopes shareholders will approve. In theory only shareholders have a beneficial interest in deciding at what price a merger or sale of the corporation can be effected. In practice management may use the corporation's resources to fight a takeover at the proposed price even though it has no beneficial interest in the corporation (the shares it owns or has options on give it the same voting rights as other shareholders).

In theory shareholders acquire a capital instrument giving them an owner's right to be represented to the extent of their property interest. In practice shareholders only acquire a right to vote on the basis of a political concept of representation (the notion of one vote for one share of stock being counted toward a simple numerical or constitutional majority is political). Furthermore, whereas in politics the constituent may cast his vote for the losing party and still be assured of minority representation, this is not true for the shareholder. As Abram Chayes put it, the shareholder is not "the governed of the corporation whose consent must be sought."[11] Only management, which is entitled to decide how the corporate assets are to be used, is the governed.

A person who owns a share of a partnership is in quite a different position. When he is asked to cast his vote, he does so among equals. Whether he has voted for or against the majority, he always retains the power to protect his equity interest. As long as he remains a partner, he does not lose this right. If a shareholder disagrees with the majority, the most he can do is sell. Furthermore, what is the meaning of this voting right when control is vested in a controlling block of shares? (In this connection, it is interesting to note that the Belgian government, in a not entirely successful attempt to right the economic deficiencies of shareholder voting, prevents a controlling block, no matter how large, to account for more than 20 percent of the vote.)

In the days when a limited number of stockholders met to vote, they were essentially extending their mandate to a management that they themselves had chosen and could rely upon to fulfill what the vote defined as the common good. Today a similar situation exists with the privately held corporation, where a minority stockholder has access to direct confrontation, persuasion, and negotiation of his interests with management. By contrast, the function of a public shareholder's right to vote is so difficult to define that Adolf A. Berle, among others, views it as a legacy that continues because "no one has come up with a better scheme."[12]

The right to vote can be and has been misused. In 1956 Robert Young, through control of about 5 percent of the shares of the New York Central Railroad, was able to convince other shareholders to approve his takeover on the basis that his new management would lead to increased profitability. Ten years later, the railroad was bankrupt due to what was euphemistically termed "mismanagement." In 1976, the management of Marquette Industries approved a takeover of its stock by the Gulf + Western Corporation at a price equal to one-half its book value. After the takeover was effected, the salaries and benefits of some of Marquette's managers who did not own any stock were substantially increased, as stated in the proxy material.

Can one really believe that a stockholder's right to vote against these takeovers would have benefited him, in spite of controlling blocks of stock? Some, like Bayless Manning, contend that even the right to vote, when the shares have been "improperly acquired solely for the purpose of corporate raiding, ought to be suspended by management,"[13] and such powers to restrict the right to vote are actually included in most trust agreements of publicly traded trusts. Ultimately, though, a stockholder's right to judge management's exercise of power is best expressed by his decision to buy or sell.

Although voting doesn't contribute much to a stockholder's real property rights, especially if he owns only a few shares or owns them in trust, it is remarkable how little these rights have been abused by management. Most directors, though nominated by management, act as if they are genuinely motivated by their responsibility to the stockholders. A peculiarity of the American system of political voting within corporations is that, although it is far from perfect, it has also been far from producing the worst kind of abuse. This is probably due not only to the "enlightened self-interest" of those wielding economic power but also the the requirement of disclosure and dissemination of information without which any voting right would be entirely meaningless.[14]

Information

In the American system, a stockholder's claim confers upon him the right to receive all information that could in any way materially affect the value of his equity. He has a right to know everything about how management is using the corporate assets to produce an income from them. He has the right to receive all financial information, all information concerning the ownership of controlling or insider blocks of stock, all information describing who the corporation's managers and directors are, and all information about extraordinary intentions of management should these result in actions affecting either the corporate assets or the income produced from these assets. The disclosure and dissemination of information by management is considered so important that the main function of the Securities and Exchange Commission is to continuously monitor it.

However, most of this information is available not only to shareholders but to the public at large. One doesn't have to be a shareholder to have access to all publicly disclosed information; one only has to have the will and time to seek and interpret it. Furthermore, some of the information that is theoretically a privilege of shareholders is in practice rarely made available. For example, although only shareholders have the right to inspect the corporate register of shareholder names at annual meetings, this right is hardly ever exercised. Management is reluctant to allow shareholder inspection of its register, not only because of the information this places at the disposal of corporate raiders, but because these lists have been used by brokers in soliciting the sale of blocks of stock.

There is one instance, however, in which a shareholder's access to information actually places him in a privileged position. This is the derivative suit—a legal device intended to protect shareholders against fraud and other misdeeds of management and directors.[15] It enables a shareholder to file suit not as an individual seeking personal recovery of damages but as a shareholder seeking recovery on behalf of all other shareholders. Thus his rights are derivative to the extent that they arise out of the collective shareholder interest and not his personal interest. The possibility for a derivative suit arises when a shareholder claims that he, along with all other shareholders, was denied access to information that could have led him to sell his shares, or that he was given misleading or fraudulent information that resulted in a loss of share value.

The derivative suit is a dismal and not very efficient shareholder right. It is expensive. Only lawyers seem to benefit from it. All money recovered must be paid to the corporation (and therefore will come under the control of management) prior to distribution to the stockholders. Furthermore, management generally uses corporate funds in defending itself against its stockholders.

Nonetheless, the shareholder's right to information is extremely important, for information provides the sole basis for judging the worth of a shareholder's property. Obviously, there are many people who buy and sell common stock solely on the basis of their own analysis of the day's market, presumably because they believe that interpreting management disclosures, while theoretically necessary for an efficient market, is a practical waste of time and an abuse of intelligence. The fact is, however, that no sound value judgment can be made without an attempt to assess the significance of the information disclosed by management.

Valuing Equities: Exchange Value versus Utility Value

There are, of course, limitations on the extent to which value judgments can be made. The most important of these is that a judgment about the value of common stock must be concerned only with its exchange value and not its utility value.

A share of common stock has no utility value. It cannot be consumed. It has no caloric value. The only pleasure or satisfaction it may give derives from a hefty increase in market price. In short, common stock is property without utility.

Even though wealth may be used to describe the degree to which a person can afford to enjoy the "necessaries, conveniences, and amusements of human life," as Adam Smith put it, a person's capital stock can be responsible for his well-being only when it is spent. It is, like any other capital instrument, a measure of his savings and not of the degree to which he spends, consumes, and, hopefully, enjoys. Of course, gambling may provide a good measure of enjoyment, but its utility is not above suspicion.

The notion that common stock is intangible property without

utility is not self-evident. In the following chapter we shall trace the development of this idea in an attempt to show how the value of common stock is dependent upon a judgment not of its utility but of its exchange value.

There was a time, especially during the days of the seventeenth-century trading companies, when the ownership of common stock was judged to be of value primarily because of its utility. For example, those businessmen who could afford it bought shares in the Dutch East India Company, not because they were primarily interested in reaping capital gains from the sale of stock, but because they were interested in receiving dividends. Dividends, in those days, were largely paid out in kind—in the spices, silks, and sundries that each merchant ship brought back to Holland. Virtually all the net income was paid out in goods useful to the Dutch shareholders in the course of their business.

Under these circumstances it is obvious that information disclosed by the management of the Dutch East India Company was of very limited value to shareholders. What the shareholders were primarily concerned with was whether or not a ship was able to make its return journey to Holland safely. Disclosure of the finances, capital investments, and possibilities for growth were not especially significant, because they did not contribute to the utility of the dividends received by the shareholders.[16]

Today, then, any judgment about the value of common stock has to be limited to describing its exchange value and not its utility. Exchange value is not, as Adam Smith conceived it, the "value in exchange" of one commodity for another—that is, the ratio of exchange between goods that have utility. Exchange value is not even market value. It is, rather, a description of that quality of capital that provides for the very possibility of a market. Exchange value is an expression of the judgment applied to common stock which, although property without utility, represents ownership in a claim on income. It is a judgment about the relationship between the capital, the realized past income, and the expected earning power of the corporation. In short, it is a judgment about *intrinsic value.*

Although it is difficult, if not impossible, to define precisely the extent of the claim to which a shareholder holds title, there can be no doubt he owns a share of a capital instrument and not just a happy "convenience" that he can buy and sell irrespective of his independent judgment of its value. Although capital is property without power, utility, or responsibility for its management or direction, it is property invested with the expectation, however tenuous, that one will receive more for it than what one paid. This expectation is the consequence of a claim on income. It means that one expects one's property to be worth more because it produces income that is either paid out as dividends or retained by the corporation. As a shareholder one may not be able to dictate to management how much income is either retained or paid out, but one is entitled to expect that there will be income and that this income will either directly or indirectly benefit one's own property interest.

What allows common stock to be a legitimate form of property is the possibility each shareholder has of making a judgment about its value. What makes this judgment possible is the disclosure of information by management of the income the corporation has earned and is expected to earn. This judgment, however much it differs between shareholders, is a description of exchange value.

Perhaps it would be helpful to include the following description of exchange value given by John R. Commons in his classic, though now generally neglected, book *Legal Foundations of Capitalism.*

> The concerns "owns" its going business in the sense that it owns the liberty to continue in business through access to markets, and it "owns" its gross income in the sense that its board of directors has power to acquire, use, and dispose of that gross income. But when once the gross income is distributed according to priorities, the residual net income as determined by the board of directors becomes not an asset of the concern, but a liability of the concern owing to its stockholders.
>
> Hence the going concern owns two types of assets, its physical, incorporeal, and intangible assets which are the parts of the whole, and its going business which is nothing else than all the expected transactions by which the parts are bought, sold, and distributed to the several participants . . . and it is this gross expected income of the concern as a whole that constitutes its "underlying life," "immeasurably more effective" than all its physical assets . . . [its] assets are, in substance, the present value of the expected purchasing power of things now owned or used. Consequently, the ownership of exchange value is more than the ownership of a mere ratio of exchange—it is the ownership of expected purchasing power. . . . The meaning of property, in the business sense of assets, is a shift from things to the expected purchasing power of things by way of expected transactions on the commodity and exchange markets.[17]

The Principle of Prudence

The principle of incorporation describes the formal context in which judgments about the value of a share of common stock must be made. We have seen that such judgments must be based on an analysis of exchange value. There is, however, another aspect of valuation that is a consequence, though not a necessary one, of what it means to own common stock. This is the principle of prudence.

I have pointed out that a shareholder holds title to a claim whose validity is not a direct consequence of what we would normally assume to be a property holder's right to control or have power over what he owns. A shareholder doesn't even have the right to specify or define the income that is the object of his claim. What income is, how much will be paid in dividends, how much will be retained by the corporation—all these are decisions made by management, even though it may be effectively monitored by directors acting on behalf of shareholders. In spite of this, what he owns is still his property. He can sell it or add to it. He can expect it to increase in value. In short, he can always judge how much it is or should be worth to him.

This ability to judge (rather than control or produce) is a passive activity when viewed from the perspective of the productive forces in the economy. One could say that an investor doesn't contribute anything other than his capital or savings. Yet from the investor's point of view, the anticipation of a return on his common-stock holdings in excess of what he could expect from bonds or a savings account is justified, not by inactivity or judgments without consequence, but by his willingness to take risks and make judgments that will have real consequences.

Prudence, in our context, may be viewed as a principle that guides or limits our judgments in situations where we are powerless to control our destiny. It is an attitude, then, that goes along with active judging, not gambling or, what is worse, a belief that any attempt to form value judgments is futile. When an investor buys shares of common stock, he becomes the owner of property, albeit a special kind of property. He becomes the owner of a special kind of financial claim about whose value he has the right to entertain certain expectations. These expectations must be based on a desire to interpret whatever information management discloses concerning the company's financial prospects that may affect the production of current income or the disposition of retained income.

Whatever significance one attributes to the behavior of the market price of the company's shares, the principle of prudence demands that the shareholder make an independent appraisal of the intrinsic value of his property. In other words, a shareholder is acting prudently only to the extent that he makes a conscious and continuous effort to determine what his property is worth to him. Neither the marketplace nor management can make this appraisal for him. Management has the obligation to disclose all pertinent information, but it has no control over how this information is interpreted. This is a limit to its power, and the basis for the shareholder's power of ownership.

What I am saying is that the shareholder's right to make an independent value judgment is as much a power as management's right to exert a certain influence on how this judgment is arrived at. Just as management may use the technique of induced optimism, so can the shareholder use the technique of prudence. Ultimately neither source of power is totally impervious to the checks and balances of the other.

The concept of prudence will be discussed in greater detail in a later chapter. To summarize what is said there, prudence is a discipline guiding value judgments rather than a result of valuation. It must be based on what I call an *expectancy,* which in turn must be derived from an analysis of the stockholder's equity (that is, the book value of his stockholdings), an estimate of a reasonable rate of return on this equity, and a determination of the minimum opportunity cost applicable to his investments.

In establishing a reasonable expectancy value, furthermore, market price is far less important than a careful analysis of all information disclosed by management. Finally, the principle of prudence suggests the importance of recognizing—and, if necessary, using—one's rights as a shareholder. The full power of prudence becomes evident only when all these factors are taken together.

It may be too much to imply that prudence is a power, just as it may be too much to say it of any activity involved with interpreting relevant information for the purpose of making a decision. We normally associate power with the use of coercion and the benefits of honor. Yet in America power is only to a limited extent based on privilege or government largesse; it is to a great extent the consequence of liberty, specifically, of the right to transact business without undue interference. Nobody can be forced to buy or sell or, worse, restrained from selling a share of capital stock, except under the gravest economic circumstances.

The American economic system allows people to form expectations on the value of their property and to act on these expectations. Prudence, therefore, is a consequence of the right to own property in the form of capital.

3

Exchange Value

In the preceding chapter we began our inquiry into the valuation of common stock by examining some of the implications of owning it. There we were primarily interested in understanding the object of valuation—namely, the modern corporation—in order to arrive at a relevant procedure for valuing. In this chapter we will concentrate on the issue of valuation itself; in particular, we will be concerned with the notion of *exchange value* and its significance for a rational valuation process.

In discussing valuation, one might draw a distinction between *proof of value* and *evidence of value,* as lawyers are wont to put it. Evidence of value is usually taken to be the market price of a share of stock at a specific time, but proof of value is quite a different matter. The old adage "the worth of a thing is the price it will bring" is a helpful idea here, as long as it is not taken too seriously. Obviously, a round lot of common stock has some value even before it is sold. Even if one were to say that it is worth only what it could be sold for, this is one thing when it actually has been sold and another when it is only marked for sale.

The Fallacy of Market Price

Evidence that IBM is worth $160 at one time and $400 at another is not necessarily proof that it is worth one or the other at any one time. Market price is an evidence of value, but there is no proof that it is the only basis for valuing stocks. There are many reasons for this.

First of all, value is a subjective concept. It describes a benefit to a particular owner at a particular time under specific circumstances. The value of a controlling block of stock, for example, may be greater or smaller than the value of a simple round lot to a minority shareholder, and value under depressed economic conditions will generally be lower than under conditions of unbridled confidence and stability.

Second, the view that the market price of a unit of shares bought and sold ought to describe the value of those shares still held in the portfolio involves an assumption that may need justification. While this assumption may be more readily accepted for IBM or AT&T, it is much more apparently inapplicable to corporations with smaller market capitalization.

Third, an owner of common stock may use a variety of procedures for determining what an equity is worth to him. He may value shares in terms of the present value of anticipated future income in the form of dividends or retained earnings. He may understand value only as the expectation of an increase in market price. If he planned to make a tender offer for all the shares of a company, he might understand value in terms of the original cost or the replacement cost of the firm's assets. If he suspects fraud or deceit on the part of management, he may consider value not only in terms of the damages to him, but in terms of a general notion of reasonable value applicable to other minority shareholders. Finally, if the government can be considered an "owner" to the extent that it owns a claim against corporate income, it will value in one way for the purposes of taxation, another for the purposes of eminent domain, and still another for controlling the rates that a company may charge the public for its services or the prices it may set for its products.

Most of what has been written on valuing equities in the past twenty years by business economists is really concerned with analyzing the significance of the evidence of value to no one in particular. The value of the firm itself is often confused with the value of its shares owned by minority shareholders. Furthermore, as we will see in the next chapter, many of these writers consider it irrelevant to analyze the kind of claim or property right that is bought and sold.

Perhaps one of the most discouraging aspects of these studies has been their continual confusion of value with market price. Although the evidence they use may indeed support the hypothesis that there is no difference between what a share is worth and what price it is selling at, one would have expected these studies to demonstrate a less naive and more critical concern for the theory of valuation itself. They make no attempt to put into a proper perspective the admissability of the evidence they consider using. Perhaps this reluctance to discuss the concept of value independently of how it is applied is the "dismal" legacy of economic science.

Forty years ago James C. Bonbright, in a work that is now usually left in library stacks, expressed his dismay about this trend: "This identification of value with market price, for which the classical economists are perhaps primarily responsible, does such violence to the spirit of the word that its abandonment might well be urged, were it not too late to hope for success in this direction."[1] However inappropriate this statement may be when applied to the classical economists, it seems to be entirely appropriate to those modern business economists who insist on confusing price with value. Market price may indeed be a most convenient indicator of value, but even if this is found to be a fact, we cannot deduce from it that market price is identical with value. This is why we have begun our inquiry into the valuation of common stock with an analysis of the nature of the kind of property created by corporate equities.

Furthermore, our statement that equities don't have utility is useful in understanding the substance of equity ownership. Beginning with Adam Smith, the classical economists have always distinguished between value and utility. But a share of common stock is quite different from a diamond, a commodity which, though valuable, was thought then to have scarcely any utility. A share of common stock represents a claim against income. It is in view of this capacity or expectation that we must discuss its value, and not in terms of the utility of what we may be able to purchase and consume with the money received from the sale of each share of common stock. This is why we introduced the term exchange value in the preceding chapter. Exchange value refers to the substance of ownership in its capacity as a claim against income. This is the basis for our efforts to understand value.

Exchange Value

The term *exchange value* is currently very much out of style. As James Bonbright put it: "One looks in vain through most of the early English economic treatises for use of the term 'market value.' Almost without exception, the older economists chose the alternative phrase 'value in exchange' or 'exchange value.'"[2]

Even if the classical economists did sometimes tend to confuse value with market price, they at least recognized that market value is not always identical to market price because market price reflects a unit price at a specific time and place. Thus when they wanted to express the value of all of a specific commodity in terms of the price of only those goods actually bought and sold, they used the term exchange value. Market price can reflect market value only in terms of the actual, not the possible, outlay of money. Exchange value was never thought to describe the actual conditions of a sale. It was a theoretical price that could be used to describe value by the marketplace.[3] Exchange value could not be used to describe value to a specific owner at a specific time and place; to do so would be to speak not about value but market price.

Exchange value also came to be used as a theoretical term describing a possible, not actual, transaction between a willing buyer and a willing seller. It is in this sense that the term *market value* is often used today when it is assumed that the market is composed of willing and, I might add, informed buyers and sellers. This may be true or it may not be. It is not an easy assumption to test. Certainly it involves using the market as a theoretical justification for a convenient imputation of value. To what extent are the short sellers of Pabst on November 19 at $28 willing buyers of Pabst at $34 on November 20? To what extent is a seller willing to sell his stock to cover his margin requirements in a prolonged bearish market?

To believe, as do many contemporary business economists, that since the market is efficient, because it consists of responsive, willing, and well-informed buyers and sellers, it is an adequate evidence of value, may be a convenient but not necessarily valid assumption. It is an impossible assumption to verify. As James Bonbright put it, years before the identification of market price and market value was so rigorously and mathematically postulated, "We are convinced that the willing-buyer, willing-seller incantation is a great bar to clear thinking in the law, and that it has no more place in legal opinions than it has in the literature of economic theory."[4]

Historically, the term exchange value was used as a theoretical construct describing not actual value but possible value. One spoke of the exchange value of marketable securities in the sense that one could relate value to market price. It was often used as a means of avoiding the confusion of completely identifying value with price. It served as a reminder that market value is not always and under all circumstances identical to market price.

In this book I use exchange value to describe the value of a share of common stock in its capacity as a claim on income, however this claim is defined by a shareholder. Some shareholders may define exchange value—mistakenly, as we shall see in the following chapter—as the present value of future income or, more specifically, of future dividends. Others may define exchange value as the marketable or replacement value of income already earned and retained by the corporation. A more appropriate approach, as will be shown in the following chapter, is to define exchange value for the minority shareholder as the relation of expected to retained earnings. This definition views exchange value as what may be called an *expectancy.*

My use of the term exchange value is heavily dependent on, though not identical with, John Commons's definition quoted in the preceding chapter. He defines exchange value as the capacity or expectation for producing or earning income. In the following chapter we shall further explore how he interpreted the significance of exchange value and how this concept should clarify our thinking about the nature of owning common stock. There we shall see how Commons traced the development from utility, or use value, to exchange value in the definition of property. He didn't limit exchange value to the corporation but extended it to any business endeavor. (Thus he could also speak of the exchange value of labor as supported by a labor contract.) However, here we will be concerned only with applying exchange value to the valuation of common stock.

John Commons was not unfaithful to the classical economists who spoke of exchange value as the value in exchange of one commodity for another. He wanted to emphasize that under modern American capitalism, property can be bought and sold—that is, exchanged—not only when it has the capacity of being used but also when it has the capacity of producing income. One may be able to deprive a business of using its assets in a particular way—for example, by imposing pollution controls—but one cannot deprive nonregulated business of its capacity to produce income.

In the last analysis the right to negotiate, buy and sell, and transact business is important only to the extent to which it produces income. When a business is sold, its value will depend not on the specific right or permit to use a specific property in a specific way but on the value one gives to the expectation of income produced from it. That is, the exchange value of a business depends not on a monopoly right but on its earning capacity. When a business is sold for money, it is as if it were exchanged for the right to purchase another business of comparable earnings capacity. It is in this sense that John Commons speaks of the exchange value of business.

We can go so far as to state that the exchanges or securities markets exist only because businesses have exchange values that serve as a basis for negotiating a market price for all or part of their shares. Thus the concept of exchange value bears directly on what John Commons calls *reasonable value.*

Exchange Value as Intrinsic Value

It could be argued that my use of exchange value adds confusion to an already confused vocabulary. After all, in the last analysis, isn't exchange value really the same as intrinsic value? To a certain extent it obviously is.

Graham, Dodd, and Cottle speak of the "attempts to value a stock independently of its current market price. . . . This independent value has a variety of names, the most familiar of which is 'intrinsic value.' It may also be called 'investment value,' 'reasonable value,' 'fair value' (in some legal proceedings), and 'appraised value.'" They go on to say:

> A general definition of intrinsic value would be "that value which is justified by the facts, e.g., assets, earnings, dividends, [and] definite prospects, including the factor of management." The primary objective in using the adjective "intrinsic" is to emphasize the distinction between value and current market price, but not to invest this "value" with an aura of permanence.[5]

I would, of course, agree that my use of exchange value is entirely in keeping with the above definition of intrinsic value, and in fact, both terms will at times be used interchangeably in this book. However, I have wished to imbue the term intrinsic value with the notion of exchangeability, as measured by the value one attaches to the claim on income. That is, I want to express the idea that not only is the value of a share of common stock independent of its market price but, furthermore, the securities market functions precisely because of the existence of an exchange value (or intrinsic value, if you will). In this respect, as we shall soon see in this chapter, the securities markets are conceptually quite different from the commodities markets.

If we were talking about corporate bonds rather than common stock, the meaning of the term exchange value would be more obvious. A bond with a 6 percent coupon maturing in ten years should have the same exchange value, which in this case will be its present value, as any other 6 percent bond with the same rating. The market price of bonds exhibiting the same characteristics may differ, but their exchange value is the same. Not only is the intrinsic value of these bonds the same, but they can also be exchanged for one another without any loss in value to their owners. Many bond traders actually rely on this disparity between market price and exchange value.

This also holds true for common stock, except that it is not so simple to calculate exchange value. Some business economists would like to calculate the intrinsic value of common stock on the basis of the present value of future dividends or even income. This is nonsense. As I will show in the following two chapters, the two essentials necessary for the calculation of exchange value are the return-on-equity ratio and the individual shareholder's opportunity cost.

Common stocks not only have intrinsic values, but their intrinsic values can be compared to each other. As long as one owns a minority position in the shares of a specific company, he will always have to compare the value of these shares as a claim against income with the value of the shares of other companies, whether or not in the same industry. The intrinsic or exchange value of IBM can and always should be compared with the shares of AT&T, and to a less obvious extent to Eastman Kodak and General Motors. Since a minority shareholder has forsaken any utility or use value of his property, he must always be concerned with the intrinsic value as a measure of its exchangeability with other stocks as well as with bonds and other short-term obligations. This is why I prefer the term exchange value to intrinsic value.

Furthermore, I should add that the term intrinsic value has fallen into disfavor with many business economists. For some, intrinsic value is "the value that asset 'ought' to have as judged by an investor. Discrepancies between current value and intrinsic value are often the basis of decisions to buy or sell the asset."[6] By "current value" I suppose we are to understand market price. By "ought to have" we are supposed to understand the possibility of different judgments made by different analysts, and also the possibility that these judgments have no measurable relation to the stocks involved. They are expected values that can, in fact, never be realized because equities just do not have intrinsic value.

This last statement—that equities have no intrinsic value—may seem surprising, to say the least. However, there is a tendency among modern business economists like James Lorie and Mary Hamilton, who produced the preceding definition, to deny the existence of intrinsic value simply because it can never be objectively proven or demonstrated. Put another way, they believe that the fluctuation of market price is as good an indication of intrinsic value as any other. Since judgments about future income, retained earnings, and the financial structure of a company are subject to error, they should be avoided.

Once again we are reminded of the saying that the value of a thing is the price it will bring. Evidently, business economists assume that only prices, not subjective values, can be scientifically studied.

Furthermore, they believe that insofar as the purpose of judgments about intrinsic value is prophecy, these judgments ought to be avoided, because statistical analysis proves security analysts to be false prophets.

The needs of prophecy aside, capital stock does have intrinsic or exchange value, because it involves the expectation, though not necessarily prophecy, of income produced by assets that exist, whether or not they are visible. The reason why the term exchange value is preferable over intrinsic value is that it emphasizes the idea that intrinsic values not only can but must be compared. That is, it emphasizes the element of choice that is the peculiar characteristic of any market society.

Exchange Value and the Close Corporation

A privately held company has an exchange value even if it has no market value. Furthermore, to the owners of the common stock (but not to management) it has *only* exchange value and no use value.

This last distinction is not always apparent, because most owners of the shares of a close corporation are also its management. Nevertheless, the owner who is not also engaged in running the business still has some rights. Even if his vote is insignificant and he is not entitled to benefit from the use of the corporate property, he still has a right to expect increased wealth rather than impoverishment from his property.

Nonmanaging owners of minority interests in close corporations have often felt that the value of their property was entirely dependent upon the largesse and generosity of the other controlling shareholders. Yet they, too, have a right to appraise the worth of their property, even if they don't intend to sell. They have a right to believe, and perhaps demand, that their claim on income is not entirely illusory. For example, they have a right to any information that would naturally affect the value of their shares. Also, there is a limit to which the corporate assets can be appropriated and wasted by management, and to which salaries can be increased and dividends withheld.[7]

In short, there is a limit to which minority shareholders in a close corporation can be oppressed, as it were, because even though there may be no market for their shares, they are still entitled to appraise the value of their property. This is an appraisal of their property's exchange value as opposed to its use value—although in speaking of a closed corporation, it may be more appropriate to use intrinsic rather than exchange value, because for shareholders of such companies the possibility of selling is not always very appealing or even probable.

Valuing Commodities, Real Estate, and Options

Commodities have a market price but no exchange value. Gold, wheat, cotton, and silver have no exchange value because they are not incorporated means of producing income.

Here it must be remembered that we are speaking of exchange value not in the classical sense of a value in exchange but as the value of expected income produced by a corporation. Commodities do have an intrinsic value if by this we mean use value, but they do not have an intrinsic value in the sense of an incorporated capacity to produce income. The market price of commodities is a function of their utility and availability or scarcity, as the classical economists would say.

To put it differently, commodities are capital goods, but they are decidedly not capital assets. They can be exchanged one for another in the sense that they can be bartered. Gulf + Western can decide that it will purchase sugar with silver. The Arabian Emirates can negotiate to sell oil for gold. In spite of these exchanges, commodities have no exchange value separate and independent from their market price, because there is no basis for measuring their exchange value other than their market value. Silver can be exchanged for sugar and gold for oil only because the sellers prefer the use of these commodities to money. These commodities may offer greater stability or a larger number of alternative uses than money (for example, they can be used for minting coin, as a reserve store of value, and, of course, for jewelry and industry). Commodities have no exchange value because they have a utility value. The market gives this utility value a price.

Recognizing that commodities have no exchange value, economists speak of their *marginal rate of substitution*—that is, the price at which one commodity could be exchanged or substituted for another by a consumer who might prefer to use one rather than another if the price of the second justified the substitution. For example, sugar made from corn may be preferred when the price of sugar made from cane and beets becomes too high.

Like commodities, land that produces no income has no exchange value. Its utility value can be measured only by the real estate market. The price one pays for a particular piece of land will depend on how much one desires it, how much the seller wants for it, and, frequently, whether an adequate mortgage can be obtained. As a result, comparing prices for similar parcels of land is of limited use in determining value.

To a certain extent it is possible to speak of the exchange value of income-producing real estate in arriving at some notion of market. The gross and net income, amortization, depreciation, taxes, and so on, of a 200-room motel in Cincinnati can be compared to a similar one in Atlanta. But the peculiarity of real estate is that different properties have their own singular characteristics, which may outweigh their similarities. This is the reason why a marketplace in real estate does not really exist. One just cannot sell apartment 11A and 12B in the same way one sells two round lots of a real estate investment trust. (The recent successful attempts to auction condominium units are examples of a marketing technique rather than of a viable, continuing real estate market.)

Prior to the creation of the Chicago Board Options Exchange, options on stock, puts, calls, and their various combinations had neither an exchange nor a market value. Prices had to be negotiated with dealers on the over-the-counter market. Even though the option writer was always able to write the options he desired against his position, he still had the problem of how to represent the current value of the options he had already sold. Indeed, it was because of this difficulty, together with the desire to provide an orderly and continuous market, that the CBOE came into being.

Today, listed options do have a real, though often erratic, market value, but they still do not have an exchange value. It could be said that a deep-in-the-money option with little or no premium has an exchange value based on the exchange value of the underlying stock. A call on IBM, expiring in January, at a striking price of $220, selling at $42 when the stock is at $260, has a premium of only $2. To the extent that the remaining $40 represents the differential price of a share of IBM that one has already paid for if one were to call the stock, there is some sense in analyzing the exchange value of IBM in any decision to buy or sell. This would be especially so if one also determined that the $2 premium was substantially less than the interest one would have to pay, less dividends, if one were to buy the stock. An out-of-the-money January call on IBM, at a striking price of $280 priced at $10, is quite a different matter. Here the price of the call is simply a reflection of the expectations of market risk and volatility.

Specialists in the art of pricing calls—such as Fisher Black and Myron Scholes or Richard Brignolli—do have a notion of the intrinsic value of a call based on risk, volatility, and cost of money.[8] However, since this notion has nothing at all to do with the expectancy of the underlying corporate earnings, it would be improper to equate it with exchange value. What their concept of intrinsic value essentially implies is that there is some price at which it may be cheaper to buy the call than the stock and that there is some price at which it is more sensible to buy rather than sell a call, or the converse.

The Go-Go Years

One of the main characteristics of the go-go growth years of the fifties and sixties was that many stocks had a euphoristic market price and little, if any, recognizable exchange value. There is perhaps little point now in playing the archeologist by excavating the remains of buried and forgotten expectations. It is difficult for me to write down the names of those corporations known to most by the apology of their prospectuses and the evangelism of their underwriters. There were often no earnings. Indeed, losses took the place of earnings. The bigger, the better; they meant greater expectations, which, of course, meant higher expected prices.

Venture capital, as some of these exercises in deceit were called, does have some justification, although I doubt that the public interest has really been served by the creation of a public market for it. Certainly the sale of stock to the public at prices that bore no relationship either to the amount of capital employed by the firm or to the earnings this capital could reasonably be expected to produce created a situation in which the only concept of value derived from the "greater fool" theory. It is a dismal recollection that some of the greater fools happened to be some of our financial institutions entrusted with public fiduciary responsibility. I suppose it would be more charitable to say that they were really adherents to the intrinsic-value theory to the extent that they believed their purchases "ought" to be worth more than they paid.

There is no doubt that our securities markets, through the principle of negotiation, have an enormous importance in providing us with a convenient and ready appraisal on which we can base the value of untransacted securities. There is no denying the convenience of being able to mark a portfolio to market, hypothecate shares on the basis of market value, and speak of market "averages" and indices of performance. To say, for example, that in 1968 corporate equities had a market value of about 1,000 billion dollars—an amount equal to one quarter of this country's total financial assets—is a statement of some significance. Nobody can deny the convenience of market price in providing a source for valuing equities in an appraisal or damage remedy. Yet it would be unwise to confuse the arithmetic and statistical convenience offered by the market with the complicated process of appraisal or, worse, to substitute the former for the latter. The market only provides us with one source for the evidence of value. That it is often the most convenient source should not make us believe that it is the only source.

Market Price and Coercion

The comfort and stability we derive from the belief that ours is a market economy in which we are free to transact business can easily be converted into a source of conflict and displeasure with the realization that the market for the goods we are dealing in is devoid of any notion of value other than price. Market price, when it is used as the principal judgment of value, can easily become an insidious instrument of coercion. Our ability to negotiate becomes severely impaired because our judgment about what we want cannot be influenced by what we think we ought to pay.

Coercion is introduced into a business transaction as soon as we are forced to pay the price somebody else establishes, without recourse to other alternatives. This can occur through bilateral negotiations or through the competition of the marketplace. Competition is supposed to provide the comfort of an equilibrium, because it is supposed to be conducted by many reasonable, well-informed buyers and sellers, none of whom has the power, or at least the right, to manipulate prices.

It is in this sense that the market has been used as an indicator of reasonable and fair value. However, this use of market price as an indication of a concept of equity is itself based on the notion that buyers and sellers have a concept of value independent of the market. Otherwise, what would be the sense of talking about "reasonable" and "well-informed" participants, if it were not to say that they have a sense of value that enables them to arrive at an informed judgment about fair price?

The significance of an economy based on a free market rests in the presumption that people who have a sense of value will be able to negotiate free from the restraints of government and manipulation. The significance is not in the view that the market itself is the initiator and sole judge of value. Prices are a behavioral phenomenon. Neither our legal system nor our economic institutions in their analysis of the causes and purposes of people's actions adhere to a purely behavioristic interpretation of society.[9]

Coercion in the commodities market

The use of prices as an instrument of coercion can be most readily understood in the consumer and commodities markets. The recent escalation in oil prices as a result of the embargo and in sugar prices as a result of manipulation are obvious cases in point. Although a free market does not exist in oil, it does in sugar. Both private and industrial consumers were forced to pay the price or not use sugar made from beet and cane.

Sugar as a commodity has a value because of its utility. It will be bought as long as consumers can afford to use it—that is, as long as they cannot or will not substitute some other sweetener. Apart from its utility, sugar, like other commodities, has little or no economic value. The market prices of commodities can become the instruments of coercion to the extent that specific commodities must be used by consumers or industry.

The development of the futures market was undertaken precisely as an attempt to limit the coercive forces the markets could have on consumers and, in turn, on producers. Specifically, the Commodity Futures Trading Commission was established with the goal of maintaining stable and orderly markets and keeping price fluctuations to a reasonable minimum. This commission is concerned with monitoring information such as forecasts about weather, crop yields, and economic trends. However, the purpose of such monitoring is not to predict the use and availability of commodities but only to prevent pertinent information from being withheld from the public so that a few privileged buyers or sellers may take advantage of the public at large.

Despite these regulatory efforts, there is a sense in which the buyer of commodities, if he is a user rather than a trader, is coerced by market price. Because of the peculiarities affecting the use or consumption of each individual commodity, not to buy may often mean not to do business or to transact business under adverse conditions. For example, while soybean meal may to some extent be substituted for animal and fish protein meal, aluminum will be substituted for copper (in the production of wire cable) only because the high price of one may force industry to use the other.

In short, there is no way of establishing the value of a commodity other than by reference to its market price, which presumably is a function of the relation between its scarcity and its utility. The concept of exchange value is inapplicable to commodities because their value can never really be expressed in terms of alternative commodities. This is why the commodities markets are beneficial only to successful traders and users intent on establishing a stable long-term cost for their commodities.

Exchange value as a force against coercion in the securities market

One of the important consequences of the notion of exchange value is the degree to which it limits the securities markets from being used as a means of coercion. In this respect, the securities markets differ markedly from the commodities markets.

This is a difficult idea to convey, because if we were to express it in practical legal language, it would appear that I believe that an appraisal remedy is an effective means of protecting minority shareholders against "squeeze-outs." But we all know that appraisal remedies, although becoming increasingly effective, have been of very limited benefit to the majority of affected shareholders.

To the extent that an appraisal remedy is based on the value one gives the corporate assets and earnings capacity, it is indeed concerned with exchange value as opposed to market price. However, the idea I'm trying to express is not restricted to appraisal remedies but is of a more general nature. It is simply this: since the capacity to value equities is not entirely dependent upon market price, the degree to which the market can coerce one into buying or selling is extremely limited. Valuing equities essentially means interpreting information about a firm's financial resources and prospects. Except in the case of a squeeze-out (where an owner may be "coerced" into selling because he decides that an appraisal remedy would benefit his lawyers more than himself), one never really has to buy or sell if the market doesn't present the possibility of a price one believes fair and reasonable.

This holds for stocks as well as for bonds. Like the stockholder, the owner of a bond—that is, somebody who owns an indentured claim against income—can never be coerced into either buying or selling. He always has the possibility of establishing the worth of his claim independently of the market. The peculiarity of financial capital is that it must have an exchange value. It is anonymous to the extent that it is exchangeable, at least in theory if not always in practice (one may not always want to establish a real loss in order to exchange one capital instrument for another).

Appraisal, then, which is inextricably tied to exchange value, is an important safeguard against coercion in the securities market. Whether we own stocks or bonds, we can always judge the value of our property independently of its market price. If it has risen in price, we may decide that it has not risen enough for us to sell it; if it has fallen in price, we may consider it more valuable to the extent that we can buy more at a cheaper price. To forgo the right of appraisal is to deprive ourselves of an essential means of protection against manipulation by the market.

Weighing Investment Alternatives

There are always alternatives to stock ownership. The very concept of stock ownership, since it precludes any measure of its utility value, must always be evaluated in consideration of alternative investments. It is true that stock ownership involves a particular claim on the earnings of a particular corporation. However, this fact—say, that it is Texas Instruments and not Motorola in which we own stock—is important only insofar as it permits us to form a judgment about how much each has earned on the capital employed, what the prospects for future earnings appear to us to be, and how much of a dividend each is paying its stockholders. Apart from these concerns with the quantity and quality of earnings, there is no advantage to ownership in one rather than the other.

Similarly, the decision to invest in one industry rather than another is fundamentally a decision made about the earnings potential. Thus we may decide to invest in Sears rather than in Giddings and Lewis because we believe that at present the prospects for the machine-tools industry look rather worse than the prospects for an increase in consumer spending. This decision is fundamentally different from the decision to buy one commodity rather than another. The decision to sell a particular stock because the reported earnings or the resignation of key management presented us with unexpected and undesired expectations is fundamentally a recognition that we have nothing at stake in our stock ownership other than our money and our expectations. The extent of our sorrow is measured only by our loss, all the more so because we could have invested our money elsewhere.

The art of security analysis is in choosing one investment over another. Whether the basis for the choice is correct or not, at least the possibility exists. No investment decision, and indeed no portfolio, is irreplaceable. There always exists an alternative. Even the traditional composition of portfolios according to industry groupings may be given up in favor of homogeneous cross-industrial groupings based on similarities other than industry function.[10]

The alternatives available to the shareholder are not confined strictly to common stock but include bonds and short-term paper. All capital instruments are subject to an interpretation of value by an analysis of their exchange value. It is foolish to try to value stock ownership without regard for the value of bond ownership. Apart from contractual limitations on how much of a portfolio may be invested in common stock, the decision to choose a specific stock must be weighed not only against other common stock investments but also against ownership of debt instruments.

For example, if we contemplate ownership of shares in GM, we must consider not only the alternative of other common-stock investments but also the option of investing in GM bonds or GM Acceptance Corporation (GMAC) paper. Furthermore, the decision to choose one over the other is never final but is constantly subject to an evaluation of the exchange value of these different alternatives. It is simply not sufficient to define risk as a measure of market volatility without regard for the priority and quality of the claim over corporate earnings. There are times when it may make more sense to accept the greater risk of investing in common stock at a price that would yield a historic rate of return of 15 percent rather than accepting the reduced risk and prior claim of buying the bonds of the same corporation whose yield is less than 10 percent. Although the market will present these alternatives to the investor, a sound decision can be made only after an examination of their exchange value.

"Security Exchanges as Appraisers and Liquidators"

In 1932 a work of great significance appeared, *The Modern Corporation and Private Property,* by Adolf Berle and Gardiner Means. Not only did this work become one of the pillars of the uniquely American brand of economic thinking known as institutional economics, but its third volume, entitled "Property in the Stock Markets: Security Exchanges as Appraisers and Liquidators," actually provided the foundation upon which the Securities and Exchange acts were formulated. The actual enactment of the various laws and their administration by the Securities and Exchange Commission have not invalidated either the significance or the scope of that book. It still merits our attention because the philosophy underlying the securities markets which it helped formulate is the one, where still applicable, guiding the Commission.

The subtitle "Security Exchanges as Appraisers and Liquidators" emphasizes the authors' view that the public market is a "meeting place" where corporate stock is rendered liquid by a public that is given "adequate" information for its transaction.[11] In a public and "open" market, appraisal of value—and hence liquidity—is made possible by information contributing to intelligent and informed judgments. Thus the "mechanisms of dissemination must be so well developed that any facts bearing on values can become common market property almost instantaneously."[12]

Berle and Means appear to accept the view that the marketplace can provide a fair and convincing measurement of value. It would appear that they do not think the distinction between exchange and market value of any practical benefit. Since liquidity is dependent on a marketplace for buyers and sellers who have access to information, market value really becomes a public expression of exchange value. Exchange value is dependent on an analysis of information, but when this information becomes a part of the public province, it is automatically or instantaneously reflected by the marketplace. In a word, exchange value becomes market value because the market is efficient.

The significance of these ideas becomes all the more pertinent when we realize that modern proponents of the efficient market theory essentially make the same claim. However, unlike modern theorists, Berle and Means were beset by "the difficulty of defining 'worth.'"[13] Their main objective in defining the function of the public market was to show that the disclosure and dissemination of information provided the possibility for the liquidity of private corporate stock through the activity of a public marketplace. By liquidity they meant the ability of shareholders to borrow against their holdings conveniently, quickly, and without personal guaranties. Thus a lender would not have to resort to an analysis of exchange value but could rely on an appraisal of value based entirely on market transactions.

Liquidity was a convenience based on the further convenience of market value. Thus Berle and Means were aware that the securities markets provided a "totally different function" of appraisal whereby "they serve as a yardstick by which security values are measured not only in respect of the floating supply but also in respect of tremendous immobile holdings throughout the country."[14] They realized, of course, that the market couldn't fully reflect the value of corporate stock, since only part of it was, or could be, transacted.

Furthermore, they realized that precipitate drops in the value of a common stock, while allowing a banker who has extended a loan on it to sell or demand more collateral, never really are a fair indication of the underlying value of the stock. Although the market provides the banks and brokerage houses with a convenient appraisal on which to judge the value of collateral, it cannot provide a complete and always fair appraisal of value.

When Berle and Means say that "the values accorded to securities on the force of market quotations are only 'paper' and perhaps ought not to be invested with any great amount of significance," they are simply repeating the idea that market price provides a convenient appraisal of value and no more. It may very well be that the shareholder has good reason to believe his shares are worth more, even though his broker may be forced to sell them as a consequence of his collateral agreement. Today, the very possibility of margin accounts rests on the convenience that market price affords the brokerage firms. Indeed, it is sometimes more advantageous to seek a loan against stock which does not conform to federal margin requirements, because then the lender has to look to the financial statements of the company in deciding how much more than the federal margin requirement of 50 percent he may be willing to lend the purchaser.

Sellers, Buyers, and the Concept of Liquidity

Berle and Means brilliantly analyzed the role of liquidity in a public market. Since liquidity implies a concept of value and since a dollar value is applied to securities at the "paying teller's window," they reason that this selling price is arrived at as a consequence of the buyer's appraisal of information concerning the company—information that is available to everybody simultaneously, at least in principle. When somebody, of his own free will, sells a block of stock, its price is a fair estimate of the stock's worth because the buyer was in possession of all pertinent information when he made his decision.

Berle and Means, then, write from the perspective of the security seller, not buyer. They are saying that in an efficient and orderly market, a person who has willingly sold part of his holdings has received a price that is a consequence of the appraisal made by the buyer. They are very quick to point out, however, that if the seller is forced to sell (say, in order to provide collateral for a loan), the appraisal may not be so just. Furthermore, they are aware that disorderly markets or ones beset by panic or euphoria are also not just appraisers of worth.

Liquidity is a convenience primarily for the seller, not for the buyer. Berle and Means clearly distinguish between the function of information for the buyer and for the seller. This can be seen in their chapters on "surplus value" and "flotation and banker's disclosure."[15]

In this latter chapter they question the extent to which the offering price of a new issue of stock can really be said to be a representation of value. They conclude that an investment banker has an obligation to offer new issues at a price that "may be held to be a direct representation that the security is worth the price asked, based on the market standards of the time."[16] This price can be considered fair in the sense that "if it does not advance, at least it will not decline."[17]

In effect, this may be interpreted as an admission that with respect to new issues, a buyer may pay too much, in spite of an underwriter's expertise. Much depends on the uses to which information is put, and those uses are not the same for a buyer as they are for a seller, especially when the seller is a controlling stockholder or underwriter. In a purchase, market price provides the basic opportunity, but only information provides the possibility of judging whether this opportunity is worthwhile. One doesn't buy because others buy, but one may decide to sell because there are buyers. The decision to buy always involves a judgment which, to some extent, is independent of a market appraisal. Otherwise the notion of an investment banker's expertise in new issues would be nonsensical. (The subject of new issues is dealt with in more detail in Chapter 6.)

The Principle of Self-Regulation

The Securities Act of 1933 and the subsequent seven laws which provide the legislation governing the securities markets as a whole have as their main purpose the control over the dissemination of information. This control is exercised, for the most part, not directly by Congress but by the Securities and Exchange Commission, which is a part of the judiciary. The function of the SEC is to supervise rather than judge; the power to judge is still in the hands of the courts.

The supervisory powers of the Commission are administered through the principle of *self-regulation*. In essence, what is meant by this principle is a cooperative effort between the legislative and judicial branches of government on the one hand and between the business community on the other. Indeed, "self-regulation is the foundation upon which the operating mechanism of the securities market rests."[18] However much the NYSE has been criticized for being a private club with the monopoly over the harassment of nonmembers and for the inefficiency of its members, it has to a remarkable extent fulfilled its regulatory functions of cooperation with government.

In retrospect it is easy to see why our government, concerned with maintaining the concept of freedom as the right to transact business, has chosen self-regulation as the principle guiding the greatest marketplace the world has ever known. Direct intervention sooner or later means the granting of monopoly rights and government control over the pricing mechanism. Although the granting of monopoly right by the federal incorporation of exchanges was considered, it was rejected because of the confusion and added burden that would be placed on the federal courts.[19]

Until now self-regulation as administered by the securities markets has been primarily concerned with the control over the dissemination of market information, specifically, with the effect such information has on security prices. Self-regulation has not been concerned with the control over the reasonableness of prices themselves. The reason for this was not only the desire to maintain free and continually open markets, but also the difficulty of defining fair and reasonable value.

For example, rather than enact principles by which new issues of common stock may be considered overpriced, the SEC and the securities exchanges have preferred to place the burden for this judgment on the underwriters themselves. Thus our government has refused to intervene as marketmaker (a practice that is not unknown outside the United States), preferring to let the public judge for itself and bear the consequences.

The prevailing attitude has always been that if the dissemination of information is thorough, speedy, and precise, people will be able to make up their own minds. Nobody will have an edge over other market participants because of privileged knowledge. Therefore, the SEC and the exchanges have been preoccupied more with the pricing mechanism of securities than with the fair and reasonable values of the stocks traded.

However, the SEC has long realized that stock prices not only are a leading indicator of the public's confidence in the national economy, but also tend to exaggerate perceived trends of despair and prosperity. Although nobody has yet been able to state with undisputed precision the degree of the relationship between stock prices and the national economy, the securities exchange acts do recognize this relationship in stating that "national emergencies, which produce widespread unemployment and the dislocation of trade . . . are precipitated, intensified, and prolonged by . . . sudden and unreasonable fluctuations of security prices and by excessive speculation."[20] The Commission is concerned not only with market breaks, where it has the power to suspend trading, but also with checking the speculation inherent in an unreasonable market advance. The main reason why it has not been able to fulfill its function in this latter area has been the lack of any clear guidelines as to what should be considered unreasonable speculation.[21] For example, it has rejected the price-earnings ratio as an inconclusive indicator of excessive speculation.

The NYSE not only shares these concerns of the SEC but has on several occasions used its power to suspend trading on all stocks. It has, furthermore, quite often suspended trading on individual stocks when it has determined that information already made public or about to be made public would have an unorderly and unstabilizing effect on the stock's price.

Subsequent to Berle and Means' presentation of liquidity as a function of the market, both the Commission and the NYSE have been primarily concerned with the supervision of market sell orders rather than of market buy orders.[22] Again it seems that it is easier to evaluate the effects of market price for the seller than the buyer of securities. In particular, it is easier to determine that a seller may be subject to an unreasonably low price as a consequence of the market's liquidity than it is to warn a buyer that the price he is willing to pay is too dear. I suppose that this difficulty is caused in great part by the public, which often tends to confuse high prices with greater opportunity.

Market "Freeness" versus Fairness and Orderliness

We have seen that the SEC, in its concern for the pricing mechanism of securities, has been primarily interested in the orderliness of transactions. Orderliness is a concept used by the SEC to modify its notion of *fair dealing*. Fairness, as Sidney Robbins suggests, describes a situation in which "no participant in the marketplace should be given an undue advantage over another, and to the extent differences in opportunity exist because of required differences in function and responsibility, such advantages should be held to a minimum."[23] This concept of fairness, based on a Paretian ideal of equilibrium, makes for orderliness to the extent that it limits successive differences in price changes to as narrow a spread between bid and ask as possible (or as speculator or trader can reasonably get away with).

Yet, as Robbins points out, another concept, the concept of a *free market*, is to some extent at odds with the concept of a fair and orderly market.[24] Market freedom, or "freeness," is the result of negotiation, without the restraint of manipulation or the intervention of monopolistic forces. To whatever extent it can be said to exist, it is the result of the unrestrained interplay of supply and demand. The concept of a free market is based on the right of an investor to determine the price at which he can best liquidate his holdings. Yet it is precisely because of this that the concept of market freedom can be at odds with the concept of a fair and orderly market. There are obviously times when a free market must be maintained even though the conditions it creates are something less than fair and orderly. Senator Corcoran recognized this when he said:

> We balance the advantages of liquidity in the market from the standpoint of having a place where banks can lend liquid funds and where investors can realize on securities. I am not trying to make that balance. For me there would be no choice. If I had to sacrifice liquidity of the market in the sense that sales had to be within a quarter of a point rather than within two points to prevent 1929 from occurring again, the decision would be easy for me; but that is a question of policy.[25]

Sidney Robbins sums it up thus:

> The principles of self-regulation guiding the securities market in espousing these two sometimes conflicting concepts definitely would decide in favor of maintaining a free market should the situation present itself. For self-regulation, ultimately freedom is more important than fair dealing and order. Thus the theory of the securities markets, as it originally evolved and still pertains today, rests in the principle of "freeness" where prices are determined by the forces of demand and supply.[26]

How can this be if there is not at the very basis of a free market a concept of value independent from the market itself? If there were no concept of exchange value underlying the market, wouldn't it have been more sensible for Congress and the Commission to have preferred a fair and orderly market to a free market? Here we are not talking about the commodity exchanges, where it is quite evident that the concepts of fairness and orderliness take precedence over freeness. All the commodity exchanges have some principles limiting the extent to which commodity prices can vary within any given period. This is not the case with the securities markets. As President Franklin D. Roosevelt stated in a letter to the chairman of the Committee on Banking and Currency:

> So far as possible, the aim should be to try to create a condition [so that] fluctuations in security values more nearly approximate fluctuations in the position of the enterprise itself and of general economic conditions —that is, tend to represent what is going on in the business and in our economic life rather than mere speculative or "technical" conditions in the market.[27]

Even though presidential pronouncements on values and timing have had a tendency to be wrong or misleading, it is regrettable that Roosevelt's advice has not been heeded more.

How can one entertain the idea of a securities market where capital-producing income is bought and sold without also realizing that this capital is subject to an economic judgment of its worth independently of the market for it? Isn't it evident that the market, in its role as liquidator, provides liquidity and just that? Why should liquidity be the sole and ultimate arbiter of worth? Does not liquidity provide a value primarily for that quantity of shares sold, and only to a limited degree for the remaining unsold holdings? Isn't liquidity sometimes desired for reasons having little do do with value? To quote Sidney Robbins again:

> Underlying forces in the securities markets, however, tend to distort the relationship between stock prices and values. Thus, transactions in a particular stock on any one day are likely to involve only a small number of shareholders, some of whom may have peculiarly urgent needs to liquidate a position. The resulting sales could cause sudden price variations induced not by changes in intrinsic worth or general economic conditions, but rather by the vagaries of supply and demand at a particular moment. More particularly, such distortions could arise if the seller is an institution disposing of a large block of stock for portfolio reasons entirely apart from the security's basic value.[28]

It should be clear why the principle of the self-regulation of the securities markets, based on a cooperation between government and business, should give precedence to the maintenance of a free market even if this should in some cases be at the expense of an orderly market. Corporate stock has exchange value, and it is the disclosure and dissemination of information about this value which contributes to the very possibility of our securities markets. Freeness is a direct consequence of the liberty to negotiate and transact. Without the possibility of forming independent value judgments, there is no negotiation and no transaction. Freeness, or liberty, is a direct consequence of the belief that people have the right to negotiate on the basis of their own interpretation of information and judgment of value.

4

Expectancy

For a property owner an expectation is the right to anticipate some benefit at some time. Sometimes this right is equitable. Sometimes it is fantastical or, at least, the result of wishful thinking. When what is owned is financial capital—that is, property without utility—one cannot reasonably entertain an expectation about its utility. There are a number of other expectations an owner of financial capital can hold. He can hold expectations about the future market value of his property, the present value of its income or return on investment, the effect of management on his claim on income—in short, anything other than how he can personally benefit from the use of the assets behind his claim.

I will call an expectation about exchange value an *expectancy* in order to distinguish it from other expectations. I believe that if we understand the evolution of the concept of property in the United States, we shall be able to acquire an important perspective on what kind of expectations are most relevant in the formation of practical judgments about the value of common stock.

Expectancy is the basic principle of valuation, because without an awareness of what it involves, no consistently meaningful and equitable concept of value is available. Expectancy is not a descriptive but a normative principle. Of course nobody *has* to use it in order to profit, but it provides a basis for understanding when a minority position in capital stock is over- or undervalued by the marketplace.

The desire to even think of such a principle runs contrary to the prevailing ideology of our nation's business economists, who believe that the magnitude and efficiency of our securities market has tended to obliterate the distinction between intrinsic value and market value. Yet I believe that businessmen, management, the judiciary, and Wall

Street, when convenient, believe in the enduring validity of this distinction.

To some the securities market is a game either to be played by applying probability analysis or merely to be enjoyed, whether one loses or wins. To others the securities market is a place for investing the savings of one's labor or fortune. Considering that over 25 percent of American industry is owned in trust by labor and over 50 percent of it is managed in trust by institutions, the degree to which the "game playing" attitude prevails is surprising. Even today, the majority of investors seems to equate the desire for an equitable and reasonable concept of value with a desire for a winning performance.

Institutional Economics and the Concept of Property

My analysis of expectancy is based on the concept of property provided by John R. Commons's momentous studies, *Legal Foundations of Capitalism* (first published in 1924) and *Institutional Economics* (published in 1934). Commons attempted to define capital in view of the repeated attempts by the Supreme Court of the United States to understand the concept of property as it arose for litigants defending their rights. Commons believed that an understanding of the business transaction and the negotiations and disputes it involved could clarify the meaning of capital better than any analysis of economic and political ideology. Ideology is relevant, he thought, to the extent it elucidates the judgments and attitudes of the various social and legal institutions governing the practical business transactions of daily life. For him an understanding of business values could be derived only from an analysis of the negotiations between business and labor, business and government, and business and management. The court was, so to speak, the ultimate interpreter and equitable appraiser of the validity of those values.

Although Commons's "institutional" attitude toward economics has been largely neglected by the mainstream of neoclassical economists, who have been primarily interested in arriving at a coherent, quantitative understanding of economic data, it is still shared today by some scholars of law and economics. If they would not take offense, perhaps we could understand men like Sidney Robbins, James Willard Hurst, and Henry G. Manne, to mention only three, as the contemporary heirs to that original American study of economics begun by Thorstein Veblen and developed by Commons. Kenneth Boulding is at least one economist who is not ashamed to be called an institutional economist.

Although one can see a European counterpart to institutionalism in the historical economics of men like Max Weber, the course of American institutionalism was uniquely pragmatic. It is as unique as the pragmatism of American philosophy, which, as John E. Smith has pointed out, has been uniquely concerned with the *relevance* of knowledge "for the solution of specific problems" rather than with the "ideal of total knowledge" or the construction of a system for knowing.[1]

The Evolution of the Concept of Property

John Commons begins his analysis of property with the *Slaughter-House* cases, which attracted attention about a century ago. For him the significance of these cases was vested in the different interpretations of the meaning of property given by the majority and minority opinions of the court. The majority held to the classical, Lockean definition of property as something held for the exclusive use of its owner; under this definition, the value of the property was to be measured by the benefits derived from using it.

The state of Louisiana, after having granted a monopoly to a corporation in New Orleans to maintain a slaughterhouse, decided that it was also empowered to regulate the rates this company could charge the city's butchers. The owners and management of the corporation thought this was an infringement on the corporate right to own property and a deprivation of its right to liberty. The majority opinion of the Supreme Court said, in effect, that since the rights of the company to use its property had not been impaired, Louisiana had not infringed upon its property rights. The minority opinion, however, expressed the view that "property is everything which has an exchangeable value, and the right of property includes the right to dispose of it according to the will of the owner."[2]

Several years later, in the first *Minnesota Rate* case of 1890, the Supreme Court reversed itself and adhered to the aforementioned minority opinion. Property was no longer understood exclusively as something held for the use of its owners but as something that had an exchange value. In John Commons's words:

> The title of ownership or the possession of physical property is empty as a business asset if the owner is deprived of his liberty to fix a price on the sale of the product of that property . . . not merely physical things are the objects of property but the *expected earning power* of those things is property; and property is taken from the owner, not merely under the

> power of *eminent domain,* which takes *title* and *possession,* but also under the police power, which takes its *exchange value.*[3]

As a consequence of the majority opinion of the court in the *Minnesota Rate* case, the power of government to restrict property by controlling rates or to confiscate property on the basis of eminent domain was severely curtailed. The state legislatures could no longer arbitrarily limit the expected income of a going business, in this case a railroad, without due process of law, because the earning capacity of a business was as much its property as were its physical assets. Nor could the states confiscate property according to the right of eminent domain. They had to pay its owners a price based not on their unilateral interpretation of value but on a negotiated understanding of the property's exchange value. The owners were entitled to receive a price that enabled them to retain an earning capacity comparable to that enjoyed before the takeover. Thus the court abandoned its definition of property as physical assets held only for the use of its owner. Property now came to be understood as something that produced income. The value of property now became the consequence of its exchange value.

In 1897 a further step in defining property as something that has exchange value was taken by the court in the *Allegeyer* case. In this case the court extended the concept of exchange value from expected earning power to free access to markets in which one could buy and sell capital without restraint. To say that capital, which is income-producing property, has an exchange value is meaningful only if it can indeed be bought and sold. Hence the liberty of negotiation and transaction of property is essential to the definition of exchange value. The court now said:

> The liberty mentioned in that Amendment [the Fourteenth Amendment] means not only the right of the citizen to be free from physical restraint of his person, but . . . the right of the citizen to be free in the enjoyment of all his faculties; to be free to use them in all lawful ways; to live and work where he will; to earn his livelihood by any lawful calling; to pursue any livelihood or avocation, and for that purpose to enter into all contracts which may be proper, necessary and essential to his carrying out to a successful conclusion the purposes above mentioned. . . . His enjoyment upon terms of equality with all others in similar circumstances of the privilege of pursuing an ordinary calling or trade, and of acquiring, holding, and selling property, is an essential part of the liberty and property guaranteed by the Fourteenth Amendment.[4]

Commons traces the next inevitable decision to the *Adams Express* case of 1897, in which intangible property, the capital stock of the Adams Express Company, was given a value based on its expected earnings capacity and not on the mere physical assets of the corporation. The court did not, of course, deny that physical assets were indeed used in producing earnings; rather, it denied that the value of a business could be reduced to almost nothing in a judgment, independent of what this business was really capable of earning. As Commons observes:

> The next significant step in recognizing intangible property as a value entirely different from the economists' meaning of corporeal property was in the case of *Adams Express Company* v. *Ohio.* This was a taxation case, and the Supreme Court, against the protest of the corporation, raised the value of the property in question for purposes of taxation in the State of Ohio, from $23,000 to $449,377. The corporeal property of the economists and the common law were horses, wagons, safes, pouches and similar tangible property. The intangible property was the whole market value of the stocks and bonds based on the expected earning capacity of the corporation as a going concern, of which Ohio's proper share among the states was $449,377. In this case the intangible property was eighteen times as much as the corporeal property. The court said, on rehearing, that "it is enough that it is property which though intangible exists, which has value, produces income and passes current in the markets of the world."[5]

With this decision, the Supreme Court established that the primary consideration governing the valuation of the capital stock of a corporation must be its exchange value, which is based on its earnings expectation and not on what the corporation claims its assets to be worth.

Interestingly enough, a few years later the Supreme Court upheld a similar decision in a case with different circumstances. In the *Stanislaus County* case of 1904, a water utility company claimed a very high value for its physical assets because the state of California had authorized it to base the rates it would charge its customers for the use of its water on a return on its invested capital. The company naturally gave a high value to its physical assets. In its decision, the court said, "The original cost may have been too great; mistakes of construction, even though honest, may have been made, which necessarily enhanced the cost; more property may have been acquired than necessary or needful for the purpose intended."[6]

The court here reduced the value of the company's physical property to an amount it thought would justify a reasonable rate of return. It was not the physical property itself which gave a value to this monopoly, but that portion of its property on which it could expect a reasonable income. Whatever the value of the company's physical assets may have been, the value of its intangible assets, or capital stock, had to be derived from expected income, which in this case had to be reasonable because it was a utility serving the public.

Neither the *Adams Express* case nor the *Stanislaus County* case implies that the physical assets of a corporation cannot be used in determining its exchange value. What they mean is that corporate assets only have value in a going business to the extent that they are used to produce income. The court adopted the position that return on investment is not irrelevant to exchange value. In the *Adams Express* case, where the value of the investment was reduced by the owners to avoid taxes, the court realized that it would be only reasonable to increase its stated value to a value commensurate with its earning capacity. In the *Stanislaus County* case, where the value of the corporate assets was increased in order to justify higher rates, the court reduced the value of these assets to a level that was in keeping with a reasonable rate of return.

John Commons tried to show how the definition of property evolved from the concept of physical property having only utility to its owners to the concept of property as assets used by management to produce income. This new definition of property is what we understand as capital. Capital is dependent on management's opportunity and expectation to produce income and on the opportunities and expectations the shareholder has in buying and selling his common stock. Both opportunity and expectation are a consequence of legal liberty.

Liberty of opportunity has, of course, been the subject of government intervention and supervision for both management and shareholder. There are numerous government agencies today that seek to limit liberty of opportunity to what is best for the public welfare. The liberty of expectation is an economic right dependent upon a judgment of exchange value. One is of course free to expect anything. However, it is John Commons's contribution to have shown that expectations follow from the definition of economic liberty only insofar as they are concerned with exchange value.

Conflicts of Interest

The preceding analysis of the evolution of the concept of property was undertaken by John Commons in an attempt to arrive at an economic rather than legal definition of capital. Today not all lawyers would agree that "legal capital" is necessarily dependent upon a notion of income, because the concept of legal capital is not unequivocally defined by statute. In a very general manner we could say that economic capital is concerned primarily with the determination of income, and legal capital with the determination of capital assets as determined by the balance sheet and cash flow statements of the corporation. Yet when called upon to determine what part of our property is also our capital, we would normally include only what produces or is expected to produce income. This is, at least, how the IRS views it.

John Commons's interpretation of capital is useful not only for its analysis of the transition from utility to exchange value in determining the worth of property but also for its distinction between three concepts of property generated by incorporation: (1) the corporate property, (2) management's property, and (3) the stockholder's property.

The corporate property (sometimes referred to as *the enterprise*) is represented by the title to the net assets of the corporation. The value of the enterprise must be considered differently for management and for the stockholder. To management, which enjoys the power and benefits usually associated with the control of production, the value of the enterprise lies in the possible uses of its assets. To the shareholder, on the other hand, the enterprise is valuable either as an asset capable of being liquidated or as an asset on which he may wish to impose his own management. To talk about the value of the enterprise in the abstract is meaningless; corporate property must always be viewed in relation to either management or stockholders.

The second type of property is based on the concept of utility value. Its sole beneficiary is management, which has the right and the responsibility to use the corporation's assets in order to produce income. This is true both for close corporations, in which management typically contributes most of the capital, and for public corporations, in which the source and the control of capital are separate. One might argue that management's right to use the enterprise cannot be considered a legitimate "property"; but the fact remains that only management, not the stockholder, has the power to control the use and disposition of corporate assets.

The third type of property is the shareholder's title to a claim on the income produced by management's use of the corporate assets. This income can either be paid to the stockholders as dividends or be retained by management in the corporation. When it is retained, it becomes a residual asset for the stockholders and, at the same time, an increased liability for management. The more income management retains in the corporation, the more income it has to produce to maintain the same return on equity.

These three types of property give rise to a conflict of interests. A shareholder's property has exchange value but no utility value. Management's property has utility value but no exchange value, unless of course we consider the exchange value of employment contracts or stock options. Accordingly, the value of the enterprise (the corporate property), which may be viewed as the intersection between management's and stockholders' property, will differ depending on whether it is assessed by management or stockholders.

The suggestion that there is an inherent conflict of interests between value concepts employed by management and shareholder may be unacceptable to some, especially to those who do not realize that dissension is the necessary basis for judgment under the democratic process. The balance-of-power doctrine in the Constitution presupposes that a conflict of power interests is necessary and not just tolerable to the American concept of government. Another way of expressing this balance-of-power doctrine would be to describe the American democracy as *endocratic.* This perhaps unhappy neologism has also been used to describe the possibility for the conflict of values between the different property interests in the modern business corporation.[7]

This inherent conflict between the values of management and stockholders does not, however, justify the pursuit of private business opportunities by management and directors at the cost of the corporation's opportunities for profit. The doctrine of corporate opportunity that has evolved has been instrumental in protecting the shareholder from the worst kinds of abuse.[8] Yet this doctrine has nothing to say about the decisions management makes in trying to produce a profit for the corporation; it does not even demand that management be concerned primarily with maximizing profits.

It is sometimes thought that the purpose of the corporation is to maximize profits. Yet viewed from the different perspectives of the different property interests inherent in the endocratic corporation, what does this really mean? Even if we assume that a shareholder's interest in buying stock is to maximize his wealth, this does not mean that management must share this goal or even conceive of it in the same way. Today, I doubt that the managements of the largest corporations could really publicly adhere to the view that they are concerned only with maximizing profits in complete disregard of their social responsibility to the public.

An interesting perspective on this issue can be gained from the

Dodge v. *Ford Motor Company* case of 1919. The Dodge brothers, who owned 10 percent of the stock of the Ford Motor Company, sought to compel the Ford management to pay a dividend equal to three quarters of the corporation's accumulated cash surplus, which had increased greatly in the few years preceding the suit.

Defending his retention of earnings, Henry Ford said, "My ambition is to employ still more men to spread the benefits of this industrial system to the greatest possible numbers, to help them build up their lives and their homes. To do this we are putting the greatest share of our profits back in the business."[9]

Clearly, Henry Ford's interpretation of profit maximization differed sharply from that propounded by the Dodge brothers (who, incidentally, won this case). In particular, his view of profit maximization was tempered by what he saw as his social responsibility.

Whether the control of the corporate assets by management and directors is viewed as a power in trust for the sole benefit of maximizing profits for the stockholders as beneficiaries of this trust, or whether this power in trust carries with it a responsibility to the public, is an issue that has generated some controversy.[10] Whether the power going with control is itself a corporate asset or a particular right that management can value as it pleases is another controversial issue. Certainly, control appears to have more value than a lack of it.

The *Perlman* v. *Feldman* case of 1955 is a classic example of the controversy over the value of control. Feldman, who was president of the Newport Steel Corporation and with his group controlled 37 percent of its stock, sold his controlling interests to the Wilport Company for $20 a share. The market price of the shares on the OTC market never exceeded $12. The stated book value was $17.03 per share. Perlman, a minority stockholder of the Newport Steel Corporation, brought a derivative suit against Feldman, claiming that "the power to control the allocation of Newport's product was a corporate asset, and . . . part of the price the Feldman group received for its stock was in reality a payment for conferring that power on Wilport."[11]

Perlman sought to recover about $5 per share of the control premium on behalf of the corporation, ultimately to benefit minority stockholders. The district court initially upheld Feldman's property right to receive a premium for control. This decision was reversed, however, and a share value of $14.67 was established, based on an appraisal that ignored the benefit of control.

This case has been the source of much controversy, as both the majority and minority opinions and the literature analyzing this case show. Who really should benefit from the sale of controlling stock—

the controlling stockholders or the corporation itself? If we agree with the court of appeals in the *Perlman* v. *Feldman* case that it is the corporation which should benefit, to what extent can this be understood to benefit its management more than its stockholders?

Years ago Adolf Berle suggested that control is a corporate asset, because what is sold is power and not just stock. Although the issue is still not entirely settled, the prevailing view today insists on the equal rights of all shareholders, who should benefit, at least to some extent, from whatever offer is made to purchase controlling stock.[12]

Important as this issue may be, it is to some extent peripheral to an understanding of how to value stock. Whichever side the law actually happens to be on—that is, whoever is legally the "owner" of control—the fact remains that the value of control is not the same for the minority stockholder as for management.

It is the stockholder, not management, who must demand an appraisal. Stockholders are free to accept or reject any interpretation of value given by management. It is a measure of their liberty, however, that they are not bound by statute to accept management's disclosures, even if they must largely rely on them to arrive at an independent judgment of value. Since the corporation is an endocratic enterprise, conflicts of interests and value between management and stockholder are as necessary to it as negotiation between Congress and the president is for the democratic process.

Expected Value and Maximization of Profits

Business economists, although they may accept the theory of the endocratic corporation, do not accept its significance for the process of valuing common stock. It is commonly assumed that *management's objective is to maximize the market price of the corporation's stock.* I must admit that I have always had difficulty understanding this assumption, in spite of the mathematical disguise in which it is usually presented. Unless we assume that management is free to use manipulative devices such as stabilizing the market price of its shares, we would have to make the further assumption that the market is an efficient and adequate judge of management's performance. Although this undoubtedly often is true, it is not true for all companies at all times. Was IBM's management twice as "good" in 1977 as it was in 1974, when its shares sold for half of what they were selling in 1977? Should we argue that IBM's management would better maximize shareholder wealth by paying higher dividends than by buying in its shares? What does it mean to say that management is responsible for maximizing market price when it cannot have any direct influence on market action?

Economists say that, however profits are defined, the maximization of profits by management will maximize wealth for stockholders, whether this wealth is defined as dividends, retained earnings, or market price. However, as we have seen, management is not always solely interested in maximizing profits; it may also be interested in fulfilling its social responsibility, however interpreted. Even if we accept the proposition that maximizing income will maximize shareholder wealth, very few managements today will accept the maximization of income as their sole responsibility as trustees for the shareholder interest.

Of those business economists who still believe that the valuation of common stock is a worthwhile activity, a vast majority propose the *expected value* method of valuing equities. The reliance on the expected value method is a direct consequence of the belief that management will always act so as to maximize value for the shareholder. Without this belief in maximization, the ability to arrive at an expected value becomes severely curtailed.

The notion of expected value is basically an attempt to measure the value over time of a future stream of income. One must therefore be able to know the amount of time involved as well as the amount of money one expects to receive during each period of time. If one is interested in knowing how much these future receipts are worth at the present, one will have to discount them according to some acceptable rate of interest. When they were first proposed by the neoclassical economists, expected values were hailed as a great and useful innovation enabling the businessman to understand the real value of his expected income in view of his expected costs in obtaining it.

Expected value is expressed as *present value,* or *discounted present value* (DPV), when one is primarily interested in determining the actual present value of a future stream of income discounted at an acceptable rate of interest. It is expressed as *internal rate of return* (IRR) when one attempts to equate all expected income to all the costs involved in obtaining this income. The IRR is also known as the *marginal efficiency of capital* or the *investor's discounted cash flow yield.* These methods are indispensable in determining the value of any future income in cases where one has either control over the investment or a contract specifying the amount of this income.

Expected value formulas essentially consist of five variables: (1) present value, (2) future value, (3) the investor's desired rate of discount or yield, (4) the amount of each individual expected payment or receipt, and (5) the number of periods over which one expects to receive these payments. Knowing any four of these variables, one can determine the fifth.

It is obvious that no decision to buy a note or bond can ever be made without using expected values. Thus if a 4 percent bond maturing in ten years sells for 78⁵/₈, the expected yield ought to be about 7 percent. This market price of 78⁵/₈ is actually the discounted present value of the bond, reflecting a 7 percent market rate of discount. If one desired a higher rate of return, one would have to pay less for the bond. The calculations are simple. Most financial pages of bond prices include them.

In a sense, the expected value method is merely the reciprocal of the replacement cost method of appraising value. It implies that an owner could replace his property without loss by acquiring a comparable capital instrument with the same discounted present value. In fact, this is why the method is indispensable for the appraisal of notes and bonds.

However, expected values are almost entirely useless when applied to common stock, because a shareholder holds no contractual claim over future dividends or future income. It is for this reason that it has been described by James Bonbright as a "psychic value." It shows more about the zeal of the valuer than it does about the nature of the property he is valuing. As he so piquantly put it, "like the cynic's concept of gratitude [it] is a mere anticipation of favors to come."[13] How can one possibly hope to determine the DPV of a share of common stock if one does not know (a) the amount of each individual future dividend payment with certainty, (b) the number of future periods over which one hopes to receive such payments, and (c) the future value either of these dividends or of the future price of the stock at some arbitrary date? Surely, it requires a psychic mind to use this approach.[14]

Yet there has been a tendency for business economists to assume that DPV is useful to shareholders in determining the current, intrinsic value of their shares. Victor Brudney and Marvin Chirelstein, two eminent professors of law, accept this view when they state that the "calculation of present values is central to the valuation process" by shareholders.[15] The idea is that since a stockholder owns a claim on income, all he has to do to determine the present value of his claim is to calculate future income for some appropriate period in some appropriate way and discount it according to some appropriate rate of interest. It is assumed that if he pays X dollars for his shares and can expect Y dollars in income over five years, his shares are worth today

X plus the discounted present value of the expected income Y. DPV, in other words, is claimed to be a measure of intrinsic value.

However, it may be that the stockholder has paid altogether too much for his shares. (My principle of expectancy will serve to clarify what "too much" means.) What disturbs me about the use of DPV is the degree to which it forces the stockholder to measure future income. In so doing, he has to rely on the assumption that management will indeed maximize income. If he cannot rely on this assumption, what sense would it make to measure future income? Perhaps a reliance on the minimum income management might be expected to produce would make more sense. But then a stockholder would, perhaps, have to rely on an analysis of past and not future income.

A more reasonable use of DPV is to take into consideration only dividends and not the whole income of the corporation. John Burr Williams was one of the first to develop the idea, about forty years ago, that future dividends, not earnings, should be discounted in arriving at the present worth of the corporation to stockholders. His attitude was that a "stock is worth only what you can get out of it."[16] What you can get out of it is really what you can dispose of, that is, the dividends that put money into a shareholder's pocket.

Williams's attitude toward DPV makes a lot of practical sense, especially when it is applied to bonds, preferred stock, and utility stocks. These are all capital investments in which management, if it does not have the contractual obligation of paying out a fixed amount, at least has a historically implied obligation to pay out a substantial amount of its income in dividends. Williams's approach is particularly applicable to utility stocks, not only because the dividend payout ratio is higher and because the investment in new plant and equipment is usually lower than for industrial companies, but also because the accounting principles of the public utilities are controlled by law. In this case, "maximization of profits" is fairly clearly defined.

The DPV of dividends is useful under those circumstances in which the stock of a public utility is selling at a price under or not much over its book value. Under these circumstances the investment value at the start of the discounting period allows an investor to anticipate a fair return on his investment. Unfortunately, the DPV of dividends is not very useful when the opportunity cost to the investor exceeds the dividend yield, as it does for most industrial companies and often did for public utilities.

Like any approach to common-stock valuation that relies on an expectation of future performance rather than on past accomplishments, using the DPV of dividends presupposes that the investment value at the start of the discounting calculation is fair and reasonable. While this may often be the case in the calculation of the DPV of utility stocks, whose market prices in recent years have generally not commanded a premium over book value, it is not always true for industrial stocks. It is precisely because of its reliance on the validity and reasonableness of the initial investment value that is the basis for the DPV calculations that the scope of this valuation method is so limited. How are we to estimate the initial investment value of IBM—on the basis of its book value of $90 per share, or $150, or $280? Or are we to ignore the initial investment value altogether and discount its income or dividends over perpetuity?

The theory that it is only dividends and not retained earnings which can properly be said to contribute to the maximization of shareholder wealth has been disputed in a now classic article by Merton H. Miller and Franco Modigliani.[17] They suggest that it is net income—both dividends and retained earnings—which contributes to the maximization of shareholder wealth. Although their conclusions have generated much controversy, I do agree with the theoretical substance of their position that income retained by the corporation contributes as much to shareholder wealth as income paid out in dividends. Of course, I am not comfortable with the supposition that the decision to retain a major portion of earnings invariably, or even usually, represents a maximum effort by management to increase shareholder wealth. For me, all it means is that management has a greater incentive to maintain its historic return on retained investments when it chooses to retain more than it pays out.

The Alternative: Expectancy Value

In the preceding section I have tried to explain why the use of expected values, especially the use of any formula for arriving at DPV, is not very useful to the shareholder in determining how much he should pay for, or expect to benefit from, common stock. Expected value, whether in the form of IRR or DPV, is intrinsically more useful to management, which is in a position to decide how the corporate assets will be used, to what extent it will maximize corporate profits, how it will measure them, and how it will allocate them.

If only the shareholder knew when the future begins and when it ends, and if only he could be reasonably sure of all the costs involved in calculating IRR or DPV, perhaps the expected value of a discounted present would be of more benefit to him. In the absence of such knowledge, a value based on past earnings may be more relevant to him.

The *Perlman* v. *Feldman* case discussed earlier illustrates that when earnings are taken as the substantive basis for common-stock valuation, stockholders and management may frequently disagree sharply on how these earnings are to be measured. Depending on the situation, stockholders may have an intrinsic interest in basing their appraisal on historical earnings while management may stand to gain by using discounted projected earnings. This was exactly the situation in the *Perlman* v. *Feldman* case, in which the minority stockholders attempted to set a lower price on the company's stock by basing their appraisal on historical earnings and book value. The appraisal expert for the defendant naturally tried to justify a higher price by discounting the projected earnings he thought could be derived from the improved steel-production facilities in the hands of management.

Delaware law requires that when an appraisal is made of stock values, only historical earnings (usually an average of the preceding five-year period), not prospective earnings, be used. Although other state courts (and, within states, different judges) take a different view of the matter, there seems to be at least a general recognition of the basic conflict between stockholders and management in this area.

The efforts by the courts throughout the land in resolving litigation about the value of common stock, usually between the controlling interests of management and the minority shareholders, have largely concentrated on determining the *enterprise value* of the corporation itself. This trend is based on the fact that a corporation exists as a separate entity and therefore has a value as a going concern. However, the assumption is also made that whatever the enterprise value of the corporation is determined to be, it should be just as relevant to the stockholder as to management. Enterprise value is, so to speak, a compromise establishing the "objective" or intrinsic value of the firm.

However valuable this approach may be in resolving a litigation, it is not very useful to a stockholder who wants to determine the value of his shares outside of a court of law. For him there really is no such thing as enterprise value. Stockholder valuation of stockholder property must always be based exclusively on the benefits and values to him, not on values in the abstract. If his concept of value is identical to enterprise value, so much the better. But one cannot assume that enterprise and securities values will always be identical if one accepts the endocratic nature of the corporate structure.

How then should an ordinary shareholder value his property if he cannot base his judgment either on the expectation of what his claim will produce or on the compromised, "objective" enterprise value of the firm itself?

It is my view that any judgment a stockholder makes for investment (as opposed to trading) should be based on the value he gives to income already produced from the net assets of the corporation. In other words, it is the return on stockholders' equity (ROE), or return on net invested capital or book value, which ought to be used in forming any judgment about the value of his property.

ROE and Expectancy Value

ROE is the basis for common-stock valuation because (1) it ties the measurement of income directly to the measurement of the net capital assets used to produce it, (2) it is a historic and not an expected value, and (3) it takes into account the endocratic nature of the corporation. ROE always sets income produced by management against income retained by it. It recognizes the increase in liability to the enterprise against which management must compare the income it is in the process of producing. Should the ROE persistently be seen to decrease, shareholders will have a good indication that management is failing to perform its service to them adequately.

Just what should be regarded as income and how it should be measured is as open to interpretation as what the stockholder's equity consists of. Should income be net income, net operating income, income before or after taxes? Should the shareholders' invested capital include intangible assets, surplus produced by public offerings, preferred shareholders' equity? These are matters that each stockholder will have to determine for himself as best suits his purpose. As long as ROE is consistently derived from comparable sources, there should be no problem. Much has been written about which sources of measurement are most appropriate to the shareholder's particular purpose.[18]

One important thing to keep in mind is that earnings and ROE must always be analyzed *in conjunction with book value.* If management overstates earnings, this will in turn lead to overstated retained earnings and thus to a higher book value. Overstating earnings will not by itself produce a higher ROE figure. By the same token, an overly conservative earnings statement will not by itself lead to a consistently low ROE figure, because there will be less retained income against which to calculate ROE. Thus, as long as neither book value nor earnings are analyzed independently of each other, it is always possible to derive meaningful figures for book value and ROE, no matter how inflated or deflated the book value.

Of course, the way management presents the firm's income is interesting in that it reflects management's basic attitude. A management of an airline which depreciates its airplanes over a period longer than their useful life, or a builder which chooses to include uncollected receipts from sales in its current income statement, is obviously more intent on preserving an impression of profitability than on accounting for the kind of retained earnings that can be expected to provide continuing financial strength.

The purpose of using ROE is to enable a shareholder to arrive at an *expectancy value* of a particular investment. This expectancy value takes into account the book value of the shares, the return on stockholders' equity, and the investor's opportunity cost. Specifically, an expectancy value (EV) is equal to book value (BV) times the return on equity (ROE) divided by a particular opportunity cost (OC), or

$$EV = BV \frac{ROE}{OC}$$

For example, let us assume that 10 percent represents a fair expectation of Johns-Manville's ROE, on the basis of the firm's historical ROE. If its net tangible book value is $30 per share and a particular investor's opportunity cost is judged to be 10 percent, its expectancy value will be $30 per share. This price will give the investor a fair and reasonable basis for ordering his other expectations, whatever they are. If Johns-Manville were selling at $50 per share, he would have to justify the difference in price in terms of his additional expectations, whatever they may be.

Applying the same reasoning to Coca-Cola with an approximate book value of $13 per share and an approximate ROE of 21 percent, we can see that in order to satisfy his opportunity cost of 10 percent, the investor would have to buy the stock at a cost of about $27. Should the stock be selling at double this price, he would have to justify his investment on the basis of expectations having nothing to do with ROE.

How ROE is calculated and how differing ROE ratios for a number of years in the past are averaged is also a matter of personal preference. It is undoubtedly more difficult to determine what the average ROE is for an automobile manufacturer or other companies with cyclically fluctuating sales than it is for a drug company. The measurement and averaging of ROE should be confined to past performance; extrapolating ROE from one or two extraordinary years is an imprudent practice. Normally one will have to cover at least five and perhaps up to ten years to determine a meaningful ROE figure.

The formula for expectancy value given here, it must be pointed out, should never be used mechanically as the sole basis for value judgments. It must always be used in conjunction with all other expectations the investor feels are reasonable or prudent. Furthermore, its three variables—book value, return on equity, and opportunity cost—are open to different interpretations. Yet these interpretations will not be so conflicting as to be irreconcilable. (In Chapter 9 we shall discuss the different perspectives that can be taken on defining BV, ROE, and OC.)

One of the values of the formula is that it allows reasonable and informed dissension on the definition of each of these variables. Expectancy values depend to some extent on the specific needs and interests of the individual investor, and the formula is flexible enough to accommodate these differences. On the other hand, it is sufficiently restrictive to exclude bizarre and unreasonable expectations from entering into the value judgment.

Expectancy Value and Shareholders' Property

A stockholder, as I have repeatedly pointed out, owns a share of a claim on income and not a share of the assets of a going business. His claim entitles him to appraise all the information disclosed to him by management. In forming his judgment he can, of course, use other information about the company, such as information about the market behavior of its shares or about the general economy, but such data will generally complement rather than replace the information made available by management.

I have also shown that a stockholder's property has a value, not because of its utility, but because it can be exchanged. Its exchange value is based on the earnings capacity of the corporation. As we have seen, exchange value cannot be simply equated with the expected value of future income, but it must be understood as a measurement of income in relation to the corporate assets used to produce it. I have also indicated that the measurement of exchange value, however much it differs from market value, is vested in a very basic right of the shareholder to expect value from his investments. Without this basic expectation of value, which I call an expectancy, the shareholder's ability to appraise the value of his property is severely curtailed.

In law, expectancy usually refers to the value of a property a claimant thinks he is entitled to recover from the party who has either breached a contract or otherwise caused his property to decline in worth. In other words, an expectancy recovery normally arises when the claimant has been financially injured in some way. However, an expectancy is not really a damage remedy but an equitable remedy, for it aims to measure the value of the claimant's property before it was misused (or of his contract before it was breached). The fundamental purpose of an expectancy is to reaffirm and reinstate a claimant's concept of value.

I believe that such an equitable principle is applicable to a shareholder's claim on income. I believe it can be used to describe the stockholder's substantive right to an expectation of value independently of whether the value of his property has been depleted by fraud, unjust enrichment, or even misleading or incomplete information by management.

The principle of expectancy I am describing is not properly a legal principle, but an economic principle. It is not restricted to litigation but is applicable to stock ownership in any continuing and responsibly managed corporation. When there is litigation the stockholder will, of course, try to use any concept of value of which he can take advantage.

No shareholder would invest if it weren't for the expectation that his investment will leave him wealthier than he was. This increased wealth is derived from his claim on income and can be realized either from dividends or retained earnings. Increase in market price may be a reflection that others share his judgment, but it is not essential to his claim. Management, which has the power and the right to produce income from the corporate assets, cannot directly influence the market price of his shares.

The principle of expectancy, therefore, describes, from the point of view of the stockholders, the economic value of the relationship between management and the net assets of the corporation. This is why it is an expectation based on ROE. It allows for a fair and reasonable judgment of value to the extent that it is based on an analysis of how management has used and allocated the income it has produced for shareholders in the past. The principle of expectancy reaffirms that every shareholder has the equitable right to appraise the value of his property and to determine whether management's conduct is beneficial to his property interests.

The starting point for determining the expectancy value of stock in an industrial corporation always has to be its book or net asset value, even if the ROE and opportunity cost justify establishing an expectancy value of double or even triple the book value. In the case of Coca-Cola, the basic expectancy value may be $27 per share, even if the book value is $13 per share. In the case of the Chrysler Corporation, which has a book value of about $46 per share, the expectancy value would probably be much lower, since its ROE has been so erratic in the past. Probably the current market price of about $20 per share is very close to the basic expectancy value of most shareholders.

When the market price per share is substantially above expectancy value, the shareholder must realize that he is at the mercy of the market. The behavior of management becomes largely irrelevant to the measurement of the stockholder's claim on income; his shares are worth what others are willing to pay for them. Under these circumstances he loses all possibility of acting prudently, because he relies merely on the behavior of others and not on any independently established investment criteria. In my opinion, therefore, one should invest only when the market price per share does not exceed its expectancy value.

Expectancy is an equitable principle. It is a consequence of the notion that every stockholder has the equitable right to form a judgment about the value of his property. It is, in effect, an appraisal right to which he is entitled by the fact that he owns property in the form of a claim on income.

One would normally think of the appraisal right only in connection with a litigation between minority shareholders and controlling shareholders or management. In situations of mergers, freeze-outs, or takeovers, minority stockholders always have the right to dispute the value given to their shares by management and demand an independent appraisal. The value of this appraisal right has sometimes been disputed. It has often been judged to be expensive, not very effective, and a general nuisance to those other shareholders not insisting upon it. Dean Manning, for example, has strongly disapproved of the appraisal remedy for shareholders on the grounds that it denies shareholders other kinds of relief. The appraisal remedy should only be used, he says, "to provide a way for an unhappy investor to get out when he has no other feasible way to get out."[19]

There is no doubt that appraisal rights have been abused by minority shareholders, but I also think that they serve as an effective check on management's concept of shareholder value. It has also been said that "appraisal rights represent the most firmly established compromise between the policies of assuring freedom of action for the corporate majority and protecting the investment of the minority."[20] Perhaps Melvin Eisenberg has best summed up the situation:

> In short, while it would not be irrational to eliminate appraisal rights as to shares which are traded under conditions which are likely to insure the existence of a continuous market, it seems more advisable to retain the appraisal right in such cases, partly to protect the fair expectations of those shareholders whose legitimate expectations center on the enterprise rather than on the market, and partly to serve as a well-designed emergency switch to check management improvidence.[21]

The very contention that an appraisal right, however misused, is inextricably connected to a stockholder's property right is based on the presumption that his property is as much subject to the principle of fairness and right governed by the law of equity as any other kind of property. As Berle and Means put it: "In fact, if not in law, at the moment we are thrown back on the obvious conclusion that a stockholder's right lies in the expectation of fair dealing rather than in the ability to enforce a series of supposed legal claims."[22] Indeed, one could say that the appraisal right is necessary precisely because it is so difficult to determine the exact extent and significance of a stockholder's property.

The Securities and Exchange acts have been conceived not only to protect the small stockholder from fraud or manipulation but also to ensure that he has at least the possibility of forming fair price judgments on the basis of accurate and timely information. It is, therefore, lamentable that these acts, conceived under the law of equity, do not also attempt to establish some criterion of reasonable value that would give the shareholder some measure of confidence in the validity of his judgment.[23] One of the principal reasons for the low level of public confidence in our market is the feeling that common stock is not real property but something whose value is determined arbitrarily by somebody else's expectations of what it may be worth.

The principle of expectancy I am discussing is a normative principle. It can be employed or it can be ignored by the investing public. However, it offers the only criterion I can think of which allows a stockholder to form a reasonable and prudent judgment about the value of his property without having to rely exclusively on market value. It acknowledges that the corporation is an endocratic enterprise; that is, it acknowledges the intrinsic conflict between management and shareholders, instead of assuming that management's main purpose is to maximize the value of the shareholders' property.

The value of this principle in establishing a legal appraisal is limited, because legal appraisals are determined by many other considerations. Its principal purpose is to give a minority shareholder a basis for understanding when he pays too much, and for putting into the proper perspective all the expectations he entertains when he buys stock. In short, it is the basis for differentiating between prudence and speculation.

5

Opportunity Cost

In this chapter we shall depart somewhat from our main subject of analyzing the value of common stock. Here we shall be concerned not with the concept of value but with what we may call the obverse of this concept: the concept of cost. Just as value normally refers to benefits, cost refers to sacrifice. We value something for the benefit we expect from it, but, when we attribute a cost to it, we are concerned with what we have to give up in order to obtain it.

Before proceeding, I should mention that economists differ in their use of the term cost. They normally refer to cost either as an *outlay* or as an *opportunity cost.* The first refers to cost as the sacrifice of disbursing money in order to acquire property. The second refers to cost as a measure of this sacrifice.

Until now we have been concerned with the theoretical aspects of valuing common stock—that is, the benefits, rights, and expectations involved in owning it. We have seen that one of the peculiarities of valuing common stock as opposed to valuing other kinds of property is that we are primarily concerned with its exchange value and not its utility value or even its market value.

The term market value is to a great extent misleading. If it means the value of stock given to it by the market, it is not a very useful concept of value. Value is usually taken to mean a benefit to the owner and not to others. The market, therefore, does not really "value," it prices. It determines the cost of buying and selling a specific number of shares at a specific point in time. What is usually meant by market value is market price.

Market price, like any indication of cost, is only an indication of what would have to be given up under similar circumstances to buy or sell a similar number of shares. The market is said to "value" to the extent that one can *infer* that those shares not transacted have a value similar to the price of those shares bought and sold. In short, market value is only inference. In Chapter 3 we have seen to what extent the market, as a source of value, can become both an instrument of coercion and a basis for wishful thinking.

The discussion in this chapter will take on a special significance when it is understood that the notion of valuing common stock is integrally connected to the notion of costs as a measure of the sacrifice one has to make in order to acquire the value or benefit of ownership. We shall be concerned not only with understanding the function of outlay cost determined by market price but also with clarifying the concept of cost by which we have to measure the sacrifice of acquiring common stock. Since the benefit of acquiring equity lies in its exchange value—that is, in the claim on income it represents—its cost must be measured in terms of the income one has to sacrifice in order to acquire it. One would not pay par value for a bond yielding 4 percent if one could buy other bonds of equal quality yielding 7 percent. Nor would one ever buy this bond at a 7 percent yield if one thought the sacrifice imposed by a 10 percent inflation rate too great. By the same token, one would not buy a stock yielding 12 percent total return on market price if one thought the ravages of the economy, as well as the uncertainty of this particular yield, posed too great a risk.

In other words, it is important that a commitment to an investment in common stock be preceded by an analysis of the sacrifice one is willing to make. This sacrifice is sometimes referred to as the *cost of capital.* I refer to it as opportunity cost, because, as we shall soon see, I do not think that a shareholder's concept of cost is subject to the same type of analysis economists apply to capital costs. For me, opportunity cost cannot be mathematically derived from an analysis of capital costs. It can only be derived from an understanding of the level of confidence in the conventions of society that allows a person to sacrifice his savings for the purchase of specific amounts of common stock. As each investor's level of confidence is to a great extent personal and arbitrary, so is his determination of opportunity cost.

Outlay Cost

Outlay cost comprises all the expenses and disbursements needed to acquire an unencumbered title to property that one expects to use for one's personal benefit or the conduct of one's business. When one acquires a house or automobile, for example, the outlay cost consists of all the disbursements needed to transfer title. A mortgage against the house or automobile, even though disbursed by someone other than the purchaser, would still be included in an analysis of outlay cost. In business, outlay cost refers to all the costs involved in acquiring the goods sold during an accounting period. That is, outlay cost refers to the expenses identified in the income, or profit and loss, statement of a firm's financial report.

Whether it applies to a consumer purchase or the cost and expense of acquiring goods sold for a business profit, outlay cost defines the monetary value of all disbursements involved in acquiring ownership of property that one expects to use either for personal benefit or for business profit. It is, therefore, a measure of the cost of acquiring the *utility value* of property, and hence not strictly applicable to the purchase of stocks and bonds, which have no utility value.

One could acquire the title of ownership of an automobile on the promise to pay, but one wouldn't really be free from the inconveniences and encumbrances of the former owner until one paid. Likewise, a baker has the free and unencumbered right to use the sugar he has purchased only after it has been paid for in full. Credit is only a convenience offered by his supplier, which allows him to use the sugar with a reduced initial outlay of funds. The cost of acquiring the utility value of property is really a function of the total outlay involved, irrespective of whether it comes from the purchaser or creditor.

Ultimately the calculation of outlay costs serves only two purposes. First, it serves as legal evidence that an acquitistion of property, with all the right to use it, has been made. Second, it allows calculation of the disbursement of funds so that one may know the extent to which one's revenues, or capital, have been diminished. Calculation of outlay costs is not very useful to the economist or anybody interested in determining which of two alternative purchases is better. This is because outlay cost measures only the sacrifice necessary for a purchase, not the benefit that may be expected from the purchase. Nor can it be used by a businessman in determining which of two projects will be more profitable.

Opportunity Cost

When an economist uses the concept of cost as a means for determining the benefits that are forgone in order to acquire a specific property, he is involved in analyzing opportunity costs. The purpose of calculating opportunity costs is to permit comparison between the costs of different opportunities. The concept is normally applied only to the acquisition of capital goods or financial capital. Comparative costs of consumer purchases are normally analyzed through the use of marginal and indifference analysis. (These concepts are discussed in some detail in Chapter 7.)

The opportunities relevant to an analysis of opportunity costs have to do with profit and not with psychological utility. A businessman will consider manufacturing nuts instead of bolts only if he expects an increase in revenues from this decision. Since his supply of capital will always be limited, he will have to forgo part of his production of bolts if he also wants to produce nuts. If he can make the assumption that his capital will yield 10 percent from producing bolts, he will not manufacture nuts, or anything else, unless he can expect a higher rate of return. We could say that his opportunity cost would be close to 10 percent. It may be higher or lower because there may be certain subjective considerations to which he may choose to ascribe some arbitrary value. For example, he may not want to borrow money or allocate his own funds to a new project which, though expected to be more profitable, would entail an additional risk.

Since opportunity cost refers to an investment in property which is expected to produce income, it is expressed not in terms of outlays but in terms of the expected profitability of the investments being compared. The profitability of different investment opportunities can be most conveniently compared in terms of their respective investment yields, or rate of return on investment. An opportunity cost thus is a ratio of an outlay cost to revenue, conveniently expressed as a percentage.

However, an opportunity cost must be applicable to at least two possible investment opportunities. At the very least one must have the choice between saving, or even hoarding, and investing in capital. If one had only the choice of saving at 5 percent or investing at 10 percent, one would probably choose to invest. Yet the opportunity cost involved is greater than 5 percent in this case, because one must take into account the additional risk the investor incurs when he opts for stock or bond ownership rather than saving.

The numerical value one applies to the risk inherent in investing is usually very subjective. It depends not only on the confidence with which the investment yield of a portfolio of stocks can be calculated but also on the current economic and political climate. One can, of course, delude oneself into thinking that the financial risk of investing can be anticipated according to some notion of objective probability. (In Chapter 7 we shall see to what extent actuarial risk differs from financial risk.) It is usually very difficult to take anything more than an arbitrary attitude toward financial risk. We hardly ever have all information at our disposal, nor is it always clear how we should use what little information we do have.

Since opportunity cost is concerned with the choice between at least two investment opportunities with differing ratios of profitability, it must also reflect the risk of diverting funds from one investment to another. Whatever statistical methods are used to calculate this risk, the resulting figure is essentially subjective and, to a great degree, arbitrary. Therefore, opportunity cost is best thought of as an arbitrary, ideal investment ratio against which specific, practical investment choices can be compared.

Opportunity Cost, Discount Rates, and Capital Outlay

Since we are primarily concerned with understanding the concept of opportunity cost as it may be used by a shareholder in determining his commitment to invest in common stock, it should be useful to distinguish it from other concepts that are often used synonymously.

The discount rate by which expected income is discounted to present value is often referred to as an opportunity cost. Sometimes this discount rate will be equivalent to the basic rate of interest one would expect to receive for short- or long-term government obligations. This is often referred to as the *risk-free rate of return*.

Sometimes the basic rate of interest may be adjusted to reflect the acceptance of risk. This adjustment for risk can be made either intuitively or on the basis of an actuarial analysis of the probability that the expected income will conform to actual income.[1] However, even if we decide to calculate the riskiness of investing by analyzing the frequency with which actual income has conformed to expected income in the past, there is no single well-established discount rate available for expressing risk. Thus it is difficult for the practical investor to account for risk through a constant risk-adjusted rate of discount.

Business economists, in speaking of the discount rate applied to future dividends, will sometimes refer to the *market rate of discount*. By this they mean the rate of interest that would equate the present value of future dividends with the market price of the stock.[2] In other words, the market rate of discount is equivalent to a market valuation of the opportunity cost of investing in a particular stock.

However, it is difficult to see how one can find the market rate of discount for Massey-Ferguson, for example, with a dividend of one dollar and a market price of twenty dollars. It is impossible to derive the market rate of discount with any certainty unless one also knows what the future value of these dividends will be for any specific, generally agreed-upon future period of time. Although one can and always does refer to the market rate of discount for a bond, it is nonsensical to use it in analyzing the rate of return from an investment in common stock.

However it is derived, the discount rate is not what I call an opportunity cost. It is what economists sometimes refer to as the *explicit cost of capital.*[3] The explicit cost of capital is equivalent to the rate of return by which the future income from an investment would have to be discounted to make this amount equal to the original cost of the investment. It is a way of measuring the returns that would be forgone if one were to liquidate the investment. Put another way, explicit cost of capital is the discount rate used to calculate the internal rate of return. However, it is not an opportunity cost, because it does not attempt to compare the rates of return of alternative investment possibilities.

Comparing the rates of return from different investment opportunities is equivalent to measuring the *implicit cost of capital*. The implicit cost of capital is equivalent to the highest rate of return that would have to be forgone in order to seize a particular investment opportunity. The notion of implicit capital cost is useful to management interested in determining the best financial decision it can make for a specific outlay of funds, provided there are alternative uses for the firm's funds.

Generally, management is interested in the implicit cost of capital in order to determine how best to use the firm's retained earnings as well as funds raised from outside the firm. In practice, however, management is likely to use this notion as a guideline rather than as a rigid financial tool. One may question, in fact, whether managements, in embarking upon a new adventure or the acquisition of the shares of another company, are invariably motivated by the desire for an optimum financial decision.

As it is generally understood, the concept of opportunity cost is associated with implicit rather than explicit capital costs. Its purpose is not to measure the rate of return of an investment but to establish the highest rate of return that can be derived from whatever possibilities for investment seem to exist. In this sense, the concept of opportunity cost is not as independent from the cost of real capital outlays as one might think. In their desire for measuring the profitability of alternative investments, economists tend to ignore outlay costs. They might insist, for instance, that it is economically more efficient to invest in

Project A with an expected return of 20 percent than in an alternative Project B with an expected return of only 10 percent, even if Project A requires an initial cash outlay of $1 million, compared to $100,000 for Project B. The amount of money spent sometimes appears to economists, especially when they are employed by government, to be less significant than the anticipated rate of return.

Yet, to a very real extent, the concept of opportunity cost defined as the implicit cost of capital is meaningful only when the possibilities for alternative investments are supported by the availability of actual funds that could be used for one of several investment alternatives. It is unrealistic to talk of opportunity costs when the opportunity to spend a specific amount does not exist. An analysis of the optimum allocation of funds can be a useful exercise in urging management to raise funds from the capital markets or from the sale of assets, but it cannot be applied blindly to the situation of the individual investor.

I am not trying to criticize the application of opportunity costs by management in its analysis of how it should best invest corporate funds. The analysis of explicit and implicit capital costs on the basis of financial ratios can be a very important tool in the hands of management. However, I am suggesting that the concept of opportunity cost that ought to be used by the shareholder in valuing his property cannot be derived by the same logic used by management for corporate investment decisions.

A shareholder can, of course, decide that an investment in Eastman Kodak at $40 per share is cheaper than an investment in Polaroid at $25 per share. He may also believe that Pabst is cheaper at $24 per share than Anheuser-Busch at the same price. These decisions may be based on an analysis of the return on book value and the relationship of market price to book value. At any one time, one of each of these pairs of alternative investments ought to be better than the other. However, an investor cannot derive his opportunity cost just from an analysis of market prices and financial statements, nor from his expectations of earnings or even return on book value. It may very well be that none of these investments satisfies his independent definition of what constitutes an opportunity.

Even if an investor had access to a computer readout of 1,000 stocks giving him an analysis of all the financial ratios he thinks relevant to his investment strategy, he still could not derive his opportunity cost from it. It may very well be that his estimate of opportunity cost is more, or perhaps less, than the implicit costs of the best investment opportunities available. For example, in 1972 he may have decided that the best return from a list of 20 investment possibilities selling at an earnings yield of 8 percent (a price-earnings ratio of 12.5) was insufficient for him to divert his funds from long-term bonds. In 1974 he may have concluded that although the earnings yield from these same stocks had risen to 12 percent, he still should not invest in common stock unless the earnings yield could exceed the 15 percent opportunity cost he then needed because of his anxiety over business conditions.

Since a shareholder's concept of opportunity cost cannot be derived from either the market price of stock or internal financial ratios (such as return on book value), it cannot be derived by an analysis of explicit or implicit capital costs. The analysis of capital costs, insofar as it attempts to define opportunity as an optimum investment decision, is of no practical value to the investor. Indeed, in valuing common stock there is no way of defining an optimum decision.

If the desire for optimality must be pursued, it ought to be restricted to the minimum rate of return an investor would need to divert his funds from short- or long-term obligations to investments in common stock. In this case it would become a measure of the extent to which funds ought to be diverted from other forms of financial capital. A shareholder's opportunity cost can serve as an indication of when he ought to invest in common stock rather than remain liquid. It ordinarily cannot serve as a basis for comparing the performance of the stocks already in his portfolio or for deciding whether or not to sell a specific stock.

The Subjective Nature of Opportunity Cost

Whatever else it may be for management, for a shareholder, opportunity cost is an expression of the sacrifice he must be prepared to make if he is to forgo the liquidity and relative safety of government and corporate obligations in favor of common-stock investments. This sacrifice is expressed, not in terms of the return of his money that he will actually have to forgo, but in terms of the minimum return he would expect from owning common stock.

The investor's preference for common stock may be based on certain calculations of risk, the discount rate, and his assessment of inflation and prospects for growth, but it cannot be derived from these calculations with any presumption of mathematical certainty. An investor who refuses to invest in common stock unless he can expect at least a 12 percent return on his cash outlay may justify this percentage in a variety of ways. He may say that the inflation rate is 7 percent and the treasury bill rate 5 percent. He may say that the corporate bonds yield 8 percent and he needs an additional 4 percent "risk premium" to accept the uncertainty of buying common stock. The number of possible rationalizations is endless.

A practical investor does not base his preference to invest in common stock on an analysis of the cost of capital. He does not try to determine the market rate of discount and invest in those stocks whose present value of future dividends is the highest. Indeed, he would look upon this approach to investing as just short of the ludicrous. He might very well purchase General Motors at $67 per share on the grounds that its current dividend yield of 9.5 percent satisfies his basic desire for a higher-than-average income from dividends. He would not calculate the present value of future dividends, because he knows that he has not much of a basis to assume that these dividends will continue to be paid out forever. He realizes the uncertainty of his decision, but he may also think that a 9.5 percent current dividend yield from one of the financially most solid corporations in the world is worth his commitment. He will not justify the validity of this investment solely on the basis that it offers the best available return exceeding the discount rate established by treasury bills or even General Motors' bonds. In other words, he will not analyze his opportunity cost solely in terms of his implicit cost of capital.

Even if an investor were to consider the price-earnings ratio as his most important criterion for evaluating investment opportunities (and in a later chapter I shall show why he should not base his primary expectations on this ratio), he is still not going to base his opportunity cost solely on the lowest price-earnings ratios available from comparable stocks. The fact that Levi-Strauss and Iowa Beef Packers are selling at lower price-earnings ratios than Collins & Aikman and Kane-Miller is not in itself sufficient for him to judge that they are "better" investments. A comparatively low price-earnings ratio may cause an investor to become interested in a stock, but it cannot provide the basic criterion for his investment decision.

If an analysis of the cost of capital seems to be so irrelevant to how a shareholder formulates his opportunity cost, why am I spending so much time discussing this issue? Wouldn't it be more to the point just to say that an analysis of cost of capital, while possibly contributing to management's understanding of how it could make an optimal financial decision, is useless to the individual shareholder? Perhaps. However, I think it is important to understand the widely accepted academic basis for valuing common stock. An investor ought to realize that what academicians say about valuing common stock is based on certain assumptions that are legally, economically, and empirically misleading.

The fundamental academic error, as we shall see, rests in the basic assumption that a shareholder's interests are identical to management's interests. A shareholder just cannot proceed to value his property on the simple presumption that management is doing all it can to maximize his wealth. Even if it were, this is not an assumption on which a responsible shareholder should base his expectation for increased wealth.

The Performance Cult

The days of the go-go, growth-oriented, performance-minded investment manager are gone forever—or so it seems. However, history sometimes has a tendency to repeat what we would most like to forget. I, for one, would like to forget the days when the investment community seemed dominated by men more interested in outperforming their competitors than in protecting their clients' money.

One might ask why business economists didn't warn the investment community of the dangers inherent in this performance cult. To some extent they did. The development of the theory of the efficient portfolio, the consequences of which we see today in the index funds, can be understood as such an attempt. Yet an index fund, while it does not try to outperform the market, is not really concerned with avoiding losses but only with avoiding losses in excess of general market losses. The criterion is still performance, albeit market performance.

Someone familiar with the academic literature would have realized that business economists didn't issue the warning they perhaps should have because they too are subject to a performance cult. The name of this performance cult is the *optimal financial decision.* By this business economists mean a decision with the promise of the highest profit, taking into account only those elements of risk that are reducible to actuarial principles.

It is fairly easy to see that the desire for an optimal financial decision can be useful to a businessman contemplating buying or building a new plant. It is not so evident how it can be of use to the shareholder. A shareholder doesn't make financial decisions that affect the value of the corporation's property. He does not decide to build plants or increase product price. However much he may think he knows about running a corporation's business more profitably than management, he can't do anything about it other than taking over control and ousting management.

How, then, can business economists believe that a shareholder is able to make an optimal financial decision—that is, a decision that will maximize his wealth? Quite simply, they equate the interests and objectives of management and shareholders. This identification is accomplished by the "maximization of shareholder wealth" theory that we have examined in the preceding chapter. This is the theory of value that provides the basis for most of the discussion about the cost of capital developed by business economists today.

The "maximization of shareholder wealth" theory

In its most general form, the maximization of shareholder wealth theory pretends to be a theory of the firm. As such it tries to encompass three distinct value concepts: the value of management's decisions in maximizing income, the value of the corporate enterprise itself, and the value of a shareholder's claim on income. Although business economists normally emphasize one or another of these objectives over the rest, most are confused in the discussion of the three objectives.

Myron Gordon begins his now-classic book on *Investment, Financing, and Valuation of the Corporation* with a restatement of this theory: "In neoclassical theory the objective of the firm is to maximize its value: the value of a firm is a function of its future income, and its future income is a function of its investment. With knowledge of these two functions, the value of the firm may be predicted, given its investment; and given its value maximization behavior rule, its investment may be predicted."[4] (In this context, the word *firm* refers to the corporation as an enterprise, but it also refers to management's use of the enterprise; the word *investment* refers to the outlay costs involved.)

The maximization of shareholder wealth theory is stated primarily as a theory of entrepreneurial behavior. However, it is claimed that it can also be used as a theory of valuation by shareholders, as long as shareholders discount the firm's future income by a discount rate allowing for risk.[5] This would imply that one of the major differences between the valuation processes used by shareholders and by management rests in the discount rate each uses to determine the present value of future corporate income. Presumably an investor's discount rate, or opportunity cost, should always be higher because of the element of risk.

Proponents of this theory sometimes suggest that shareholders should be engaged in valuing only dividends, not total corporate income. Even in this restricted version, however, the theory claims that the value of future dividends can be determined only if it is assumed that management will maximize the dividend payments to shareholders. Even economists who assume that "the value of a share of stock is the discounted present value of the dividends expected to be paid to the owners of that share"[6] feel that this assumption can only be made on the further, more basic assumption that the *objective* of management is to "maximize the value of the firm to its stockholders."[7]

The maximization postulate enjoys the support of most economists even if they do not agree about what management is trying to maximize. Some say it ought to be concerned with maximizing current earnings. Others say future earnings. Some say earnings before depreciation, taxes, or interest expense. Others say after one or all of these.[8] But almost no economist rejects this theory entirely.[9]

The "satisficing" theory

There are some economists who realize that management is not always concerned with maximization of the firm's value. Management may define its optimum financial decisions as those which will enable it to maintain a satisfactory share of the market it believes it is functioning in. This theory was first referred to as the "satisficing" theory of value by Herbert Simon.[10]

Basically, this theory tries to establish the value of the firm not as a function of the highest profits attainable by management but as a function of maintaining a capital structure that will enable the firm to perpetuate its competitive strength and historic profit margins. Management will try to make not the best decisions but those which will be sufficient to maintain the status quo of the company. The satisficing theory of the firm could be interpreted, I suppose, as a realistic explanation of the behavior of corporate bureaucracy. However, even though it may offer valuable insights into the typical behavior of management, it is useless if we are interested in determining the value of the firm to stockholders.

I have no reason to dispute the maximization theory of value when it is applied to understanding the optimum financial decision of management in defining its cost of capital. However, it should be clear by now that I find little merit in the use of this theory to help a shareholder value his property.

"Maximization of shareholder satisfaction"

In one of its variants, the maximization theory proposes that just as management's purpose is to maximize the economic welfare of the firm's owners, the shareholder's valuation is based on his desire to "maximize his satisfaction."[11] This view is misleading on two accounts. First the definition of "satisfaction" will differ between shareholders.

One may prefer a higher dividend. Another may prefer higher retained earnings, as we have seen in the preceding chapter. Second, as I have repeatedly pointed out, it is not very prudent for a shareholder to assume that he can always equate his interests with management's interests. For one thing, the corporate property, which has only exchange value for the shareholder, has at least utility value for management.

If a shareholder indeed is involved in maximizing his wealth or satisfaction, he doesn't also have to presume that management has the same objective. All he has to care about is that the price he has paid for his shares is cheap according to his own standards. What possible sense does it make to invest in IBM, General Motors, or Avon solely on the belief that their managements are engaged in maximizing wealth? It would be far more reasonable not to make this presumption—or even assume a "satisficing" theory—and buy the shares at a price one believes to be cheap enough. After all, it is perfectly possible that the shares of a corporation whose management is known to be stodgy and overly conservative may make as good an investment opportunity as the shares of an aggressive, performance-minded corporation—as long as the price is right! Indeed, the theory of maximization has given credence to the performance cult in one important aspect: that purchase price paid is only relevant as long as the selling price is higher.

Perhaps another way of understanding the reliance of business economists on the maximization theory is to see it as their attempt to provide a basis for forecasting the price of common stock. Forecasting would tend to lose much of its validity if shareholders assumed that management is not actively engaged in maximizing earnings or dividends.

It is disturbing to be exposed to a theory of valuation that accepts the postulate that management is engaged in maximizing shareholder wealth as defined by market price. If there is one aspect of the firm's economic behavior over which management does not have much control, it is the market price of its shares. Why then should a shareholder define the value of his property according to that aspect of economic behavior over which management is relatively powerless?

The maximization theory of the firm denies the endocratic nature of the modern business corporation. That is, it ignores the fundamental conflict between the value concepts of shareholder and management. This, as we have seen in the preceding chapter, is a dangerous oversight, and it is the primary reason for the invalidity of the theory.

Opportunity Cost and Gordon's Valuation Model

I have emphasized that the concept of a shareholder's opportunity cost cannot be derived from the financial structure of the corporation whose stock is being considered for purchase. Opportunity cost is not a function of the company's income and growth patterns, nor is it related to the firm's cost of capital. Rather, it is a subjective figure based on the individual's confidence in the economy and his willingness to assume financial risks.

Myron Gordon has constructed a simple stock-valuation model essentially based on four variables:

r = the return on the corporation's invested capital
b = the fraction of income retained by the corporation
Y = the current earnings per share of the corporation
k = the rate of return investors require on their shares (analogous to *opportunity cost*)

The model presupposes that only future dividends and earnings can be used by the investor in establishing the theoretical price of a firm's shares. Futhermore, Gordon assumes that the model also serves as a model of the firm itself, since what is of value to the investor should equally be of value to the firm.

Gordon states that the dividend D at any period t is defined by

$$D_t = (1 - b)Y_t$$

He then asserts[12] that the value (or price) P of a share of stock at any time period t should be computed according to the formula

$$P_t = \frac{(1 - b)Y_t}{k - rb}$$

which by definition is equivalent to

$$P_t = \frac{D_t}{k - rb}$$

In other words, the price an investor should put on a share of stock is equal to the current dividend divided by the dividend yield investors require on their shares, where the required dividend yield corresponds to the difference between opportunity cost (k) and the dividend growth rate (rb).

It is obvious that for this model to work, k must always be greater than rb, or the stock price derived from the equation will be totally meaningless. Indeed, although it would appear that the opportunity cost k cannot be derived from the financial behavior of the corporation, Gordon attempts to show that k must in some fashion act as a function of rb. This is necessary for him not only because he must ensure that k is always greater than rb, but also because he assumes that k can serve as both the investor's opportunity cost and the firm's cost of capital. This assumption, as I have shown, is not only unnecessary but also unwarranted.

To use his theory as an investment model of the firm, Gordon solves his equation for k, as follows:[13]

$$k = \frac{D_t}{P_t} + rb$$

In other words, k, as the corporation's cost of capital, is equal to the dividend yield (D/P) plus the dividend growth rate. Thus, as long as the dividend yield is greater than zero, k, by this formula, must be greater than rb.

The kind of dubious results Gordon's theory can produce when it is used as a valuation model for the shareholder rather than as an investment model for the firm can be readily illustrated by applying his formula to a real company. Consider Avon, for instance, with D = \$2.20, r = 29.3 percent, and b = 33 percent. If we assume an opportunity cost k of 10 percent, the theoretical stock price becomes practically meaningless:

$$P_t = \frac{\$2.20}{10\% - (29.3\% \times 33\%)} = \frac{\$2.20}{.002} = \$939$$

Applying this approach to stocks like McDonald's, where D = 0.15 cents, r = 21 percent, and b = 96 percent, would yield equally meaningless results unless we are ready to choose an opportunity cost large enough to offset the inherent flaws of the model. But if we are forced to derive a different opportunity cost for each company on the basis of its dividend yield and dividend growth rate, the concept of opportunity cost can no longer serve the investor's need to compare available investment opportunities. Opportunity cost would become a matter of compliance and not choice.

Opportunity Cost and the Price-Earnings Ratio

The reader may reasonably ask why opportunity cost should be such an important concept for a shareholder to use in valuation if hardly anybody in the investment community refers to it. Even if it is an arbitrary number differing between investors, this would seem insufficient to explain the general indifference to this concept.

Perhaps a partial explanation for the obscurity of this concept is the traditional reliance of the investor on the price-earnings ratio. The P/E ratio has fulfilled the needs of the investment community, at least for the past twenty years, to understand opportunity cost.

Business economists have occasionally even tried to use the P/E ratio, or some variant of it, for determining what the implicit cost of capital ought to be for management.[14] This use of the P/E ratio stems from a desire to arrive at an opportunity cost for future investments that is not entirely determined by the firm's financial structure but to some extent is based on shareholders' expectations, which may influence the cost of capital.

Managements have sometimes tried to use the P/E ratio as a justification for its investment decisions to its shareholders. For example, when Control Data bought Commercial Credit Corporation, the prevailing attitude was that the purchase of a company with a low P/E ratio by a company with a high P/E ratio would tend to considerably increase the P/E ratio of the former.

Management has always seemed to be particularly attracted to using the high P/E ratio on its shares as a justification for purchasing control of a company with a lower P/E ratio. On the other hand, management will also use a low P/E ratio on its stock as a justification for repurchasing part or all of it back. In other words, in defending its decision to purchase common stock, whether or not for control, management has usually used the P/E ratio as it has seen fit and not as an implicit, derived cost of capital.

The P/E ratio has been used by investors as a substitute for opportunity cost. Who hasn't heard the refrain, "This stock is cheap; it's selling at only ten times earnings, and all the other companies in the industry are selling above fifteen times next year's earnings." In fact, however, the P/E ratio is a very poor measure of opportunity, especially if it is above ten. Somehow stocks with low P/E ratios have tended to perform better than those with high P/E ratios.[15]

There are many reasons why an investor should not use the P/E ratio as a measure of his opportunity cost. (We will discuss the price-earnings ratio in more detail in Chapter 6.)

First, the P/E ratio is a measure of what other people will pay for realized or expected earnings. Thus it defines an opportunity solely on the basis of how the market has defined it. Second, although it may be used to define opportunities within a specific industry, it usually cannot be used to compare opportunities between industries, which may have widely divergent ROE ratios. Third, it defines an opportunity by comparing current or expected earnings only to market price and not to return on book value. Since earnings are considered without reference to previously retained earnings, the ultimate criterion of value is market price. Fourth, it fails to relate an opportunity to the sacrifice one must make to invest in common stock. For example, if we require a 10 percent return in order to invest, a stock selling at five times earnings may still not satisfy this requirement. It may very well be that the company's return on equity is only 5 percent.

Perhaps the principal reason for the obscurity surrounding the concept of a shareholder's opportunity cost is the lack of any generally accepted shareholder criterion of value other than current or expected earnings and market price. We have seen some of the limitations of market price as an indicator of stock value in Chapter 4. The issue of earnings and their questionable significance for valuation will be taken up in more detail in Chapter 6.

The Proper Meaning of Opportunity Cost

How then are we to establish a specific opportunity cost against which we can measure the value of an investment?

First, we must recognize that a shareholder's opportunity cost is not a function of the corporation's cost of capital. It is not derived from the financial structure of any company he may wish to invest in. If anything, it is derived from the state of confidence he is able to maintain in the general economic conditions. To this extent a shareholder's opportunity cost is a function of his belief in being able to make long-term commitments.

In our context, "long-term" is a difficult expression to define. It can be one year or five. It is, of course, dependent on the capital resources of the investor. It is an indication, so to speak, of his staying power—that is, his ability to resist consuming his savings. Theoretically, institutional investors ought to have the greatest staying power. Practically, their conduct for the past 20 years has shown anything but this. As David Dreman has pointed out in his recent book, ***Psychology and the Stock Market***, institutional investors are no less subject to the rapidly changing fashions in investment attitudes than anybody else.[16]

Second, an investor must be able to express his opportunity cost to reflect the extent of the sacrifice he makes in forgoing alternative opportunities for investing his savings. These alternatives will include many financial instruments, not just common stock. Generally his opportunity cost will be greater than the yield for long-term bonds of a quality or "rating" comparable to the stocks in which he is interested. I say "generally" because it is conceivable that his opportunity cost is lower, especially if he believes inflation will reduce the value of debt more than that of equity. Obviously, the opportunity cost will always be greater than the return from short-term obligations. Today I do not see how any investor could accept an opportunity cost of less than 8 to 10 percent for investing in common stock. How much more will depend on the needs of the individual investor and his assessment of the economic and political uncertainties of the times.

In calculating a shareholder's opportunity cost, the error is sometimes made of adding up all the possible costs of all the sacrifices that are made. Using such a procedure, one might arrive at the following calculation:

10% base cost (equivalent to 6% yield from tax-free A-rated bond)
2% risk premium
1% transaction costs (broker's fees)
5% loss in value due to inflation
18% total opportunity cost

Although an 18 percent yield might be the minimum return a shareholder desires from a common-stock investment, this figure is clearly too far out of line with the yields that may reasonably be expected from alternative financial instruments. In other words, opportunity cost is not a wholly arbitrary figure but must provide a realistic measure of the sacrifice of forgoing alternative investments.

In a *Fortune* magazine article, Warren Buffet argued that inflation is diminishing the value of the 12 percent average rate of return on book value that corporate equities have tended to generate in the past.[17] He seems to believe that it would be unwise to invest in stocks at book value if their return on equity is less than 12 percent. However, he also implies that opportunities still exist if we will seek stocks yielding considerably more, I suppose in the vicinity of 20 percent.

Although there are many opportunities for investing in stocks whose current market price could justify a yield of 20 percent or more, I do not think that one ought to adopt this high a yield as an opportunity cost. One ought to adopt it only as an objective. In general, one should adopt an opportunity cost with which one can live in good times and bad. An opportunity cost ought to provide an investor with the minimum rate of return that will continue to satisfy his criterion for investing in common stock.

Some investors may feel more comfortable adopting high opportunity costs in times of great economic anxiety and low opportunity costs in times of increased confidence and prosperity. Unless one's foresight of the business cycle is very sharp indeed, this approach cannot be recommended. To lower opportunity costs continually as the market becomes more bullish is to court disaster. (Perhaps one of the best indicators that the market is overbought is if the expectancy values of the equities in a portfolio, based on a predetermined opportunity cost, are appreciably lower than their market prices.) On the other hand, to increase opportunity costs continually in a bearish market may be to forsake genuine opportunities.

Furthermore, even if the business cycle could be predicted with reasonable accuracy, few investors are flexible enough to be in or out of the market at the right time. Thus, even if an investor wishes to change his opportunity cost, he must set it in such a way that it will be compatible with his long-term investment objectives.

In Chapter 8 we will discuss how a shareholder ought to structure his expectations so as to maintain a continuing state of satisfaction from his investments. One of the main prerequisites for being able to maintain a minimum level of satisfaction is choosing an opportunity cost that will be high enough to justify forsaking the benefits from non-equity financial instruments and low enough to enable the investor to choose among a reasonable number of alternative stock investments. That is, I am taking a "satisficing" attitude, so to speak, to the formulation of opportunity costs. The optimal financial decision for a prudent investor is not that decision which promises the highest rewards but the one that will assure him of the greatest number of alternatives for investing, for it is primarily by assuring oneself of continuing alternatives that one can protect oneself against the greatest losses.

An opportunity cost, then, really should reflect a minimum acceptable return rather than a maximum possible return. Practically, this means that a minority shareholder should probably be satisfied with an opportunity cost between 10 percent and 12 percent, even though he may not wish to consider making any initial investment yielding less than about 20 percent. I should again emphasize that the actual yield figure an investor uses will be arbitrary to the extent that it reflects his relative confidence in the general economy and in the investment opportunities available to him.

In determining the yield an investor will use as his opportunity cost, there are two practical considerations that should be kept in mind.

First, as I have pointed out, the investor must be prepared to abide by whatever yield he chooses. An opportunity cost should reflect the shareholder's long-term investment commitment. It can be a very costly and self-defeating attitude to lower one's opportunity cost as the market appears to become more definitely bullish. Similarly, increasing an opportunity cost after the market turns decidedly bearish is not particularly conducive to maintaining a happy state of affairs. Once an opportunity cost has been accepted, it cannot easily be reinterpreted, unless one wishes to float on bubbles of confusion.

Second, only one opportunity cost can be posited for a portfolio of common stocks. It would be self-defeating to have a different opportunity cost for each different stock or group of common stocks. There is no reason why the opportunity cost of investing in computer or fast-food stocks ought to be any different from the opportunity cost for machine tool or textile companies. To adopt a multitude of opportunity costs would be to deny the minority shareholder's power to choose from a wide range of opportunities. If the price is right and the market exists (and if capital gains are not a consideration), there is no reason why any investment should not be substituted for any other that promises more.

This is not to say that different opportunity costs cannot be assigned to different kinds of portfolios or investment objectives. An equity portfolio primarily geared to generating dividend income might not be based on the same opportunity cost as a portfolio for which dividend income is not the main concern. However, the practice of applying a different opportunity cost to each stock within a specific portfolio in my view is a great mistake. In determining an opportunity cost, the primary concern is not to take account of short-term price fluctuations of specific stocks but to establish a reasonable basis for comparing available investment opportunities.

Used intelligently, a shareholder's opportunity cost can become a powerful instrument for defining investment objectives and ordering expectations. Obviously, the use of an opportunity cost presupposes that the investor has an independent criterion of value. An opportunity cost is useless to anybody who believes that the market price of common stock is identical to its intrinsic value. It is also useless to anybody who believes that the purpose of valuation is to predict the price of common stock within a specific period of time.

Generally, when anticipated earnings become the main criterion of value, independently of the capital and retained earnings that make these earnings possible, no proper use of opportunity cost is possible. Specifically, one will never be able to determine whether an investment is over- or underpriced. Even if the investor's earnings forecast is correct and leads to an accurate prediction of market price (and in Chapter 6 we shall see that these two things do not necessarily go together), forecasting still is not concerned with establishing a criterion of value that justifies the ownership of common stock.

Conclusion

In the preceding chapter we have seen that the basic principle of common-stock valuation is expectancy, which was defined as an expectation about the exchange value of an investment. The concept of expectancy is intrinsically related to the concept of opportunity cost; one is irrelevant without the other. Since the criterion for prudence is dependent on the formation of a reasonable expectancy value, it should be evident that the investor's ability to form prudent investment decisions is grounded in his definition of opportunity cost.

Opportunity cost, as we have seen, is a largely arbitrary, ideal investment ratio against which specific investment choices can be compared. As applied to common stock, it generally measures the sacrifice of forgoing the liquidity and safety of government or corporate obligations. Although it may involve various calculations of risk, discount rates, growth prospects, and other factors, it ultimately is a subjective value and cannot be derived with any mathematical certainty.

In summary, I have tried to show that an opportunity cost

- Must be based on at least two alternative investment opportunities.
- Must reflect the investor's confidence in the investment yield and in the general economy.
- Is not a direct function of the corporation's explicit or implicit cost of capital.
- Should not be based on P/E ratios.
- Should be the same for an entire investment portfolio rather than differ for each stock considered.
- Should reflect a long-term investment commitment and thus be chosen so as to avoid having to change it frequently.
- Should be high enough to justify forgoing the benefits of non-equity financial instruments, but low enough to provide an adequate choice among alternative investment opportunities.

If used in conjunction with an intelligent interpretation of financial information (see the following chapter), opportunity cost can provide a meaningful basis for comparing investment alternatives and ordering the shareholder's expectations.

6

Information

Over 40 years ago Berle and Means summarized the essential functions of the securities markets as the maintenance of a free market, the disclosure of all information so as to permit a continuous appraisal of value, and the provision of liquidity.[1] We have already examined the first and last of these two market functions, and we have seen to what extent the securities industry has attempted to interpret and define them. However, we have not examined the second, even though it provides the very basis for the freeness and liquidity of our market. Information—its disclosure, dissemination, and interpretation—determines the market's efficiency as an economic instrument of a free society.

The American Plan

Our securities market is a unique phenomenon in this modern industrial world, and a good measure of its uniqueness is a direct consequence of the value our government and business place on the availability of information. Anybody who has ever tried to buy capital stock in any of the financial capitals outside the United States, whether in Europe or Latin America, knows that not only the conduct but the purpose of the majority of these markets are fundamentally different from our own. This fundamental difference is in great part due to the kind and quality of information available to buyers and sellers of capital. It is also due to the very nature and concept of incorporation outside the United States. The corporate revolution initiated by our judiciary as a consequence of its interpretation of the Fourteenth Amendment has no exact counterpart in the rest of the industrial world. Outside the United States the big public corporation is still largely a relic of medieval sovereign power testifying to the privileged relationship between management and government.

The American corporation, conceived as a sovereign right of the American people and not of the American government, is a unique expression of our concern for the right of the individual to own property, transact business, and buy and sell. Despite ever increasing government regulation and intervention, there is no government participation. Some of our new, radical economists, in advocating greater government participation in corporate life for the betterment of the public welfare, are also advocating the abolishment or curtailment of the traditionally adversary relationship between the business corporation and our government. Though there may be collusion between our government and business on the political level, this is a collaboration between two sovereign beings. Our big public corporations may have the political power to act as states albeit without nationality, but their power is nevertheless the consequence of their industrial and marketing capacity and not of government largesse.

Whatever the real consequences may be of Galbraith's much-disputed concept of countervailing power, I think we must realize that the American corporation thrives best where there is dissension between it and government and labor.[2] Dissension is the prerequisite for negotiation, that is, for a transaction in which two beings with equal rights reduce their mutual expectations in the process of reaching an agreement.

In Chapter 2 we discussed the *Dartmouth College* case of 1819, which established that a corporation's right to contract cannot be impaired by any sovereign political body. In its subsequent decisions, the Supreme Court, pursuant to the enactment of the Fourteenth Amendment of 1868, defined the corporation as a legal person enjoying the same rights of negotiation and transaction of business as the individual. The implications of these important decisions, though generally well understood, are apparently often forgotten.[3] A corporation may be a creature of the law, but it is not a creature of the government. Our government is itself in large measure subservient to the laws emanating from the Court's interpretation of the Constitution.

One just cannot rigorously maintain, for example, that because a corporation pays approximately half its pretax earnings to the federal government in taxes, it is in fact in partnership with the government, and that big business therefore is an instrument of government, or vice versa. Although the two may act together, as they have so often in the past, they do so essentially out of conflict, as equal adversaries under the law having to negotiate the terms of their relationship.

When the government collects taxes, it is not acting as a medieval sovereign exacting payment for the monopoly right of usufruct. It is acting as a collecting agent for the general public. Consequently, the amount of taxes a corporation must pay is the result of an evaluation of the corporate property and earnings "as between taxpayers."[4] The federal government does not exact a tax based on what it thinks a corporation should pay for the privilege of conducting its business. Socialism, of course, has every right to this privilege, being the *de facto* legal heir to the medieval right of sovereignty formerly vested in monarchy.

The federal government's right to tax is expressed as a claim on earnings, and it is in this respect that it is similar to a stockholder's claim. But because the government's claim cannot be bought or sold or exchanged against other capital claims, it is not a property and, hence, not a capital right. This distinction may appear superfluous, but in fact it is not. Since the government, upon due receipt of taxes, abandons its claims on the retained earnings of a corporation, it has effectively abandoned all claim to the management and exchange value of corporate property. Our government is not itself capitalist, as it were, but exists for the protection of those who are. It would perhaps not be inappropriate to recall the view taken by our Founding Fathers, who considered the function of government not as the provision of the greatest good but as the avoidance of the greatest evil. And the greatest evil was—and some still think it is—the use of sovereign power to curtail negotiation and transaction of business.

Europe's lack of comprehension of the nature of the American industrial corporation is evidenced by the widespread confusion of American political and military power with corporate power. As nations with varying degrees of nostalgia for the monarchies to which they all owe historical allegiance, they cannot readily accept the notion that American corporate sovereignty is independent from and opposed to the sovereignty of the federal government.

For example, Jean-Jacques Servan-Schreiber, in his notorious book *Le Défi Américain,* attributed the success and power of the American corporation in Europe not only to the organizational genius of the American firm but also to its collusion with and dependence on the federal government.[5] For him, the economic power that IBM wields in France is a direct consequence of government subsidization through the granting of exclusive contracts, and of government intervention in its internal affairs. That IBM is but an instrument of the federal government, to which it owes its economic and legal legitimacy, is merely an extension of his view of the relation of the big European corporation with its sovereign parent. He was unable to understand the source of the power of the American corporation, because he could not understand the source of its legitimacy. He didn't realize that the source of IBM's monopoly or oligopoly power is not dependent on the federal government's benevolent and interested bestowal of sovereignty over the manufacture and sale of computers, but on IBM's ability and authority to create and maintain this power through the support of the financial community in the face of legitimate opposition by the government.

Though IBM has entered into contracts with the United States, it has negotiated these contracts with the full force of its own independent legitimacy. IBM has been criticized and sometimes sued for its abuse of power. But I don't think IBM's critics and enemies would insist that the responsibility for its possible abuse of power should be shared by the federal government as co-conspirator. Although IBM has always benefited from large defense subsidies, it is still an independent company. Therefore, its legitimacy is fundamentally different from that of its French competition, which is at least partially owned by the French government, either directly or through government-owned banks.

Supplying Information—A Question of Self-Interest

If the American corporation is set apart from foreign firms by virtue of its essentially autonomous position in relation to government, its legitimacy is largely earned by management's disclosure of information to shareholders. How, why, and to what extent this is done is one of the features that distinguishes private from public corporations.

For a private corporation, disclosure of information is required but once a year, when it files its tax reports with the federal and local governments. Of course, if it is operating as a regulated business, such as a public utility, brokerage house, or investment adviser, it may also have to supply the information necessary to assure the government bureaucracies that it is indeed complying with the nature of the public service it is supposed to be providing. As a nonregulated business, a private corporation fulfills its public purpose by filing and paying its taxes. A private corporation doesn't have to provide its shareholders with any other information except insofar as this information would materially affect the decision of a shareholder to buy or sell.

The logic is evident. Since the public is not involved, management, as long as it pays its taxes, can do as it pleases. The legitimacy of a private corporation is based on the close relationship between management and shareholder, which is usually assumed to exceed the contract between the two stipulated in the articles of incorporation.

It would be a mistake to believe that the concern for the disclosure of information by a public corporation has arisen solely from the shareholder's feeling of remoteness from management and his inability to control it adequately. This concern developed, rather, out of the desire to maintain confidence in a truly public market for corporate securities.[6] The self-regulation of the securities industry depends on the assumption that the level of public confidence necessary for the maintenance of a free market (though not necessarily of a fair and orderly market) can be provided only if the public, whether composed of shareholders or not, is supplied with all the information necessary to form a value judgment.

Information must, of course, provide all pertinent facts concerning supply and demand, price and volume. But market information, which is concerned primarily with the conduct of a fair and orderly market, is not all the information that is required. Market information is supplied by the exchanges and not by the corporation; it is the responsibility of the market and not the corporation. No securities market can exist without the rapid disclosure and dissemination of information. The effectiveness of this information is a testament to the efficiency and public purpose of the stock market, but it is not a test of the legitimacy of the public corporation itself. Consequently, market information can never be used in and of itself as a source of public confidence. Otherwise we would have to say that the level of public confidence would remain unaffected whether the Dow-Jones Industrial Average is at 500 or 1,000. Confidence in the legitimacy and efficiency of the public market is dependent not only on the rapid disclosure of price information by the marketplace but also on the disclosure by the corporation of information relating to its finances and business prospects.

Social Responsibility versus Business Utility

Although the disclosure of information by the corporation is made primarily for the benefit of its shareholders, its dissemination benefits the public at large, whether or not intending to become shareholders. In particular, such information may be used to question the legitimacy of the corporation and its right to make a profit for its shareholders when the pursuit of this right may be in conflict with the interests of the public at large.

The basic argument is that since the public corporation is using the country's natural resources—whatever these may be and however much it may have paid for them—it is in some measure accountable to the public for how these resources are used. Does Johns-Manville, for example, have the right to abuse the land, pollute the waters, and cause a potential health hazard in its production of asbestos? Does Standard Oil of California have the right to pollute the shore line of California? Even when privately owned, natural resources such as land and water may in a sense be held to be public.

Advocates of this view contend that the potential damages caused by the misuse of private property can far exceed the costs justified by the right of ownership and thus should be subject to legislative control. The owner of private property can so misuse it that he may not only damage it beyond recovery to its natural state but also inflict comparable damage to the environment which he does not own. The courts have been continuously involved in interpreting these damages and in imposing restrictions on the use to which private property can be submitted. However, these restrictions, imposed upon the utility of private property for the sake of health, conservation, or other public purpose, are not peculiar to the big public corporation but apply to all owners of property.

The legitimacy of the public corporation, then, is not really a consequence of the uses to which it puts its own property but a consequence of its function as a going business. Its legitimacy as a going business is based less on management's social responsibility than on its ability to make a profit. After all, corporate property has a value to its public shareholder only to the extent that it produces profits. The accumulation of property without expectation of profits, socially responsible as it may be, is not the prerogative of the management of the public corporation.

The distinction between corporate utility and responsibility has been clarified admirably by James Willard Hurst, who showed its importance for corporate legitimacy.[7] One may question the corporation's response to government, labor, the environment, women and minorities, and foreign dictatorships; but if one admits that efficient production is usually better accomplished by corporate management, with all its possible abuses of economic power, rather than by government bureaucracy, it is difficult to deny the basic legitimacy of the corporation. To forsake utility for social responsibility would be to reject the modern corporation as the essential business vehicle without having a viable alternative other than perhaps government.

The increasingly popular tendency to interpret the legitimacy of corporate power in terms of its social responsibility as well as its business utility will probably take the form of new legislation. It is interesting to note, however, that sometimes legislation taken on account of the public purpose has actually had the effect of benefiting the business utility of the larger corporations involved. For example, the anti-pollution legislation to which the paper manufacturing industry has been subject has actually increased the oligopolistic strength of the larger, more established companies that were able to afford the required capital investment. It appears that this legislation, in concentrating almost exclusively on the social responsibility of the corporation, has forsaken the right of the smaller corporations to exist for the sake of making a profit.

What is disturbing about this form of response is that it attempts to establish by law what could perhaps be just as well accomplished through negotiation with each individual company. While law can hope to control social responsibility, it cannot control business utility. In a sense, such a legislative approach implies a renewal of government control or sovereignty over the corporation which our judiciary saw fit to reject a hundred years ago.

The concept of the legitimacy of the public corporation has been interpreted quite differently by our judicial branch of government. Through the Securities and Exchange Commission, it has consistently maintained that it is the disclosure of information which is the main source of corporate legitimacy. As James Willard Hurst put it, "The SEC emphasized disclosure as the prime instrument to hold private power to useful and responsible roles."[8]

Of course, the Securities and Exchange acts are a series of laws enacted by Congress. Yet the interpretation of these laws has been left, as it should be, to the judiciary. The result has been the principle of self-regulation, which is nothing more than the confirmation of the principle that the country is better served by a public market in which industry has the possibility of negotiating with government rather than having to comply with a series of injunctions. The SEC is concerned with the relation of the public to the business corporation. It recognizes that information is the only vehicle that can render this relation meaningful and reasonable.

Even the organization of the public into citizens' committees for developing public consciousness of possible abuses of social responsibility by management is not directly aimed at control, although such committees are usually formed with some hope of influencing legislation. It is recognized that only the government has the authority to enforce what these committees feel is the public interest. Thus the main purpose of these committees is to collect, interpret, disclose, and disseminate the information they feel the public at large has been deprived of, even though it may theoretically have access to this information. The assumption is that if the public knows all the facts, it will be able to decide for itself. Information will provide the knowledge on which a value judgment can be made.

Information, then, is essential not only for maintaining a fair and orderly market but also for enabling the public to determine the social responsibility of particular industries and corporations. Only information can provide the basis for alternative judgments, for conflict and dissent, and for the negotiation of dissident expectations that will ultimately be resolved in the formulation of a social policy. While this policy will probably fulfill nobody's expectations completely, it should to some extent satisfy everybody.

In our society the determination of the public welfare is not the exclusive right of government's sovereignty but a consequence of the individual's sovereign right to receive and interpret information. Information is not merely part of the procedure by which the public welfare is determined; it is its very substance. Perhaps the bewilderment of the European press over the consternation and anguish that the Watergate scandal produced in the United States is explained by its lack of understanding of the value Americans place on the disclosure and dissemination of information.

The Public's Claim on Information

Whereas the preoccupation with the social responsibility of the business corporation is ultimately the result of the relationship between management and government, concern for the legitimacy of business as a public corporation is ultimately based on its relation with its shareholders. This relation is essentially one of information. Ensuring the availability of all relevant information is the primary purpose of the Securities and Exchange acts, and it also is the main function of the securities exchanges. Today liquidity and a free market seem to be provided by the market as a whole rather than any particular exchange.

Despite claims to the contrary,[9] we have seen that a shareholder does not really own any of the capital assets to which his shares, at best, give him a residual claim. He doesn't own any of the "means of production," quite simply because these means are owned by the corporation and can only be utilized by management. His ownership is limited to his right to receive dividends and buy and sell his shares. As a shareholder he has no power to use the assets of the corporation. He can only exercise control to the extent that he can elect directors who may disagree with and, to some extent, change management. All a shareholder owns is a claim on corporate earnings, and all this claim gives him is a continuing right to information on what the assets of the corporation consist of and what management has done and is doing with them in order to produce earnings.

The rights involved in the ownership of common stock are extremely egalitarian. No purchaser of 10,000 shares of IBM, for example, can demand that he be treated any differently from other shareholders. He can demand no rights to which other shareholders are not entitled, no matter how large his stockholdings. He can only demand that he receive all the information necessary for him to maintain a continually valid judgment about the worth of his shares. He cannot even demand this information personally if it exceeds the guidelines and prerequisites established by the SEC.

A shareholder of publicly traded shares, then, can be privy to no contract not equally binding on other shareholders. The extent of his contractual relation with the corporation is, so to speak, limited by the quantity and quality of information it is obligated to furnish him. Indeed, one of the principal causes of costly stockholders' suits is information that is deficient, defective, or misleading.

A shareholder is not the only one entitled to receive information about the company in which he owns stock. The public at large has virtually the same right. Indeed, a person holding no stock is assured that he can know as much as an owner, and at the same time. This is the sense in which the securities market is a genuinely public market. Unlike the commodity markets, the securities markets are engaged not only in buying and selling, but in providing the information necessary for the independent evaluation of securities. The very existence of the stock market is predicated on the necessity of information and on the possibility that this information will be used in the evaluation of the price of a stock. To put it differently, the information provided by securities markets is based on the necessary difference—in theory if not always in fact—between market price and exchange value.

Public access to information provides for the competitive nature of a free market, because it permits easy and more or less cost-free entry to and exit from the stock market. Though commission costs are higher for the odd lotter than for the large institution, this difference is not in itself sufficient to obliterate the small investor's right of entry into the market. And although the majority of stocks traded on the NYSE are of corporations that are either monopolies (as in the case of utilities) or oligopolies, ownership of these stocks is not dependent on a privilege.

If ease of entry is one of the main characteristics of a freely competitive market, it is the free availability of and free access to information which makes for ease of entry. Whether one manages $1 billion or owns $10,000, one has the ability to buy or sell as long as there is the possibility of making judgments based on all available information.

Regulation of the commodities markets is, as we have seen, limited to maintaining a fair and orderly market with limited price fluctuations. The information needs for the proper conduct of a commodities market are limited to the disclosure and rapid dissemination of prices. No commodity market is dependent on the availability of disclosure of other information that may affect prices. Thus no regulatory agency is, or can be, concerned with monitoring what the weather is in Kansas, how much wheat was sown on Thursday, how full the silos are, or how much the Russians intend to buy.

Such information is irrelevant for the conduct of a commodities market because commodities have no exchange value but only utility value, which determines their price. Furthermore, it should be remembered that the function of the commodities markets is not to facilitate the buying and selling of commodities for immediate delivery but to assure that producers, middle men, and end users, through the use of futures contracts, can buy and sell at more or less satisfactory prices.

The situation is fundamentally different for securities markets. Information in the broadest sense is essential for the conduct of a securities market because it can provide an understanding of exchange value, not just of market prices. To permit such informed value judgments is the fundamental purpose of the disclosure rules set forth in the Securities and Exchange acts. If the SEC really believed that information is relevant only insofar as it concerns stock prices and, consequently, that independent value judgments are unnecessary, a lot of paperwork could be saved. But it would be saved at the expense of the freedom to judge whether market prices are a realistic expression of the intrinsic value of securities.

The Primary Sources of Information

The information necessary for the valuation of capital stock is essentially derived from two sources, the stock market and the public corporation, and only incidentally from government and independent comments on the state of the economy.

The stock market as source of information

Information disclosed by the stock market essentially concerns prices, bids and offers, and supply and demand. Even though the disclosure of this information is seen as the primary responsibility and raison d'être of the stock exchanges, the advent of NASDAQ and automation has greatly increased not only the disclosure but also the dissemination of this information.

To a certain extent the disclosure or price information is incomplete, because brokers in the fourth market (that is, those arranging for the private purchase and sale of large blocks of stock between institutions) are not required to disclose either the volume or price of a transaction. However, since the volume of these transactions is relatively small, it does not have a material impact on the overall validity of price information.[10] Furthermore, although information about these private transactions may not be immediately disseminated, sooner or later it has to be disclosed and thus will become part of the public province. There are also numerous technical services that provide numerical interpretations, such as the Dow-Jones Industrial Average, of the price movements of individual stocks and various groupings of stocks.

It is generally assumed that prices are facts, like coffee spilled upon a desk, but nobody is yet quite sure how to interpret these "facts" apart from any fundamental or trend analysis. Does the last trade of a widely held stock like AT&T convey the same kind of information as the last trade of a more sparsely held stock like Weyenberg Shoe? To what extent do these last trades reflect the price of stock that hasn't been traded? These are all "facts" that business economists have been eagerly trying to interpret. Information concerning prices, in its simplest, most elementary presentation as a last trade with an indication of bid and offer, whether it reflects the more realistic inside market or not, is subject to some form of interpretation. This interpretation falls outside the province of the self-regulatory mechanism of the securities market and directly into the hectic estate of the trader.

Yet precisely because information concerning prices has to be interpreted before it can be used, it can lead to serious mistakes. Errors in price judgment have an uncanny way of sometimes being induced mainly because not all the information concerning supply and demand and the expectations of buyers and sellers is revealed with the same candor as bids and offers in the last sale. Self-regulation, as it is practiced, may prevent price manipulation, but since it cannot control the disclosure of price *expectations,* the significance of price information is often far from evident.

Subsequent to an announcement by Morgan Stanley in the summer of 1975 that the investment bank would underwrite an issue of AT&T common stock, the price of this stock rose intermittently by several dollars until the secondary offering was distributed, whereupon it proceeded to lose most of these dollars in market value. It would be harsh, unrealistic, and untrue to say that the market was manipulated. What one can say is that an underwriting by the leading investment bank created an expectation of higher prices sometime in the future. Yet this expectation created the possibility for mistaken judgments, however temporary its consequence. What the effects of this can be at the hands of the unscrupulous we have all to some extent experienced.

Not every underwriter has as fair and reasonable an understanding of value as Morgan Stanley. Few investment banks can match its admirable preoccupation with pricing public offerings equitably. Not only the unscrupulous, but anyone interested in obtaining the best possible price knows that the creation of a mistaken interpretation of his expectations is a useful tactic in inducing the other party to give the best bid or offer. This is not illegal and nasty but a normal part of competitive bargaining. After all, the specialist on the exchange floor, to the extent this species still survives, is not required to reveal the contents of his book to any floor trader wanting the best price. So long as he maintains a fair and orderly market, he is entitled to disclose his expectations and his position only to the extent he feels necessary. If he can create the mistaken impression that he is on balance a buyer when in fact he is a seller, he can expect to make a profit and still fulfill his specialist role.[11]

Disclosure of price information is aimed at providing such information as is necessary for the conduct of negotiation between two parties, the buyer and seller. It is proper to refer to our securities markets as negotiated markets even though there sometimes seems to be little negotiation, especially on the part of the small buyer and seller. But even the small buyer has to choose between placing either a limit order or a market order. Even though he doesn't know the seller, he still has to decide whether to accept to buy at the market price. When he places a market order, he is assuming that his purchase is so small that he has no power to induce a mistaken account of his intentions.

Obviously, a large institutional buyer cannot buy with the same disregard for the process of negotiation. The fact that he uses a professional trader to try to interpret price information and induce a seller to meet his price is an indication of the extent to which he must bargain in order to satisfy, but not necessarily fulfill, his expectations. It is also an indication of the degree to which he can, indeed has to, make mistaken decisions, for he is also subject to misinterpreting the information disclosed by the seller. One can automate the disclosure and dissemination of price information and pay dearly for computer readouts presumably summarizing its statistical significance, yet because one will never fully know the expectations of the negotiating buyers or sellers, one is still left with the impossible, though necessary, task of interpreting the price of the last sale—that is, if one still believes that value is a consequence of negotiations and not automation.

The corporation as source of information

Disclosure of information by the public corporation constitutes the main source of its legitimacy not only as a business enterprise but also as a form of ownership without utility. That is, the requirement of disclosure of information enforces, at least in principle, responsible conduct by management. Corporate information, to put it differently, is the very substance of the relationship between shareholders, who own property without utility, and management, which controls the means of production. Because corporate information is what allows capital owners the possibility of placing a value on their property independently of the market, it contributes to the very liberty to acquire and dispose of capital. Without corporate information the sole source of value would be the market, and buying and selling would therefore be subject to the coercion of market forces.

Corporate information originates from two sources, management and the securities industry. Both sources of information are to some extent regulated and monitored by the SEC, though according to different guidelines since the function of such information is not the same for the two sources.

The primary purpose of information furnished by management is to supply the stockholders with a fair and comprehensive account of the extent to which it is fulfilling stockholders' claims to future earnings, and of the ways it is using the earnings retained from the stockholders in the fulfillment of their claim. In so doing, management must indicate why sales and earnings have taken the course they have, what it expects this course to be in the future, and what it is doing about it (for example, investment in new plants and equipment). In addition, of course, it must provide the stockholders with those financial statements required by law, such as periodic balance sheets, earnings statements, and statements reflecting the use of funds. This information is disseminated both to the stockholders directly and to the public through the periodic filing of the various financial forms required by the SEC.

In the past, discrepancies sometimes occurred between information supplied to the stockholders and that made available to the SEC. Specifically, the information given to stockholders was often less complete than that supplied to the SEC. However, the tendency now is toward maintaining consistency between the financial information supplied to the public at large and to stockholders. Thus, many companies now include form 10-K as an integral part of their annual report. The information supplied by management to the SEC tends to describe more the nature of the company than management's expectations.

A financial statement is an interpretation of reality, based on a subjective description of numerical relationships. The significance of the measures used is usually explained in the footnotes to these statements. In general, as long as some degree of historical continuity is maintained in the quality of interpretation, its validity is acceptable.

Often management will further seek to interpret the financial statements for its shareholders by using financial ratios. Financial ratios are the major tools used by management to evaluate financial statements and analyze the company's profitability, and by stockholders to determine the value of their claim.[12] The principal financial ratio used to interpret profits are earnings per share (EPS) and return on stockholders' equity (ROE). Though management sometimes also uses the price-earnings ratio, it usually omits this ratio on the grounds that it doesn't always reflect the company's accomplishments.

There are, of course, numerous other ratios management can use to explain the company's financial situation to shareholders. The purpose of this interpretative exercise is to increase investor confidence. It indicates management's desire to communicate more than required by law with its shareholders. The feeling is that a judicious use of ratios, whatever they tend to indicate, will increase the financial awareness, and hence confidence, of the shareholder. Thus, it is usually the most effectively managed companies which, recognizing the need to maintain good relations with the investing public, fill their annual and quarterly reports with the most informative collection of financial ratios.

An experienced investor will often be able to determine what management feels important, what it wants to reveal, and what it may prefer to conceal, by examining which ratios are used. For example, a company with a low ROE may tend to avoid using this ratio even though it can be easily calculated. Similarly, a company with an erratic pattern of earnings but a strong commitment to increasing its plant and equipment may emphasize its percentage increase in retained earnings.

Management has many other means at its disposal for inducing unreasonable expectations. It may devote a disporportionately long discussion in its annual report or meeting to a new product whose income potential is in fact very limited. It may use illustrations in its annual reports that do not depict any actual product line but emphasize a particular product that may not even be in production. Indeed, the annual report has become a highly sophisticated public-relations tool for corporations' stock.

Management may also heighten stockholder expectations by splitting its stock or proposing authorization of additional shares, even though there may be no sound financial reason for doing so. Or it may propose new directors with a highly favorable public image in a particular area management may wish to emphasize.

Financial analysts and experienced shareholders are rarely continuously deceived by management's fanciful and colorful interpretations of its accomplishments. Responsible management knows that developing a successful relationship means to maintain continuous shareholder interest, irrespective of the company's current earnings. Shareholders will not lose interest in a company just because current earnings are low, but they will lose interest when management makes no attempt to inform them about the actual state of the company's affairs. Management knows its relationship with its shareholders is successful when it is pestered by inquisitive shareholders and analysts, when more shareholders attend annual meetings, and when it is obliged to answer pertinent questions about the quality and quantity of earnings. Although it is not the function of management to value its own stock, it is usually quite content to know that there are many people actively engaged in doing so, thereby creating a higher market price and diminished interest from marauding, well-financed acquisitors.

One of the most startling aspects of American corporate management is the degree to which it is willing to disclose and discuss pertinent information with stockholders, security analysts, and anyone having a legitimate business interest in its company. The larger the public corporation, the more organized it is in this respect, with its director of corporate communications making access to top management relatively more difficult. Direct access to the managements of corporations with sales of less than $500 million is generally easier. Of course, managers of companies that are prime takeover targets tend to be reluctant to discuss their business, because, to a very considerable extent, their jobs are at stake. Still, one may ask why American management is so responsive to questions from the public. Why does management invite an active dialog with the investment community and its shareholders? What benefit can it derive from disclosing information it is not obligated by law to reveal?

The most obvious answer to these questions is that management is interested in obtaining a higher market price for its stock. A higher market price serves two functions: it increases the possibilities for additional equity financing, and it provides an increased measure of recognition for its managerial ability—whether in the form of public recognition or an increase in the value of its stock options. However, since the majority of corporations have tended for a good many years to satisfy their equity needs through retained earnings and not secondary distributions, and since glory and the increased value of stock options are not always as significant as the direct benefits received from salary and pension plans, I believe there is yet another explanation for management's willingness to disclose information.

As owner of the means but not the benefits of production—that is, as one having the sole right to use property that does not belong to it—management has the obligation to be concerned with the legitimacy of its power. This obligation involves not only the profits it produces for shareholders, but also the degree to which it is fulfilling whatever concept of responsibility it feels bound by. In the last analysis, the legitimacy of management's relation with its shareholders is built on the disclosure of information that enables the shareholder to judge management's behavior and the worth of his property.

In a sense, the relationship between management and stockholder is very similar to that between government and citizen. Like government, the more management seeks to keep the public in the dark about what it is doing, the more suspect it becomes and, hence, the more its right to persist is questioned.

Information about the Economy

Except insofar as it affects opportunity cost, information about the economy is irrelevant for an analysis of the exchange value of common stock, though it is certainly relevant for determining whether one wishes to own stock or not. No amount of knowledge about the status and causes of inflation, recession, growth, unemployment, the money supply, and similar factors can be used in the calculation of the value of common stock. In short, information about the general economy may determine one's confidence—or lack of confidence—in the economic system, but it cannot be used to judge the exchange value of specific stock or even groups of stock.

Information about the economy, then, is useful only for estimating the opportunity costs of alternative capital investments. Opportunity cost is a number, not an idea. It consists of the rate of return from a "riskless" investment, plus an arbitrary number corresponding to the additional margin or "interest" needed to satisfy oneself that the additional financial risk of capital investment is warranted. If we arbitrarily assume an opportunity cost of 10 percent, we would invest in capital stock as long as the return from our investment—dividends plus retained earnings—can be assumed to be at least 10 percent.

All too often, information about the economy is used not to determine a specific opportunity cost but to indulge in destructive anxiety. To say that inflation is galloping and will sometime soon run away, or that unemployment is at an alarming 10 percent, or that the money supply has increased or decreased to an intolerable degree, is merely to express the degree of our dismay or hope. Even in periods of dismay there is opportunity as long as one bothers to calculate it. Anxiety serves no useful purpose if it leads us to prefer treasury bills at 9 percent to an investment in one of the world's great oligopolies at a rate double that.

Information about the economy is always the result of statistical interpretation of a predefined reality—that is, of those facts one has chosen to present in a particular way.[13] It does not, nor is it meant to, convey the "truth," but only a set of relationships that have to be interpreted. Thus, in talking about inflation, Ezra Solomon said, "Any inflation rate which is correctly and universally anticipated by the financial markets should have no effect at all on stock prices."[14] What makes information about inflation a cause for discontent and lack of confidence is its interpretation by different people. In a sense, therefore, inflation becomes an economic problem primarily because people choose to view it as such.

Under ideal conditions one would expect that information about the economy should influence our confidence in the basic economic and political system. In practice, however, economic information has little impact on the long-term state of our confidence; instead, it tends to create anxiety over the short-term implications of statistical data. Even though we all know how easy it is to "lie" with statistics, it seems easier for people to be impressed with graphic displays of numerical relationships than to understand whether our political and economic system is viable. The only reasonable short-term use to which economic information can be put is to help an investor clarify his own subjective concept of opportunity cost.

Investment Research as a Source of Information

The research departments of the major Wall Street and regional brokerage houses are responsible not only for disseminating information about the overall state of the economy, but also for interpreting price movements (technical analysis) and information disclosed by corporate management (security analysis).

Economic reports issued by research departments are useless when they attempt to interpret the statistics issued by various government and industrial institutions in an attempt to determine the future course of the economy, because they presuppose a level of econometric and political expertise most brokerage house economists do not have. However, these reports can be extremely useful if they are written primarily to analyze opportunity costs as a function of the market value of investments in common stock. Some research departments do provide just such a service. (John Levin's "Overview" for Loeb-Rhoades is a good example.) They attempt to interpret the economy in terms of the relative value of alternative investment opportunities by analyzing interest rates, return on corporate investment, and the significance of opportunity costs as they understand them.

Securities analysis—useful or useless?

With the theory of an efficient securities market, business economists have developed an ever increasing tendency to distrust the interpretations of value disseminated by security analysts, whose judgments have met with little success in the past. To the extent that security analysts have been involved in forecasting earnings and speculating on the relation between earnings and future market price, this distrust is well founded. However, business economists have raised doubts about the usefulness of security analysis in general. Nevertheless, they have put such doubts to rest with two observations.

First, security analysis, according to business economists, is not only necessary in itself but essential for market efficiency, because market efficiency is essentially dependent on the lack of success security analysts have in interpreting information. (The efficient market theory will be examined in more detail in Chapter 7.) Business economists maintain, furthermore, that it helps if in thinking they can be successful, security analysts will also disbelieve the concept of market efficiency. Thus it appears that business economists value security analysis for the legitimacy it gives their theory rather than for its role in enforcing responsible conduct by management.

The second observation concerns what business economists think security analysts should really be doing. If analysts are not successful in interpreting publicly available information and if, furthermore, their existence depends solely upon a successful interpretation of public information, perhaps their major objective should be to "obtain information that is as yet unknown to the general public. . . . The usefulness of such inside information in producing above-average gains is clearly consistent with the efficient market theory, which refers only to publicly available information."[15]

I would like to think that this is not intended as an advice to violate the disclosure rules administered by the SEC. Perhaps inside information here means having a cozy chat with the treasurer and being led to believe that there really is gold in those yonder hills of coal. The fact is that inside information is no information, because it cannot be used with impunity and is no more reliable than publicly disclosed information. The desire to seek inside information is predicated upon the conceit that one is above being deceived in interpreting somebody else's motives. My own experience leads me to believe that the pursuit of inside information is a very costly pastime indeed. As a matter of fact, I would feel very reassured if some of the directors and officers I have had contact with knew more about their own companies than they give cause to believe.

Overreliance on technical reports

Some research departments still persist in issuing technical reports—interpretations of the price action of the market as a whole and of some stocks in particular. These reports are useless except to someone who derives special comfort from graphic interpretations of reality. It may be comforting to hear that the market is oversold when one is long, or that it will meet a "technical resistance" when one is short. But insofar as such information ignores all factors other than prices, it is without value.

This is not to deny that in principle one may use technical analysis with some success, although the prevailing theories of an efficient market, which are based on the random behavior of stock prices, would seem to contradict this. But if anybody has in fact been consistently successful in interpreting market information by technical analysis, it seems unlikely that he would ever reveal his expertise to the public, and if this expertise cannot be communicated, there is little to be gained by discussing it.

Some well-known advisory services make much to do about their technical expertise, and no doubt their talk succeeds in establishing investor confidence in their services. It is human nature to be more comforted by the intricacies of an elaborate procedure for coping with reality than by an acceptance that the future is unknowable and that the investment adviser has little to say that would make it more certain for his client.

The need for technical analysis is rooted in a reluctance to listen to the discourse of management, analysts, and government in order to arrive at a coherent understanding of what has been said. Numbers and graphs are blessed with an appearance of intrinsic relevance. They appear as if no one had compiled them. In fact, however, their relevance is anything but self-evident, for they are the results of specific, and often tenuous, interpretations of reality. It is ironic indeed that the author of one of the leading textbooks on technical analysis should also consider himself a student of "general semantics."[16]

Business economists versus securities analysts

The security analysis offered by research departments is fundamentally different from that produced by the business economists at the nation's schools of business administration or applied mathematics. By and large the main functions of analysts employed by research departments are to contact management, interpret financial reports, and record any significant changes or patterns they observe in the industry of their specialty. In most brokerage firms, research analysts also act as salesmen for the stocks they cover.

Business economists are not really security analysts, although they may write books about security analysis and construct theories and models of stock valuation. They do not contact management or try to interpret the firm's current financial information so as to reach value judgments that will enable them to buy and sell stocks, nor are they interested in understanding why management discloses or withholds certain information. They are scholars who try to determine the significance, primarily statistical, of the relationship between various pieces of information at their disposal. Their usefulness in performing this function is testified to by the degree of funding they receive from the securities industry, government, and business. But no matter how insightful their analysis may be, it cannot be used as the basis for making a decision to buy or sell.

The task of research analysts employed by the securities industry is enormously difficult. The legitimacy of their profession is usually measured by the success of their forecasts, and business economists have adequately demonstrated that research analysts have been very unsuccessful in forecasting earnings and price movements of stocks with any degree of accuracy.[17] Thus many brokerage houses prefer to measure the success of their research in terms of the commission dollars generated.

Whether they are employed by brokerage houses or investment funds, security analysts perform the task of maintaining a dialog between management and investors. The gullibility and lack of business acumen of so many of the more than 11,000 analysts should not lead us to ignore the necessity of their task. Research analysts are, in great measure, responsible for the quality and thoroughness of the disclosure of information by management. Without them the principle of self-regulation would become meaningless.

Virtually all business economists agree that the main function of security analysis should be the prediction of future financial results; in other words, security analysts must produce consistently successful earnings forecasts.[18] Having made this assumption, it is easy to conclude that since research analysts have never been consistently successful forecasters, they are performing incompetently—although their collective incompetence, according to business economists, is a necessary prerequisite for an efficient market. One of the reasons why the securities market is an efficient allocator of information and why prices quickly reflect available information is that there are so many analysts employed in interpreting this information according to a method of valuation to which they all, more or less, subscribe. Specifically, their valuation efforts are primarily dependent on the forecasting of earnings, which however are claimed to be indeterminable because they behave as randomly as stock market prices. Thus, security analysts are gainfully employed doing what, by the definition of business economists, cannot be done. In other words, the market will be efficient so long as there are fools who believe in greater fools.

What business economists overlook is that forecasting cannot be expected to produce consistent accuracy; the possibility for error is a necessary prerequisite for prediction. Rather than abandon their misguided theory, however, business economists have tended to push it to absurdity. The trouble with research analysis, they say, is that its traditional preoccupation with analyzing financial statements and interpreting information disclosed by management leads to unsuccessful forecasting. They should not forsake forecasting but become more proficient at it by developing prediction models, preferably ones that are not too expensive to use. As Baruch Lev puts it:

> Little is to be gained from acting upon financial information after its release to the general public. Action should be taken on the basis of predictions rather than on available information. . . . The orientation of financial statement analysis should therefore shift from the traditional examination designed to identify undervalued or overvalued stocks to the development and use of prediction models. . . .

> In short, the objective should be to transform publicly available information to inside information by the application of original tools and techniques.[19]

To a simple-minded investor, it might appear that the difference between a forecast and a prediction model is complexity. But if both are to be judged by the degree to which they successfully anticipate price movements, the complexity of prediction models offers no advantage over the crudeness of naive forecasts.

There is no doubt that much forecasting of earnings is a needless waste of time which research analysts should abandon, but they should not also relinquish their nonpredictive activity of interviewing management and interpreting financial statements. I would suggest that research analysts be judged by the degree to which they use their interpretive rather than forecasting skills. The most effective research reports are those which raise many questions about the financial statements they are analyzing and which cast as many doubts on management's expectations. Security analysts, in short, should be accountants working on behalf of the investing public rather than management.

Forecasting—Two Approaches

In discussing forecasting, it is useful to distinguish between two different approaches: *naive forecasting* and *regression analysis.* Both attempt to use mathematical expectations in predicting common-stock prices. Expectations that cannot be quantified cannot be used in making forecasts. There are, of course, many important expectations that appear to be nonquantifiable. Although they are not directly useful for producing forecasts, many of them at least help to determine the level of confidence that should be attached to numerical forecasts. For example, expectations about the quality of a company's oligopolistic market position or management's integrity and desire to communicate, though inherently nonquantifiable, may greatly influence people's confidence in specific financial forecasts regarding the company.

"Naive" forecasting

Naive forecasting is predicated on the assumption of historical continuity of the variable under consideration. Sometimes this approach is simply intuitive, as when the sales figures for the past three years are seen to increase by about 10 percent annually, leading to the simple forecast that they will increase as much in the coming year. Sometimes, however, this approach can become quite sophisticated, as when the time sequence of past observations is also taken into account. A forecaster may decide that he cannot evaluate the significance of all past observations equally, and that he ought to weigh the more recent observations more heavily, according to some formula he thinks pertinent. Here a forecaster may use complex time series and exponential smoothing formulas to establish the supposed trend of the variable under study.

Such an approach is naive in the sense that no attempt is made to correlate the variable under consideration with any other variable. A naive forecast is primarily concerned with determining the value of a mathematical expectation over a relevant period of time. It is not concerned with determining the correlation between two different sets of expectations.

Regression analysis

Regression analysis, the second forecasting method, is the one primarily employed by business economists in the construction of forecasting models used to predict the price or the price-earnings ratio of a stock. The main purpose of regression analysis is to determine the value of an expectation, or variable, that is presumed to be dependent on the value of other, independent, historically derived variables. Regression analysis hinges on the assumed interdependence, or correlation, between the dependent variable on the one hand and the independent variables on the other. When the forecaster is trying to establish the degree of the correlation between the independent and dependent variables rather than the value of the dependent variable itself, he is primarily involved in correlation analysis.

The relevance of the forecasting model for use in regression analysis is crucial to the desired results. It has long been obvious to forecasters that it is possible to establish mathematical relationships between variables that apparently don't have anything to do with each other. Thus, a forecaster has to believe that there is good reason for assuming a causal relation between the independent variables of his model and the dependent forecast. For example, even though it might be possible to establish a mathematical correlation between the orbit of the moon and the Dow-Jones Industrial Average, this correlation would be meaningless unless its relevance could also be accepted.

In regression forecasting it is assumed that there exists a valid and meaningful relation between what people ought to pay for a share of stock—that is, the forecast market price—and the independent variables used in the forecast model. The independent variables most commonly used are historical earnings, dividends, increase in retained earnings, debt-to-equity ratios, and other variables derived from the financial information of the company. However, independent variables derived from the marketplace are also used together with the preceding variables. These variables usually measure the volatility and marketability of the stock in question.

Regression forecasting is usually expensive, because information must be accumulated and analyzed and, of course, paid for. Yet this expense could perhaps be justified if we could at least learn from the continual failure of such forecasts. However, not even that seems possible.

In order to use regression analysis as a useful forecasting tool, one not only has to know the historical correlation between the independent and dependent variables, but also has to make the unwarranted assumption that future patterns of behavior will exactly conform to past observed ones. Furthermore, even if one could anticipate future earnings with reasonable accuracy, there is no reason to assume that the price the market will establish for a company's stock will be related to these earnings according to some mechanical formula.

In sum, regression analysis is based on what may be called a *derived expectation*—one that is crucially dependent on the future behavior of other independent variables. In a naive forecast, these primary variables—for instance, projected earnings, return on equity, or dividend policy—can be inspected separately, permitting an immediate judgment as to the sensibility of the result. Yet taken together and injected into a regression equation, their significance is obfuscated, and all we are left with is an abstract, composite value that is totally dependent on the validity of the assumed relationships.

Usually the purpose of regression forecasting is not to establish the degree of closeness between the behavior of the dependent and independent variables but to derive the dependent variable—the future price or price-earnings ratio of a stock. Thus regression forecasting is basically an attempt to determine intrinsic value, that is, what the shares ought to be selling at. Yet this concept of intrinsic value presupposes a high correlation between information derived from the financial disclosures by the company and information derived from the behavior of the stock on the market. It furthermore assumes that market value will ordinarily be the same as exchange value, even if the two can be conceptually distinguished. (Of course, this conceptual distinction is hardly ever made.) Thus the belief in market efficiency—that market price reflects the "value" of a share of stock—is at the heart of the regression approach to forecasting.

If experience has taught us anything about the market, it is that people rarely pay what we think a stock ought to sell for, even if they have indicated their willingness to do so in the past. Attempts at forming expectations about the future price of stock must also be based on expectations independent of market forces. It is often forgotten that increase in market price is only one of the criteria that can be used in judging the success of an investment. Return on investment, whether derived from retained earnings or from dividends, is another criterion, and one which has historically been just as important, especially before the emergence of the modern market with its high liquidity.

The distinction between exchange value and market value is important because it allows us to distinguish between the sources of information we must use in forming a judgment about the value of capital. The general refusal to respect this distinction in regression forecasting is part of the reason for its lack of success. Of course, not all business economists would agree with this criticism. Those subscribing to a positivistic approach to economic forecasting would argue that the objective validity of assumptions used to construct a forecast model are irrelevant to its success or failure. This, to me, is like arguing that the shortest route from Wall Street to Kennedy Airport is via the circuitous Belt Parkway because we would get lost taking another route.[20]

Another, perhaps more important, shortcoming of forecasting models is their inability to generate any concept of prudence that could be applied in the event of their failure. If the forecast fails, all is lost. There are no options to fall back on that could provide a measure of satisfaction equal to the initial expectation.

It is my belief that mathematical expectations ought to be considered only when evaluated independently of each other. The techniques of naive forecasting can be very useful in the formulation of mathematical expectations as long as expectations derived from financial sources are used independently of each other and, more important, independently of information derived from market sources. I believe that the simpler the technique, the better the results. If the objection is raised that the quantity of information is too profuse to be easily handled, my response is that only that information deemed necessary for the prudent ordering of expectations should be used. Valuation is a selective judgment, not a computerized aggregate of irrelevant information.

Present Value of Future Earnings

Both business economists and research analysts agree that the prediction of earnings is the most important consideration in determining the future price of a share of stock. Basically this attitude is a consequence of the theory of the present value of capital, which states that present value is equivalent to expected income discounted in some relevant fashion. As Irving Fisher, who was largely responsible for the development of this theory, put it, "The value of capital must be computed from the value of its estimated future net income, not vice versa."[21]

Thus the calculation of the present value of a share of common stock is predicated on our ability to predict what these shares will earn in the future rather than on a determination of how much the invested capital has generated in the past. Knowing the opportunity cost of capital is, of course, necessary in determining the internal rate of return of an investment. Only when the present value is greater than the opportunity cost will the capital investment be considered marginally efficient.

The present-value approach to stock valuation is at the very heart of the concern with the prediction of future earnings. Research analysts and business economists are not particularly concerned with determining the book value of a company or the worth of the company should it be liquidated. Valuation for them does not mean determining which stocks are selling at a discount from book value, but only estimating future income.

There are two reasons why any present-value analysis of common stock that depends primarily on discounting the value of expected income or dividends is bound to fail. First, it rests on the assumption that one can count on what the future will bring. Second, and more important, it involves interpreting earnings independently of the capital used to produce them.

By contrast, our analysis of a stock's expectancy value makes no attempt to add up discounted future receipts of income or dividends, which cannot be reasonably estimated. Furthermore, a firm's earnings, whether past, present, or future, are never analyzed in isolation from the capital employed by management to generate them. As we shall see, many of the problems in interpreting earnings tend to disappear if we consider them together with their effect on the firm's capital structure—that is, if we concentrate on the return-on-equity ratio.

Problems with interpreting earnings

Both research analysts and business economists agree that there is nothing more important than understanding the significance of past earnings in accurately predicting future earnings; in fact, without such knowledge, a judgment about future stock prices would be impossible. An understanding of what present and future earnings are is at the very basis of analysts' and economists' efforts to understand the value of common stock. The assumption is always made that if one could really predict what a firm's earnings will be, one would always be able to know what a share of common stock ought to be worth and thus what it ought to be selling at. No research analyst would be able to hold his job for very long if he didn't try to make sense out of a firm's past earnings and predict what they will be for at least the coming fiscal year. No business economist could arrive at an understanding of the present value of a firm's worth or construct an elaborate forecasting model without relying on the significance of earnings or, at least, of the price-earnings ratio.

Both research analysts and business economists agree that capital stock represents a claim on earnings. Neither are very interested in determining the legality of this claim; this would seem to be an issue more pertinent to the SEC and to stockholders filing suit against the corporation. Even though both groups of experts are ostensibly concerned with determining the value of the object of this claim, neither is very sure of what these earnings really are. First, they don't agree on how these earnings ought to be measured. Second, they don't agree on how earnings ought to be used to predict the expected value of a firm's shares. In short, when it comes to defining a claim on earnings, nobody seems to have a definition that, if not objectively accurate, is at least useful in practice for determining the value of a capital investment in common stock.

What claim does stock represent?

It is fairly easy to judge the value of capital in the form of a debt instrument, whether a long-term bond, convertible debenture, or promissory note. Even though these capital claims may be secured by a specific mortgage on real or movable property, they are still dependent on the ability of the firm to produce an income out of which the interest—and, one hopes, the principal—can be repaid. Usually there is a loan agreement negotiated by the borrower and the lender which extensively describes not only the nature of the claim but also the nature of the income that must be used to satisfy this claim. Even when there is no specific loan agreement, both the borrower and the lender generally have a clear and uniform understanding of what is involved.

Although a share of common stock is more similar to a debt instrument than to an equity interest in a partnership, there is one important respect in which it differs from the former. This is the extent to which the object of the claim is almost entirely defined, calculated and disclosed by management without intervention by the shareholder. The earnings representing a stockholder's claim are essentially what management says they are. Management's power to calculate and disclose whatever earnings it sees fit to is limited mainly by the board of directors, the directors' audit committees, and the general accounting principles governing the firm's accounting procedures.

I am not implying that management acts arbitrarily without any regard for its shareholders. If this were so, no judgment about value could ever be formed, nor would the disclosure of information have any significance; indeed, there could be no securities market. I am simply saying that it is not shareholders, research analysts, or business economists who are responsible for the definition and disclosure of a firm's earnings, but the management of the firm itself.

An earnings report describes not reality but how management has chosen to represent the extent of its liability to its shareholders. It may minimize this liability by paying out all reported income as dividends, or maximize its liability by retaining all income. Presumably, such dividend policies can be explained in terms of the concept of growth. Some firms with a limited growth potential—for instance, many of the public utilities—have a high dividend payout policy. Thus their liability to stockholders roughly consists of maintaining the return on their slowly increasing equity. However, some so-called "growth" stocks, like McDonald's, pay little or no dividends. Thus their liability is increased by the extent to which they must try to maintain a historically valid return on their steadily increasing equity. These firms are growth firms not because their earnings show great increases, but because they are supposedly able to maintain their rate of return on their increased retained earnings. Research analysts sometimes forget this when they judge a stock solely in terms of the reliability of the expected earnings increase rather than on whether the firm is maintaining its historical return on equity.

It is sometimes assumed that the responsibility for measuring earnings and other financial data is the function of a corporation's independent financial auditors. There is no doubt that the leading accounting firms impose certain restrictions on the ways in which management can present the financial information at its disposal, but these restrictions are usually concerned only with maintaining consistency in the firm's accounting procedures to comply with generally accepted accounting principles. The basic policy decisions remain the responsibility and prerogative of the firm's management. Every firm has its own accounting policy. The function of the independent auditors is but to monitor the policy and advise the firm of its propriety; they do not establish it. Interestingly enough, recent investigations by the Senate Subcommittee on Reports, Accounting, and Management resulted in directives to auditors to act more independently of management than in the past. Needless to say, the accounting profession does not fully agree with the subcommittee.[22]

Management's latitude

The degree of latitude which management has in measuring its earnings has been the subject of extensive study. Leonard Spacek published a simple and now classic study in which he showed how eight different earnings figures, from 80¢ to $1.79, can be derived from the same financial data using generally accepted accounting principles.[23] Abraham Brilloff has written an extensive and especially critical book on this subject.[24] Likewise, R. J. Charles has shown how it is possible to manipulate financial data in an almost unlimited fashion.[25] How a firm chooses to account for its pension fund assets, research and development, patents, inventory, depreciation, and so on, has a great effect on how much earnings are reported, independent of the actual cash flow generated during the accounting year.

If a firm consistently minimizes its reported earnings, this is often taken as an expression of its financial conservatism. What this conservatism really means is a desire on the firm's part to reduce its expressed liability to shareholders and to "smooth" income so that the effects of good years can be somehow carried over to offset the effects of bad years.[26]

From a shareholder's point of view, a firm's cash flow, as determined from an examination of its statement of sources and uses of funds, is more useful in judging the value of his claim than is the simple earnings figure derived from the company's profit and loss statement. Although accountants would define earnings basically as the difference between revenues and the costs involved in producing those revenues, only the cash flow statement can give the shareholder an adequate understanding of what these revenues and costs consist of. The earnings figures themselves are merely an expression of management's interpretation of its liability, which it hopes the shareholders will accept.

It is, therefore, difficult to understand why reported earnings should be so important to research analysts and business economists in arriving at a judgment about the value of a firm. If the calculation, interpretation, and disclosure of earnings is a reflection of management's prerogative to interpret its own performance and not an indication of how it has used and disposed of the firm's assets, why should it constitute the most significant factor in determining the value of a company's stock? Wouldn't it be more reasonable to judge the significance of the firm's cash flow, or the degree to which it has increased its retained earnings and its dividend payout? Wouldn't it at least be more sensible to use earnings as an indication of return on invested capital rather than as numbers to be used in the calculation of present value?

It sometimes appears that the Petersburg paradox—which says that a share of stock should have an infinite value if the growth in earnings is continuously higher than the opportunity cost—has been applied in the past not only by merchants of growth stocks but by many investment researchers in determining the value of cyclical and otherwise "dull" companies. When earnings are conceived of as totally independent of the capital that makes them possible, this seems to indicate a naive expectation that the future will continue to bring larger, more robust, and hence more satisfying numbers.

Earnings reports—to be read between the lines

It would be easy to conclude that since earnings reports are value judgments monopolized by management, they ought to be of no value whatsoever in judging common-stock values. In that case research analysts ought to ignore management's calculations and derive their own, or perhaps what is needed is a new interpretation of what earnings are. In fact, however, no such drastic conclusion is justified. It is very important to understand earnings reports in the context in which they are disclosed by a particular firm, for they show exactly how management wishes to convey to shareholders information about its performance.

Earnings ought to be understood within the context of a negotiated understanding between management and shareholder (or research analyst acting on behalf of the shareholder). This only means that earnings should never be interpreted independently of other financial information, especially net worth. Earnings are, after all, a reflection of a return on invested capital that management assumes its shareholders will accept. They are neither random numbers nor figures obeying some paradoxical principle of growth. Taken as abstract numbers they can become the delight of the mathematically inclined analyst hell-bent on discovering if there is, or why there isn't, a relation between successive earnings reports. No businessman would ever buy a company solely on an inspection of its earnings, nor would he ignore them entirely. Whether they are used to minimize a liability to the IRS, to maximize the value of a public offering, or as a means of establishing a growth pattern—which many research analysts seem to be so fond of—earnings are useful information as long as one keeps in mind that they are disclosed by management with a specific purpose.

Just because the depreciation policies of the various airlines differ, for example, this does not mean that a research analyst should make them all conform to some uniform procedure which he thinks better reflects what management ought to be saying.[27] It is sufficient that he observes that the firm pursues a consistent procedure, however much at variance it is with its competitor's procedure.

If one were to examine the per-share earnings figures for the past five years of, say, the Diamond Crystal Salt Company, they would appear to be meaningless: 1972, $1.93; 1973, $1.48; 1974, $2.54; 1975, $2.04; 1976, $4.11. I have purposely chosen a company with very erratic earnings even though it is an extremely well-run company. But if one were to compare these earnings figures with their corresponding book values, they become immediately more meaningful: 1972, $21.26; 1973, $22.15; 1974, $24.80; 1975, $26.24; 1976, $29.75. We are now able to see that management is running a business which it thinks ought to yield a return on investment of between 7 percent and 13 percent. A reasonable and, I think, prudent interpretation of these figures is to assume that as long as the lowest anticipated earnings for 1977 are in excess of $2.00, yielding an expected return on equity of under 7 percent, one could purchase these shares at any price up to $20, assuming an opportunity cost of 10 percent.

Earnings as a random variable

Business economists do not agree on the extent to which an examination of past earnings is useful in determining or even understanding a firm's future performance. Even if they concur that one cannot calculate a firm's present value without reference to its expected income, many still hold that an analysis of expected earnings based on naive forecasting methods is totally useless. Many believe that earnings are random variables, that is, that their past behavior cannot be shown to follow a consistent pattern. Indeed, some business economists attribute this to the fact that even oligopolies and monopolies are engaged in "free" competition.[28] Even monopolistic utilities may have to pay more for energy than anticipated. Almost all agree that, even if an extrapolation of historical earnings may make some sense in determining an "average," trend, or pattern, successive earnings changes appear to behave randomly and do not fall into any predictable pattern of growth.[29]

Clearly, this literature is not free of all confusion. It is difficult to understand why the firm's value should depend on its earnings if so little sense can be made of them. Witness Lorie and Hamilton: "Changes in earnings seem to follow a random walk, meaning that the simple extrapolation of historical trends is not likely to be very useful in predicting future changes in earnings. Clearly, however, historical earnings will continue to be useful in predicting future levels."[30] This is what is known as an academic straddle!

For anybody interested in understanding how the very statistical process used can actually influence the results of the extent to which earnings appear to behave randomly and historical extrapolations are at all useful, Baruch Lev offers some insight into the subject. After analyzing the effects of different statistical processes, such as a constant-expectation process and a martingale process, he concludes that it is "obvious that the identification of the statistical process actually generating corporate earnings is crucial to the construction of prediction models."[31]

Whatever conclusions one may reach concerning the relevancy of past earnings for predicting future earnings, it should at least be evident that past-earnings figures, as an expression of how management wishes its shareholders to understand the value of its use of the shareholders' equity, are not at all irrelevant and random numbers. If they were, their disclosure and the monitoring of their disclosure by the SEC and the securities industry would be a preposterous waste of time.

As it happens, the substance of the disclosure often gets confused with the function of the disclosure. One may wish that the function of publishing earnings would be different. One may want them to be more uniform or objective; one may also prefer that earnings be defined as the result of a change in asset value rather than as the figure from which one calculates that change in value.[32] But for the present, earnings must be accepted for what they are—an indication of how management wishes its shareholders to value their claim.

Use of the Price-Earnings Ratio

One of the major consequences of the need of research analysts to make forecasts has been their persistent use of the price-earnings (P/E) ratio. The P/E ratio is simply a fraction indicating the relationship between earnings per share (denominator) and the price per share that people have been willing to pay for those earnings (numerator). As such it attempts to state the relation between two heterogeneous factors that are not necessarily dependent on each other. Thus, the P/E ratio differs from other ratios in which the numerator bears some direct relation to the denominator, such as the current ratio, the debt-to-equity ratio, and numerous other ratios used in financial analysis.

When the P/E ratio is stated on the basis of past earnings, it produces a number which, though meaningless in itself, is an indicator of past performance as compared with an industry or other companies. To say that Upjohn is selling at a P/E ratio of 25, based on last year's earnings, is not illuminating in itself, but only allows comparison with other similar companies. However, British analysts often refer to this relationship between past earnings and market price not in the form of a ratio but in the form of an earnings yield. Thus, Upjohn would be selling at a 4 percent earnings yield. This figure is immediately more meaningful, because it can be more readily used in comparisons with other capital instruments such as bonds, for which earnings yield can also be calculated.

Most often the P/E ratio will be presented in the context of future earnings, in which case it is assumed that there is a relation between what people are now paying and what they will pay. In fact, however, there is no justification for assuming such a relation, and this is why the use of P/E ratios based on projected earnings has proved to be a fairly meaningless forecasting tool.[33] Nonetheless, even though the P/E ratio, like any other ratio, is supposed to be used as a standard of comparison, the securities industry has often used it as an indication of value. Indeed, there is hardly any research report that does not try to indicate value using the P/E ratio.

P/E ratios, in short, cannot be used as indicators of future value or even current value. Even as indicators of past performance their usefulness is limited. One would tend to think, for example, that portfolios consisting primarily of high P/E ratio stocks would outperform portfolios of low P/E ratio stocks. The high multiple on earnings some would pay because a company's earnings appear to be growing at a rapid rate would seem to justify a high purchase price on the expectations of a higher-than-normal growth. Yet two well-known studies on the subject have demonstrated that portfolios of low P/E stocks tend to outperform portfolios of high P/E stocks.[34]

The difficulty in using the P/E ratio to determine the value of a stock is that in focusing on a standard for an industry or some other homogeneous grouping of companies, it generally ignores alternative investment possibilities. Should one ever pay 30 times last year's earnings for a company when one can buy investment-grade bonds yielding 10 percent? Use of the P/E ratio tends to obfuscate this sort of alternative. The P/E ratio is a performance ratio; it conveys no information about the exchange value of the firm. Its use, especially with regard to future earnings, unfortunately tends to relieve the obligation of the research analysts to provide a meaningful interpretation of other financial ratios and information available concerning a firm's financial value.

The Original Offering Prospectus as a Source of Information

Less than 4 percent of the equity needs of industry in the past has been met by the issuance of stock to the public, whether from the original offering of the shares of private corporations or from the secondary offering of shares by companies already public.[35] The percentage of shares offered to the public by stockholders, and of no benefit to the company, has been even smaller. The bulk of the supply of equity capital has come through the retention of earnings. Likewise, the role of the investment banking establishment in raising new and additional equity capital has not been as significant as one might suspect. Of course, if we also consider that only 10 percent of that establishment provides 75 percent of the equity capital derived from public offerings, it adds a somewhat different perspective to the matter.

Both the original public offering of an erstwhile private corporation and (to a lesser extent) the secondary offering of a closely held public corporation can lead to much confusion insofar as the value of the information contained in the offering prospectus is concerned. This prospectus is the only SEC-authorized representation about the company one can offer a prospective buyer of its securities (meaning a "dealer, salesman, or any other person"). No other source of information can be used. The prospectus contains all the "facts," "financial statements," "description of business," "purpose of offering," "management," "controlling shareholders," and so on. It also contains information about the "value" of the shares offered, "offering price," "dilution," "risk factors," "shares offered by controlling stockholders," and so forth.

The confusion has to do with the degree to which statements concerning value support statements concerning fact, and, consequently, the extent to which the prospectus, which "does not constitute an offer to sell," is in fact an inducement to buy. The SEC does not approve or disapprove of the business or the corporation or the shares being offered to the public, but it does monitor the format, language, and kinds of disclosures contained in the prospectus. In other words, although the SEC does not approve or disapprove of the value of the shares being offered, it is concerned that the facts represented in the prospectus are sufficient for a prospective buyer to arrive at his own concept of value.

The role of the underwriter

Even though the prospectus may not be used as a means of solicitation or inducement to buy, in point of fact it has to be so used; buyers must be solicited somehow. The expectation of the SEC is that the new shares will be offered to intelligent, informed buyers who will respond to the information published in the prospectus as a disclosure and not a solicitation. The SEC believes that because the prospectus discloses all information concerning risk, an intelligent and knowledgeable reader can freely respond and is not induced thereby to make an unreasonable or uninformed commitment.

This confusion is not as unexpected as it might at first glance appear. The underwriter is not acting as a research analyst in interpreting value. He will necessarily slant information concerning fact and value, because he has gambled his own capital funds on his judgment of what the value of these shares is or, perhaps, of what he can sell them for. A successful underwriter tries to allot his commitment before he has actually made it; he also tries to stabilize or create a market before and after making the commitment.

Given the risk the underwriter takes, one must necessarily question the information contained in the prospectus. This means that the buyer, especially if he is acting in a fiduciary capacity, cannot entirely rely on the underwriter's interpretation of value. (In point of fact, the history of the performance of new issues has been dismal, to say the least.) The underwriter's pricing will reflect his interpretation of what the market will bear rather than what he would pay for these shares if they were being offered to him; and to the extent he can get away with it, he will use the prospectus as an advertising medium.

The prospectus as advertisement

It is difficult to advertise in a free and perfectly competitive market. The very number of competitors producing the same product would tend to invalidate the effect of advertising. At the very most, advertising is an inducement to buy a particular product, and at the very least it is a reminder of the name or reputation of the firm advertising. Likewise, an original public offering by any one of the top underwriting firms carries with it the prestige, wisdom, and expertise of the underwriter itself. Isn't it reasonable to assume that the thoroughness and standards of excellence are higher for a leading underwriter than for a newly formed, small venture capital firm?

Certainly, it is difficult to ignore the effect of an original underwriting managed by one of the big firms, no matter what our initial reaction may be to the contents of the prospectus. And no matter how risky an underwriting appears, the very fact that the underwriter has fixed an offering price on the cover of the prospectus psychologically offsets the chancy character of the investment. This, in a very real sense, may be construed as a form of advertisement.

Except for certain members of the underwriting syndicate, nobody is forced to buy shares of a new issue. Yet I recall, somewhat unpleasantly, the sixties when underwritings of new issues were anticipated with real fervor and greed. Fortunately, the passage of time has calmed the fervor and reduced the greed to a mere hope that the losses can be recovered. But time hasn't changed things all that much —new issues will continue to be made, and an understanding of the significance of the information contained in the offering prospectus is still mandatory, especially if we are to maintain the sanity the market has imposed on us these last few years. I suppose that as long as confidence in the market geometrically increases expectations, the desire to mint "supermoney" and to trade in it with impunity will persist. Yet even then one hopes that prudence may still retain some vestige of its ancient affiliation with caution.

A Closer Look at the Prospectus

The prospectus itself does not distinguish between representations of fact and those of value. If one reads over the table of contents of any prospectus for a new issue, one is confronted with a series of considerations that the underwriter feels the prospective buyer ought to bear in mind before judging value. The only real statement about value the underwriter unequivocally commits himself to is the offering price on the cover. Usually no attempt is made to substantiate this price directly, the assumption being that since there has been no public market for these shares, the price cannot be substantiated. More recently, however, sections concerning the "determination of offering price" and "dilution" have also been included.

Determining price

The section concerning the "determination of offering price" usually contains information about past appraisals and private transactions of the closely held nonpublic stock which show how the stock was valued before the public offering. This section is in itself informative and necessary in arriving at a clearer understanding of value, yet there is often no relation between the information contained in it and the offering price.

For example, an appraisal of the fair market value of the privately held stock of the Amdahl Corporation was made at $12 a share in May 1976. Yet in August of that year the stock was brought to the public at $27.50 a share.* Of course, some salutory financial events concurred with the public offering, the most important being the conversion of the long-term debt into common stock and the increased liquidity conferred by the public offering. Yet one wonders what kind of financial world it is when the public has to pay more than double what the underwriter thought the shares were worth only three months before because of the privilege of increased liquidity, which primarily benefited the controlling shareholders.

In July 1976, an Amdahl officer sold 2,837 shares for $17.50 per share. One might believe that the purchaser's judgment in paying more than the expert appraisal establishes a valid precedent in expecting a higher share value. According to the underwriter, "such valuations and selling prices reflected the company's substantial cumulative deficit, the absence of a market for the common stock and, in most cases, restrictions on the freedom to resell the common stock."[36] In other words, the company—and, apparently, the underwriter—believed that if there had been a public market for its stock, it would probably have been worth even more than the $17.50 received by the officer.

Regarding the final public offering, the underwriter goes on to say:

* Since the time this section was written, the stock of the Amdahl Corporation was split into two shares for every one, and a secondary offering of 1,120,000 shares, managed by the First Boston Corporation and E. F. Hutton & Co., was made in June 1977. As of this writing, the price of Amdahl common stock, traded on the American Stock Exchange, has exceeded $50 per share. The current tangible book value is about $11 per share. Since 1976, the return on equity has averaged about 26 percent, and an annual dividend of 20¢ has been declared. From the point of view of those who purchased Amdahl stock in 1976, the original public offering was thus highly successful. Clearly, it would have been easy to substitute an example of another, less successful original public offering. However, I feel that the logic of my argument holds despite this apparent exception; indeed, it seems to me highly dangerous to extrapolate from such rare situations where the public was rewarded within a reasonably short period of time for the disproportionate financial risk it took.

> Upon completion of this offering, the total number of outstanding shares of common stock (assuming no exercise of the over-allotment option) multiplied by the public offering price set forth on the cover of this prospectus would be $164,841,270. Such amount does not necessarily bear any relationship to the assets, earnings or other criteria of value applicable to the company.[37]

The underwriter is admitting here that although an investment banking firm was supposedly able to give an expert opinion in May 1976, the firm's expertise had little to do with the actual offering price.

There is no doubt that these statements were made to somehow fulfill this highly reputable underwriter's public responsibility. Yet it appears that the determination of value was made on behalf of the company, the selling stockholders, and management, and not on behalf of the purchasing public. The underwriter discharged his public responsibility by disclosing the expert and real valuations immediately preceding the public offering, which describe the financial climate in which this new issue was brought to the public. In so doing he had to act as agent for the company and its selling stockholders. Although the underwriter probably attempted to give the public the best possible price, it is obvious that the degree of flexibility he had in doing this was very limited, and it was limited because, although he had a public responsibility, he was not the public's agent.

Within the past few years, one should add, the efforts of underwriters in trying to justify statements of fact and value contained in the new offering prospectus have been greatly improved and intensified. Besides the section concerning the determination of offering price, two additional sections now commonly appear, one on "dilution" and one on "shares eligible for future sale."

"Dilution"

The section on dilution tries to justify the relationship between the amount of capital the private owners of the corporation have invested, retained, or even lost in the company, the tangible book value, and the direct increase in the book value of their shares attributable to the additional paid-in capital. This section also describes the dilution —that is, the discrepancy between the tangible book value before and after the offering—and the price the public will pay for these shares.

What is interesting about the pro forma net tangible book value after the offering is that it is often double, and sometimes more than quadruple, the original book value before the offering. In the case of the Amdahl Corporation, the original book value of $1.10 per share before the offering was increased to $5.21 per share after the offering.

Even though the real beneficiaries of this increase were the company and the controlling stockholders, the new public investors were thereby obliged to accept a dilution of $22.29 per share—the difference between the offering price of $27.50 and the new tangible book value of $5.21 per share.[38]

While the company at least quadrupled its original capital investment, the new public investors paid an offering price quadruple the value of the new tangible book value. The question is, how can the public rely on these so-called statements of fact in arriving at an understanding of value? It would appear that only the expectation of future earnings can justify such a dilution. Yet the underwriter cannot, with any degree of responsibility, say what these earnings will be even in the forseeable future. Thus, the public must have great, though vague, expectations if it is at all to justify to itself the price it will pay.

The section on dilution, for all its factual representation of the relative values of capital investment, omits one significant observation which may be important from the potential new investor's point of view. It is what the dilution signifies in relation to the current market price of the company's major competitors. For example, IBM is cited as Amdahl's major competitor. Wouldn't it be significant, especially for the public, to show that the dilution on the new offering is higher than it is for the common stock of IBM and perhaps of other major competitors? Wouldn't some effort at relating the offering price to that of comparable alternative investments be of value to the public? It would be, but if these things were included, the new offering might become an endangered species of equity financing. Most new issues are overpriced in relation to the common stock of their competitors or of other comparable businesses.

New public offerings of private business are valid if their main purpose is to generate additional funds through equity financing. After all, small, viable businesses must have a hope beyond the demands of commercial banks. But often the primary purpose of these financings is to increase the liquidity of the controlling shareholders at the public's expense. In considering an offering prospectus, it would be wise to keep in mind that the underwriter is first and foremost the agent of the corporation and the selling stockholders; one cannot expect him to play the benevolent negotiator unless all other underwriters adopt a uniform policy for the valuation of new issues.

"Shares eligible for future sale"

The section on shares eligible for future sale explains to the public the consequences of Rule 144 of the Securities Act of 1933, under which a controlling shareholder has the right to sell up to one percent of the outstanding common stock of the company during any six-month period. To the extent that a controlling shareholder does not accept any special covenant not to sell within a certain period of time after the initial offering, it is possible to evaluate the discrepancy between the value of the public offering to him and its value to the new investor.

The proceeds from most initial offerings are to some extent distributed between the company and the selling shareholders. The latter benefit not only from the initial offering price but from the liquidity their immobile holdings acquire under Rule 144. Under the most responsibly managed underwritings, the portion of the proceeds going to the selling shareholders is relatively small—less than 10 percent—but in others it is large, approaching 50 percent. The proportion of the proceeds going to the selling shareholders is important in determining the relative value of the offering. It indicates management's preferences for cash in hand as opposed to an investment in the company.

"Risk factors"

The section on risk factors has been the source of abusive confusion between representation of fact and value. The underwriter demonstrates his professional expertise in delineating all the risk factors he considers relevant for a prudent evaluation of the company's shares. However, this section often demonstrates the degree to which the disclosure of information can be irrelevant when it is given in the context of an established offering price.

It may be that the company's management has little experience, that its sales are insignificant, that there is no backlog, that the company has no special know-how or patents, that any of a number of much larger, well-established companies could manufacture and sell the product just as efficiently. If these facts were published in an analytical report, perhaps nobody would be interested in buying the stock.

Since risks are stated in an offering prospectus together with an offering price, the underwriter, in effect, has passed judgment on their significance and has said that in his opinion they are worth so many dollars.

"Use of proceeds"

The section on the use of proceeds usually shows how much the short- or long-term borrowings of the company will be reduced by the newly acquired equity capital. It thereby indirectly demonstrates the extent to which management has been able to replace the indentured claim of debt with the indentureless claim of common stock.

What is disturbing about this sort of substitution is the degree to which it can be made. For example, in an underwriting of Gap Stores, Inc., in May 1976, management relinquished only about 10 percent of its controlling shares in order to reduce a portion of the long-term debt equivalent to about 80 percent of the stockholder's equity before the offering. This means that the opportunity cost of the public shares was appreciably different than it was for the shares retained by the controlling shareholders. The prospectus does not attempt to evaluate this discrepancy, because it would then have to justify why this number of shares, and not more, was sufficient to reduce the long-term borrowings.

The Gap Stores underwriting came out for 1,200,000 shares at a price of $18 to the public; 600,000 shares were sold by certain stockholders and 600,000 shares were sold by the company. The net proceeds to the company, after the underwriting discount, was $10,152,000, which was to be used to reduce its long-term bank debt of $11,008,876.

Now, there is no doubt, especially in our economic system, that equity financing is preferable to debt financing because it increases the freedom and opportunities of industry. But the question of cost must also be considered. Is it reasonable to expect the new shareholders to give up the long-term rate of interest on a debt instrument of similar quality in order to receive only 10 percent of the Gap Stores equity? Assuming that the net earnings for fiscal 1976 would have been about $7 million (they were actually $4.4 million), is it reasonable that the shares sold by the company should claim only 10 percent of this? Is it reasonable for anyone to give up the certainty of a fixed return from debt instruments for the uncertainty of a return from equity?

Again, of course, this can be justified on the expectations of greater future earnings. Furthermore, even if the underwriter in this case had attempted to set a lower price, the controlling shareholders probably would have found another underwriter. It has sometimes been assumed that the public will invest in industrial assets only when the rate of return exceeds that from relatively riskless short- or long-term debt instruments. However, this assumption has hardly ever held true for new public stock offerings.

Another, though much less significant, example of the underwriter's lack of concern in justifying the offering price based on opportunity costs of capital is the relationship between the underwriting discount and the tangible book value of the shares before the offering. In the case of the Amdahl offering, the underwriting discount of $2.00 is almost double the tangible book value before the offering and only one-third of the tangible book value after the offering. It represents about 7 percent of the actual offering price. I am not saying that the underwriter does not deserve this fee, most of which he has to share with his syndicate anyway. I am saying that the magnitude of this relation casts a new light on how the underwriter himself can benefit from the dilution to new investors. Of course, the underwriter would reply that the dilution is irrelevant; the new investors should be willing to pay a fee almost equivalent to the tangible book value of the shares offered for their new-found privilege of owning the stock.

In the Eye of the Beholder

What the preceding analysis seems to indicate is that the prospectus, especially the new offering prospectus, is presented to the public as a form of advertisement, an inducement to buy, even though it formally stipulates that it does not constitute a solicitation. Nobody can deny the responsibility and degree of public consciousness the underwriter reveals in selecting the information he feels the public must know in order to evaluate the merits of the offering. But since he has produced a prospectus as a result of his commitment, his disclosure of information represents not only fact but an interpretation of value.

Information is to a large extent useless without clear knowledge of the intent behind its disclosure. This doesn't mean that in order to make a decision, information has to be complete. It very rarely is. But one should be able to use, and judge, whatever information one has at his disposal before arriving at a decision.

Information is most useful when acquired in the process of negotiation. When you read an annual report, you are aware that you are reading the things that management wants to say about its financial resources and prospects. Since management is not obliged, and usually not even able, to make a judgment about the exchange value of its investment, you can and should interpret the report as you wish. This is not negotiation in the sense of being confronted directly with management, but it is in the sense that you are confronted with a statement of management's intentions, which you can accept in whole or in part. You can always revise your opinion later if necessary.

An offering prospectus presents a more complicated situation:

whatever opinion you may form of the information it contains, you are not likely to have the resources to interpret it. You either accept the offering price or reject it. There is no room for the negotiated understanding of value except insofar as you can later buy or sell the shares on the open market, after the initial distribution. The fact remains, however, that the judgments of value the prospectus contains are more often the consequence of the underwriter's interpretation of what the market will bear, rather than an expression of his unbiased expertise in appraising capital instruments.

7

Uncertainty

Uncertainty is not understood by businessmen in the same way it is understood by business economists.[1] The businessman will normally rely on an instinctive acceptance of what he knows and what he thinks he does not. He thinks he knows his financial condition, his product, his market, and his position in industry. Whether this knowledge is objectively true or not is irrelevant to him as long as he can use it to make decisions and as long as it conforms to his experience.

Almost every decision the businessman makes involves a certain amount of ignorance. He refers to this ignorance as uncertainty. He is uncertain about many aspects of the future, and he is uncertain about how his competitors will act toward him and toward his market. For him knowledge and ignorance, certainty and uncertainty, are not subjects of scientific inquiry. They are intuitive, practical descriptions of his ability to act, make decisions, and continue in business.

If we were to place the businessman's concept of knowledge within the context of philosophy, he would be an American pragmatist rather than a German idealist, or even an English empiricist. The businessman knows that much of his ignorance or uncertainty is due to his powerlessness in influencing competitors, or consumers and markets, or the future. Business economists, however, don't react in the same way as the businessman to this uncertainty resulting from a lack of power to control major economic factors. Business economists try to compensate for their lack of control of these factors by insisting on their ability to predict events. They distinguish this claimed ability from prophecy by couching their predictions in quantitative terms. Whereas a prophet may know something due to a special metaphysical communication, the business economist believes that he knows something if he can quantify it and express it in the idiom of his statistical concepts. For him, knowledge consists of quantitative analysis of data which he has either produced or borrowed from other business economists.

Contrary to the classical scientific method, the business economist does not verify his knowledge or predictions by corroborating them with facts taken from his experience; instead, he is generally satisfied if his quantifications are consistent with the mathematical assumptions that he started with. The data at his disposal are relevant only in terms of the assumptions with which they were collected—that is, relevant only within the context of a specific predetermined theoretical structure forming the scope of his universe. He studies the data of this assumed universe in order to acquire knowledge of its interdependencies and interrelationships. Needless to say, this sort of intellectual pursuit is closer to religion or magic than to empirical science.

Certain versus Uncertain Knowledge

If the business economist is primarily concerned with studying interactions that never vary—that is, interactions that he assumes are invariant—he is producing knowledge under conditions of certainty. For example, if he can assume that AAA corporate bond prices will always reflect a constant relationship between their yields and the federal discount rate, he will have perfect, certain knowledge of this relationship.

Frequently, however, the business economist does not have the luxury of certain knowledge. This happens when he is studying situations which are known to have a range of different outcomes, each with a fixed (but possibly unknown) probability. In certain knowledge there is never any risk stemming from ignorance, only from poor arithmetic. However, in uncertain knowledge the business economist confronts situations where his ignorance is a direct consequence of his analysis of risk. For example, a business economist would be able to calculate the exact risk involved in buying an option if he were able to know the precise probability that the underlying stock would fluctuate either below or above the striking price by an amount equal to the option premium.

It is important to remember that both certain and uncertain knowledge presuppose the validity of the axioms the business economist uses to define the relevance of his information. When he talks about the risk–reward relationship of a particular investment decision, he is assuming that the businessman's reality will so closely approximate his own statistical assumptions that a reasonable decision can be made. Unfortunately, with respect to the stock market and the valuation of equities, this is hardly ever the case. The reason is that the data of the business economist's universe are intrinsically different from the businessman's data (which are principally new items of information in the process of disclosure).

The business economist realizes, of course, that the actual circumstances of a business decision are veiled in uncertainty. He knows exactly what possible outcomes can be produced by a particular course of action, but he cannot calculate the likelihood of those outcomes. He is faced with the need to apply subjective probability. In other words, he has to guess at what the risk would be if only he knew enough about it to define it with certainty.[2]

For the business economist, uncertainty arises when he is called upon to analyze the present value of a future cash flow without knowing exactly how much the flow will be. He doesn't even know exactly how much of it will be paid out at a specific time, and he may not even know the number of years over which it will be paid out. The confusion arising from this state of ignorance would normally impel the businessman to make an intelligent guess. If he were a corporate executive he might want to bolster this guess with a variety of pro forma projections prepared by the accounting department. These projections will present him with an orderly set of outcomes from which he can choose the result most likely to conform to his own intuition and experience.

Let us assume that the problem confronting the business economist is to determine the present value of Gleason Works. The market price of this machine tool manufacturer's stock is $13 per share. It pays a dividend of 48¢ per share, representing a payout of about 25 percent. Under conditions of certainty, where the economist would not estimate any future increase in dividends, he would say that the future value of this stock in ten years would be $19 per share. The problem is that the dividend will change, but he doesn't know when or by how much. Thus, he will attempt to assign subjective probabilities to the possibilities that the dividend will increase, decrease, or stay constant. In this way he will be able to calculate a future value for the dividend payout over the next ten years and claim that the calculation reflects uncertainty.

The absurdity of this approach lies not only in the basic definition of what constitutes value, but in the assumption that the future can be forecast by reducing it to a state of probabilistic certainty. The business economist who specializes in constructing mechanisms for decision making generally does not like the uncertain and unpredictable state of affairs in the real world of business. He would concern himself only with showing how to make the "optimal" financial decision, which is one that claims to take risk into account.[3] Thus, even though risk cannot be properly assigned in a state of ignorance, the risk is superimposed on the ignorance through the construction of subjective probabilities (that is, quantitative guesses). The business economist claims that these probabilities provide him with the "expected utility" of the outcomes of each of the anticipated risks involved in making a decision. The next step is to quantify preferences among hypothetical alternatives.[4]

It is not necessary to explain here the mathematical methods used by the business economist to arrive at a decision in the face of uncertainty. However, it is important for us to be aware that he cannot provide the mechanism for making decisions without creating a universe where uncertainty is reduced to what is sometimes called a "certainty equivalent."

The business economist confronts uncertainty and ignorance by redefining what is not known to the point where it can be "quantified" by the application of statistical analysis. Since he has been so successful at confusing the businessman and ordinary shareholder in coming to grips with the valuation of common stock, it wouldn't hurt to spend some more time clarifying the business economist's role. There are times when mathematics is useful, and there are times when it is not.

Calculating the Future

Probability is a branch of mathematics having to do with the study of events whose frequency of occurrence is known or can be calculated in advance. Frequencies are fractions less than one and, of course, the frequencies of all possible related events must add up to one. When one knows, or can calculate in advance, the frequency with which an event will occur, the probability is said to be objective. This means the event can be duplicated and the frequency of occurrence can be empirically verified. For example, in Russian roulette, the probability of firing the one bullet is generally assumed to be one out of six, assuming that each of the six chambers is equally likely. But for the man about to put the gun to his head, this is a subjective assumption. In fact, the probability of the bullet firing on any given spin of the chamber can be accurately determined only after the chambers have been spun a large number of times. Most mathematicians would rather turn their attention elsewhere than risk the possibility of being shot in the midst of determining the odds of that very occurrence.

(After all, the bullet might have a strong tendency to stick in the firing position after every spin; if so, the one-sixth probability assumed out of ignorance would represent a lethal application of subjective probability.)

When the frequency of an event cannot be empirically or theoretically known in advance, any attempt to quantify the frequency is said to be subjective. A subjective probability, then, refers to an inherently unquantifiable frequency—a state of ignorance. Advocates of subjective probability often rely on a psuedomathematical principle appropriately entitled "the principle of insufficient reason," which states that if one is ignorant of any evidence to the contrary, he can assume that events are equally probable—as in the previous example of Russian roulette.

When business economists advocate the use of statistics for the purpose of producing forecasts on which a businessman should base his business decisions, the results often can be disastrous. The main reason for this is the way business economists understand information. For them, information is data capable of being quantified; data exist independently of the source of their disclosure or the precise public for which they were intended, and are independent of the process of dissemination.

Ignoring reality

Stock prices are regarded by business economists as simply the quantified results of a transaction and not a measure of the negotiation leading to the transaction. On the other hand, for a trader, stock prices convey associations of who set them, the closeness and intensity of the bid and offer, the amount of deceit the trader thought evident at the time, and the anticipation he attached to them. All of this is valuable information that the trader uses to arrive at decisions that he hopes will lead to future profits.

Corporate earnings figures are another example of information to be converted into abstract data by business economists in their propensity for using statistics to predict future results. Successful investing is simple, they would say, All you have to do is to forecast earnings more accurately than your rivals.[5] Aside from the naiveté of the assumption that the process of valuation is limited to the process of predicting earnings, a mistake is made in thinking that earnings reports are hard numbers, all equally accurate and valid.

Using this uncritical approach, the following questions have been raised and studied by business economists: What is the relationship of earnings forecasts and the behavior of stock prices? Are quarterly earnings reports useful in updating and revising earnings forecasts? Is the study of historic growth rates and earnings fluctuations useful in predicting future growth rates and earnings changes?[6]

Used as a stimulant for yet more academic research, these questions and their answers are perhaps useful. As a guide to making business decisions they are of very limited use. No matter how often it has been proven that quarterly earnings reports are of little aid in helping the average analyst revise his forecast, they somehow still must be studied and interpreted by all analysts. Nothing, not even the failure to predict stock prices correctly, ever seems to absolve an analyst or shareholder from diligently studying and interpreting earnings as they are reported.

Perhaps the most amusing academic studies involving the analysis of earnings are the so-called "higgledy-piggledy growth" studies first produced in England and then the United States.[7] These studies have "demonstrated" that earnings data, like stock prices, follow fairly random patterns. The authors infer that trends in historical earnings reports cannot provide a clue to future earnings.

I have no quarrel with the academic usefulness of these studies. But I do think it amusing that there are people who would actually study earnings as numerical abstractions independent of the financial statements and accounting methods of the particular companies involved. Obviously, if earnings are treated as mere numbers, then the relation between them might very well appear to be random. But earnings are not just numbers to provide grist for a statistical mill. They are reports made by specific managements of specific companies at a specific time and place for a specific purpose. Only an economist could view reported earnings as hard facts rather than as messages.

If the purpose of these studies were merely theoretical with no practical consequences, it would be as pointless to fault them as it would be to fault those ancient theoreticians bent on knowing why Babylonians had flat feet. Unfortunately, such studies do have practical implications. One of these is that perhaps they ought to be ignored altogether by security analysts. If earnings behave randomly, what is the point of studying them? What is more, perhaps security analysis is a waste of time and valuation of equities futile. All of which leads this school of academicians to a final suggestion: the investor should focus his efforts on constructing an efficient portfolio of stocks or, if he doesn't have the time, buy an index fund.

One conclusion which is difficult not to draw from reading these studies is that the businessman (or decision maker, as he is called) need go no further than these studies in looking for information, certainly not to management and the marketplace. These studies do not interpret information in the context of its disclosure and dissemination, but reduce it to "scientific" data. The business economist is in the business of producing information by way of statistical analysis. He is not engaged in clarifying the structure, relevance, and ambiguity of this information. It is no exaggeration to say, then, that his efforts can at times be perceived as a kind of conceit. A businessman, however, knows that the value of information is often directly proportionate to the degree of its uncertainty. Stock prices and earnings reports can be valuable precisely because one doesn't know exactly how to interpret them. Uncertainty is a direct consequence of information when it is a communication between human beings. This is what commerce is all about.

What Is Risk?

The businessman lives with uncertainty as a normal and necessary aspect of his environment. While he constantly has to make difficult decisions in the face of uncertainty, he would usually rather live with it than totally without it. Having to negotiate prices and contracts and to compete in markets is preferable to the certainty associated with monopoly control and prices fixed by government. However, one consequence of uncertainty is risk.[8]

Risk is more often than not an indication of the businessman's state of ignorance. While he usually regards risk as a measure of the extent of his possible loss, he reacts to that risk with a corresponding degree of intuition. For him, risk is not simply an actuarial concept. An arbitrager, for example, uses as precise a concept of actuarial risk as possible, but if he doesn't have a feeling for what he is doing, he will find himself in severe difficulty. It is this intuitive response to risk which accounts for the reasonableness and adequacy of his judgment to the arbitrage at hand. What may become a discomfort to his bank account is the risk supposedly justified on paper.

Business economists do not react to risk in the same way. For them risk doesn't really exist unless it can be formally defined and quantified in advance. Thus, risk is not associated with the kind of ignorance and uncertainty that are immediately meaningful to the businessman. The business economist can only define risk in terms of probability, whether objective or subjective. Risk, therefore, describes the frequencies with which the outcomes of investment decisions can deviate from the expected or predicted outcome. Statistical risk is measured by the degree to which an outcome varies or is dispersed around some meaningful constant value such as an average or linear trend projection.

Statistical risk can only be quantified by the use of objective or subjective probability, and it can only be used to describe the possible outcome of events within a completely defined universe, that is, within a state of quasi-certainty. The business economist takes great pains to construct this complete universe, even when he is ignorant of a large portion of the relevant data or the possible outcomes of a decision. Because business economists find it difficult to calculate credible measures of absolute risk, they often resort to measures of relative risk, also known as *systematic risk.*[9]

The beta coefficient is a favorite indicator of systematic risk. It relates the variability (or the volatility) of the market price of an individual stock to the variability of the market as a whole. A stock would have a beta coefficient of one when its price fluctuations are, roughly speaking, neither larger nor smaller than, and in the same direction as, the fluctuations in the market. In other words, there must be a positive covariation between the price fluctuations of the stock and of the market as a whole.

Unfortunately, the measure used by business economists to determine the size of price fluctuations is a squared deviation from a mean trend. The squared effect causes one or two sharp spikes in the price of a stock to dominate the overall estimate of the stock's beta coefficient, resulting in misleading fluctuations in the calculated beta. In fact, business economists unhappily admit that past betas are poor indicators of future betas, an observation which leads one to suspect that beta coefficients are valuable only to the computer companies paid to derive them.

Finally, systematic risk analysis doesn't really attempt to quantify losses in absolute terms, but only relative to the market. A fully diversified portfolio constructed according to this system is defined to be efficient if it does not lose or make more money than the index of market performance against which it is measured. Money lost by such a portfolio would be justified on the grounds that nothing better could have been "reasonably" (that is, statistically) anticipated. According to the theory, the way to increase the risk of an efficient portfolio is not by increasing the number of stocks with a historical record of fluctuating more than the market, but by borrowing or leveraging the efficient portfolio; likewise, systematic risk is reduced by increasing the proportion of treasury bills or other risk-free assets.

There is more nonsense than sense in restricting the interpretation of risk to *relative* loss. Of course it is true that if you really don't know what to buy and sell, you are not going to do better or worse than the crowd if you buy and sell what everyone else does at the same time. And the idea that *absolute* loss is irrelevant to risk—because it cannot be systematically quantified—is pure nonsense. A business economist would (unfairly) describe a person who put all his money into one stock as a person who really doesn't care about risk.[10] Somehow, there is a defect in the notion that a businessman's judgment about his financial risk is insufficient in that the only academically acceptable risks must be calculated statistically from relative price fluctuations. This defect is not only a matter of semantics. It is a reflection of an attitude toward the use and value of financial information.

The use of information derived under conditions of theoretically complete statistical knowledge is really inadequate for the kinds of decisions a businessman must make. Business economists sometimes claim that the statistical concepts, such as risk, that they have developed under conditions of complete knowledge are also applicable to conditions in which knowledge is far from complete. What they really mean is that these concepts *ought* to be applicable to the real world of business decisions. In fact they seldom are. Uncertainty and incomplete knowledge are the essence of the world in which financial information is disclosed and disseminated. Uncertainty is not an accidental attribute that can somehow be eliminated from this world. There are, of course, business economists who are aware of, or profess to be aware of, the fact that statistical models do not fully account for the real uncertainties facing the business manager.[11] Yet one wonders what is the practical purpose of such models if they cannot provide a basis for business decisions.

Uncertainty and Efficiency

Viewed from its effects on the financial community as well as on the academic world, the development of the concept of efficiency in securities markets has been the most important contribution made in the last 20 years by business economists. Under this concept, the economist defines an efficient capital market to be one in which security prices fully reflect all publicly available information instantaneously. The academic literature has been primarily concerned with clarifying the meaning of the phrases "fully reflects," "all publicly available information," and "instantaneously."

Defining the efficient capital market

Three types of tests have been devised to determine the degree to which the security market "fully reflects" information. The first, or "weak form," tests were historically the first to be developed. They were concerned only with producing evidence derived from the historical behavior of market prices. These tests hoped to clarify two major issues: the extent to which historical equity prices are independent of each other, and the degree to which short-term trading techniques could be profitably used. The startling evidence produced by the weak form tests is that the pattern of successive changes in market prices appears to be indistinguishable from the path of "random walk." Successive price changes act randomly to the extent that they cannot be predicted using any predetermined pattern or formula.[12]

The business economist uses a number of standard statistical tests to look for nonrandomness in a time series of successive price changes. Unfortunately, statistics can offer no test that conclusively establishes the *randomness* of a sequence of data. Statistics can only offer tests that decide whether the data sequence is *nonrandom in some specified way*. For instance, it is easy to test whether the price of a stock is following a straight line, parabolic curve, or a sinusoidal (cyclical) pattern. However, the fact that the stock does not follow any one of these is no guarantee that it doesn't follow some subtler form of nonrandom behavior. Thus, when the business economist says that stock prices behave randomly, what he really means is that they don't behave nonrandomly in the obvious ways his statistical tests are capable of detecting. Thus, the weak form tests provide, at best, inconclusive evidence of the randomness of stock prices.

The second, or "semistrong form," tests were designed to provide evidence for how "quickly" stock prices "reflect" new information. The presumptions concerning randomness, as tested by the weak form tests, were retained. Business economists claim that, by and large, the semistrong form tests provide sufficient evidence that new information, such as annual earnings announcements, stock splits, and secondary offerings, is so quickly and fully reflected in the price of stocks that no one can profit by acting faster than the speed with which it is disseminated. There is no lag time, as it were, between the disclosure of, and the acting on, information. This is an extremely important claim, because it implies that public securities are truly competitive and, hence, efficient.

The third, or "strong form," tests were constructed mainly to find out whether the financial community had monopolistic access to information. The point was not to determine whether an insider having access to important information could profit from it before its disclosure, but to see whether individuals such as traders, specialists, security analysts, or fund managers did in fact have a competitive edge over the general public. Needless to say, these tests provided the most tentative and unconvincing evidence in support of the efficient market theory. Apparently, access to information is not what it was assumed to be. The fund manager, who supposedly knows more than the average investor, actually performed worse.

It must be emphasized that the evidence of the three preceding forms of tests is valid only if certain idealized conditions are met by the data being tested. Not only was a specific form of data frequencies (a Gaussian probability distribution) assumed in advance, but three further assumptions were also necessary: that there be (a) no transaction costs, (b) free access to information, and (c) agreement about the implications of newly disclosed information.

The fact that these conditions do not fully obtain in the uncertain world of buying and selling is, of course, recognized by business economists. Yet, as Eugene Fama has pointed out, failure of the market to meet these conditions is only potentially, not necessarily, a source of market inefficiency.[13] For example, the fact that actual trading involves paying commissions is not in itself sufficient to cause market inefficiency. Or the fact that investment bankers or management have information to which the public does not have access does not prove that securities markets are inefficient. For the markets to be inefficient, it would be necessary for this inside information to be withheld from the public while the insiders successfully translated their information into significant profits.

Finally, with respect to the third condition (agreement about the meaning of information), even though investors obviously disagree about how to interpret new information, it is still sufficient for the validity of the test that the majority will generally make the same decision to buy or sell.

This last assumption, however, is rather suspicious. What does it mean to say that investors must agree about the implications of new information if the only evidence of their agreement is buying or selling? If what is to be proven is that prices reflect information, how can it also be assumed that price is the *evidence* of the interpretation of this information?

The paradox behind the efficient market theory

It has been said that for the efficient market hypothesis to be true, "it is necessary for many investors to disbelieve it."[14] This disbelief is fostered by the investor's desire to maximize profits, to act on the basis of predictions, and to analyze all relevant information. In other words, market efficiency depends on the inefficiency of the shareholder or security analyst.

But how can this be? If it is meaningful to say that disbelief is an indication of a theory's validity, it is perhaps equally meaningful to say that belief is an indication of its irrelevance. If the majority of investors believe that market prices fully reflect all available information, why shouldn't the nonbelievers then produce extraordinary profits made possible by the market's intrinsic inefficiency?

The authors of the preceding paradox—that in order for the market to be efficient, it is necessary that the majority of investors agree that the market is inefficient—try to explain away its apparent absurdity. This paradox, they say, "is not very different from the paradox of all effectively competitive markets. Entrepreneurs continue buying to compete though the competitive process itself can reduce the rate of profits to zero. Investors continue to compete in an effort to arrive at superior judgments."[15]

I assume that by "competitive markets," the authors are speaking of markets other than the financial markets, such as the commodity markets. If the investors referred to are users or producers of commodities, isn't it their avowed intention to establish reasonable long-term prices? If they are traders or speculators, isn't it their avowed intention to cut as short as possible the losses they know they will have and to increase as much as possible the few profits they expect? For the professional trader, is not the game of speculation worth playing *only* because it is worth winning? Would any professional commodity trader seriously suggest that the only way of "playing the game" would be to subject his capital to the same variation of gains and losses as the daily prices of the commodities he trades? Could he seriously claim that if he doesn't lose more than the market falls he is successful?

Efficiency of Capital Allocation—The Pareto Criterion

If we accept that prices do indeed reflect all available information (and I shall soon show why this contention is unreasonable), why must we also believe that such a market allocates capital efficiently? What is the relation between the concept of efficient allocation to the concept of a market in which prices fully reflect information?

If business economists restricted their interest to the procedural efficiency of markets, it would be reasonable to claim that a market which immediately disseminates all information about prices and volume is efficient. Nobody would be able to obtain a competitive edge through access to inside market information. But in fact, business economists are not so much interested in the procedural efficiency of markets as in their allocative efficiency. Needless to say, economists would prefer to analyze the major issue of whether the stock market provides the optimal allocation of our country's financial resources than to investigate the much less exciting question of the convenience of the market's appraisal function. If questions of optimum allocation are excluded, procedural efficiency is then considered primarily a measure of convenience and not a prerequisite for the "best" distribution of financial wealth.[16]

Business economists define the allocative efficiency of the market according to a criterion established more than 60 years ago by Vilfredo Federico Damaso Pareto, an Italian professor at the University of Lausanne. Before examining the Pareto criterion, it would be helpful to understand why it is important to us even though we are primarily concerned with the valuation of equities and not with the economic function of the stock market.

We shall see that the Pareto criterion not only has a bearing on the relevance of information available to the shareholder, but is used by business economists to support their claim that the market is ultimately the only fair and reasonable appraiser of value. This means that exchange value would have to be based on market information, and would negate the idea that a shareholder's independent appraisal can be fair and reasonable.

What is the Pareto criterion?

Pareto developed his criterion as a way to assess group welfare in such a way that what would be valid for the good of society would also be valid for the betterment of an individual.[17] Johannes de Graaff has explained this as follows:

> The concept of group welfare hinges on the impossibility of making interpersonal comparisons of well-being. If these interpersonal comparisons cannot be made, the welfare of the group is clearly no more than a heterogeneous collection of individual welfares. If some men are made better off, and none worse off, group welfare rises; if some are made worse off, and none better off, it falls. But if some are made better off and some worse off we just do not know what has happened to the welfare of the group.[18]

The Pareto criterion states that a change in the allocation of resources which makes some people better off without simultaneously making anybody worse off has contributed to the increased welfare of society. This change is referred to as a *Pareto improvement.*[19] An economic situation is referred to as *Pareto-optimal* when no one can profit from a change in the allocation of resources without others suffering a corresponding loss. Pareto-optimality is widely believed to be, as Robert Dorfman put it, "the fundamental criterion of economic efficiency. It holds that an economy is functioning with perfect economic efficiency when there is no possible change in its operations that will benefit any consumer without hurting some other consumer."[20] When a market allocates resources according to Pareto-optimal conditions, it is an allocatively efficient market. It follows that a market is not allocatively efficient if it distributes resources in such a way that a Pareto improvement is possible.

Employing the Pareto criterion

Although Pareto-optimality is generally applied to society as a whole, it is sometimes used to describe the optimum outcome of a business transaction—that is, the best transaction that two (or more) businessmen can agree to and still be better off than they were before. The implication is that each was able to compete perfectly with the other. As a consequence, Pareto-optimality is the normative ideal of perfect competition.

Whether it is used to describe the ideal social allocation of resources or the ideal exchange of goods in a business deal, Pareto-optimality ignores differences of utility or need among individuals. This is the crux of the Pareto criterion. For example, if the problem is to distribute one loaf of bread between two people, the criterion of Pareto-optimality would state that any split of the loaf is as good as any other, because one of the two always loses by changing the split. The fact that one person is hungry and the other is almost full is irrelevant to the Pareto definition of welfare. Pareto does not recognize relative needs among individuals.

The use of the Pareto criterion to define the optimum allocation of resources is dependent on various assumptions. The first is perfect knowledge of what the allocation ought to be if all parties know exactly what is involved. The second is that all parties must have complete knowledge of the utility preferences of all other parties. (In a real business transaction, two people may arrive at an agreement which, though satisfactory to both, is not Pareto-optimal due to the uncertainty and incompleteness of the information available to each.[21]) The third assumption is that Pareto-optimality is only applicable to one point in time, which, because of the second assumption, is essentially retrospective.[22]

It is important to remember that the Pareto criterion is normative; that is, it describes how the allocation of resources ought to occur to be optimal, not how it really does occur. It is not, therefore, far removed from the lofty perspective of Adam Smith's "invisible hand"—except that, as Eduard Heimann has pointed out, the hand has been "made visible."[23]

Thus, when business economists say that an efficient market fully reflects all information quickly, they are really supporting the Pareto theory contention that the market is generally a perfect allocation mechanism. That market prices do reflect information seems to support the theory that the stock market acts as an optimal allocator of ownership of financial capital. Thus, evidence culled from a statistician's abstract universe is used to support the ethical inclinations of the theoretician of welfare economics. And all of this, in turn, is based on the economist's refusal to admit (or to understand) that he has been unable to come to grips with the inherent uncertainty of the world of buyers and sellers.

Where Pareto Falls Short

Although the Pareto criterion is of some use in characterizing the net effects of large-scale societal projects, it ignores the reality of the marketplace based as it is on an examination of transaction utility which ignores the needs and desires of individual buyers and sellers. No theory that ignores interpersonal comparisons of utility can ever be of use in helping the individual judge value, let alone optimum value.

Our explanation of value in Chapters 3, 4, and 5 was predicated on the assumption that the determination of value for the shareholder is always a function of how he thinks it will benefit him as a property owner. Yet the efficient market theory would have us interpret value not as a function of individual expectations but as a function of the market as a whole. This is unacceptable because it does not describe the market as a forum where willing buyers and sellers come together to transact business on the basis of individual expectations. It does not describe the process of commerce but the theory of what commerce could be if it was not what it is.

Shortchanging the individual

According to the efficient market theory, liberty in commerce (defined by the Fourteenth Amendment as the right to transact business as a function of an individual's personal values) would be an irrelevant concept. The right to judge for oneself the value of a share of common stock, based on one's own notion of opportunity cost and exchange value, cannot be supplanted by the notion that others, meaning the market, know what is best. If this were so, the government ultimately ought to do away with the rights of the individual. As it is, I suspect that the efficient market theory has already contributed more than its fair share in impelling the SEC to seek more power or, at least, to diminish the importance of the principle of self-regulation. The SEC's emphasis should be on the valuations from which individuals can negotiate stock prices, rather than on the valuation imputed once the negotiation has been terminated. (In Chapter 10 we shall see how the logic of the concept that the market is the ultimate judge is, unfortunately, pressing hard upon us.)

By and large the tendency of the law is to define value, not in terms of an overall welfare concept applicable to society as a whole and independent of the needs of individuals, but in terms of the adversary relationship between litigants. Remedies and equity judgments are usually arrived at as a consequence of the individual definitions of benefits lost or gained. But if we were to take the efficient market theory seriously enough to apply it as a legal principal of equity, we would have a situation in which personal estimates of costs and benefits would be to a great extent irrelevant.

Some readers may argue that in the preceding analysis of efficiency based on the Pareto criterion I overstated my case. After all, we all believe that the American stock market really does allocate efficiently, or at least much more efficiently than any other stock market. There is no other country in the world where the disclosure and dissemination of information is so thorough, speedy, and accessible. And though I explained that allocative efficiency refers not to information per se, but to the allocation of the financial capital among firms and the ownership of this capital among shareholders, the argument can still be made that procedural efficiency implies allocative efficiency and vice versa.

The view that efficient allocation of capital is somehow inextricably connected to efficient distribution of information (called "process") is based on the assumption that the pricing mechanism of the stock market will sooner or later reflect the "true value" of the stocks traded. It is therefore the procedural efficiency of the stock market which will sooner or later permit a "just" allocation of capital between corporations selling new stock and shareholders selling old stock according to their personal expectations of increased wealth. In other words, the stock market allocates efficiently because it provides the well-oiled mechanism whereby corporations are able to satisfy their equity needs at the appropriate time, and individual investors can realize profits on their undervalued securities according to the time limits of their expectations. As Sidney Robbins put it, "For an efficient process, it is important that the pricing mechanism permits the maintenance of a logical relationship between a company's financial position and the price of its shares."[24]

Is allocative efficiency a false ideal?

It is my view that ultimately statements such as Sidney Robbins' are a consequence of belief rather than rigorous systematic logic. The stock market functions in a climate of essential and irreducible uncertainty, where price is never the *only* evidence of value. Price can be the response of a few investors to any number of unrelated expectations. Trying to find the mathematical relationship between prices, politics, and profits, economic statistics and cost-benefit analysis can be as misleading as it is time consuming. The popular view of the market's allocative efficiency is based on the simpler belief that "true value will out"; however, this is not very satisfying to the model-building propensity of economists. (William J. Baumol, for one, has suggested that this belief in efficiency can be based on grounds other than the Pareto criterion.[25])

However useful this popular attitude toward the market's allocative efficiency may be in contributing to investor confidence, it is not supported by how the market actually serves industry and the investor. If, in fact, they were well served, one would expect that much of industry's need for equity capital would be supplied by additional public stock offerings. Yet, as Baumol points out, only a small portion of the capital requirements of American business is supplied by the equity market. Indeed, there are many reasons why industry might avoid the stock market, including compliance with SEC regulations, the costs associated with secondary offerings, and the desire to leave stock ownership patterns unchanged. Perhaps the most important consideration is that the equity market is often too depressed at those times when a company needs new capital the most.[26]

Management usually prefers the convenience of the bond market and the unhampered use of the firm's own retained earnings to the allocative efficiency of the stock market. Further, in spite of the popular belief in efficiency, few people believe that the stock market serves as an effective means for the distribution of wealth, or even for the allocation of corporate ownership. The recent splurge of takeovers demonstrates that it is almost always a negotiation between managements which leads to a change in ownership, rather than the simple buying of shares in the open market. Most significant changes in ownership are realized in an investment banker's office and not on the floor of an exchange. For some reason the preferred time for such a transfer of ownership is after four o'clock.

William J. Baumol has summed it up quite well:

> All in all, one cannot escape the impression that, at best, the allocative function is performed rather imperfectly as measured by the criteria of the welfare economist. The oligopolistic position of those who operate the market, the brokers, the floor traders, and the specialists; the random patterns which characterize the behavior of stock prices; the apparent unresponsiveness of supply to price changes and managements' efforts to avoid the market as a source of funds, all raise some questions about the perfection of the regulating operations of the market. But though its workings are undoubtedly imperfect it does not follow that they are beyond the pale. Rather, its operation must be judged to be somewhat on a par with that of the bulk of America's business. Far from the competitive ideal, beset by a number of patent shortcomings, it nevertheless performs a creditable job. Bearing in mind that its ramifications were never planned by organized human deliberation, one can only marvel at the quality of its performance.[27]

I have tried to point out that the concept of market allocative efficiency, whether based on the Pareto criterion or on popular attitudes toward value and price, is very fuzzy, to say the least. It seems to reflect the beliefs of certain people who use the market more than it does the actual condition or purpose of the market. At the very best, belief in an efficient market can be an inducement to invest and participate in commerce. At the very worst, it is a dogma inapplicable to the reality of buying and selling. To say that a market in which prices fully reflect all available information quickly is efficient is a confusing and needless judgment. And whether market prices do fully reflect information is something we shall examine below.

The Market Price—What Does It Reflect?

When business economists say that the market prices of common stocks fully reflect all available information instantaneously, they mean that evidence for the speedy and thorough dissemination of information is found in the behavior of market prices. This behavior supposedly provides the last word on how investors interpret the information available to them.

This claim, as we have seen, is based on the assumption that all investors agree in their interpretation of the significance of the available information. Without this assumption it would be impossible to draw any conclusions about the behavior of stock market prices. When business economists say that this assumption may be used even though it is "unrealistic," they are making a judgment about the nature of the evidence that is admissible in supporting their theory. When they claim, as did Baruch Lev, that "the question whether the efficient market model reasonably describes phenomena in real capital markets is . . . empirical and cannot be settled on a priori grounds,"[28] they are saying that no evidence is admissible other than market prices. "Empirical" thus refers to the statistical behavior of stock prices within the confines of the statistician's universe.

If one were to use market price as evidence supplied from the "real" world of buying and selling, one could use it only on the assumption of investor agreement about the use of information, In legal judgments, stock prices are not supposed to be used as the sole evidence of value, but rather as a determination of price in a specific transaction. This means that stock prices can't be used as the only evidence as to why people buy or sell.

Business economists present us with a situation in which they cannot be refuted other than in their own terms, like medical doctors who refuse to be judged other than by a court of doctors. They would have us believe that market price is the only reliable indication of value, because only the behavior of market prices can be reliably tested. The value of this reliability is defended on the grounds of its convenience. But to whom is it a convenience? The buyer? The seller? Or those shareholders who are unwilling to sell? Unless this question is answered, the "reliability" of market price is meaningless.

The debate concerning randomness

To say that prices behave randomly is, as we have seen, hardly a foregone conclusion: it really means that prices do not follow the few simple nonrandom patterns that the statistician happened to test. In other words, the claim of random behavior of prices is a nonrigorous judgment resulting from not being able to detect any one of a small number of previously hypothesized patterns of predictable behavior. Most investors, I think, would agree that prices behave unpredictably, at least most of the time. This belief is more accurate and more useful than the business economist's more grandiose claim that prices behave randomly, even though the business economist may have based his claim on vast computer data banks of stock prices and the most elaborate, expensive statistical programs available.

The problem, as I see it, lies in the kind of evidence which the three tests of the efficient market theory we looked at earlier are supposed to provide. The "weak form" tests, for example, are used to support the contention that available information is fully reflected in stock prices. Since stock prices present no patterns of behavior discernible to the statisticians, it is assumed that they must reflect information. The logic is that if identifiable, nonrandom patterns of behavior obtained, this would imply that not all people had access to this information at the same time, since some could have profited in excess by use of a simple buy-and-hold (filter) technique. In other words, randomness is the evidence used to prove the contention that all pertinent information is fully reflected in stock prices. It should be obvious that without the assumption of investor agreement about the relevance of this information, randomness would prove no such thing.

If the assumption is made that investors do disagree about the implications of information, then randomness can be used as evidence that information is not fully reflected in stock prices. One could then view nonrandom behavior as an indication of homogeneous interpretation of information, and random behavior as evidence of the intrinsic disagreement over the use of information by buyers and sellers. An efficient market would then be one that does not fully reflect information or, what is the equivalent, one that fully reflects "perfect" disagreement about its implications. From the point of view of a practical investor, I think this is a more plausible interpretation of efficiency. Extraordinary market rises or falls, like those following the assassination of a president, a declaration of war, or a large tax cut, would be evidence of investor agreement about the relevance of information.

What this exercise in rhetoric shows is that the behavior of stock prices cannot be used as evidence for anything unless the accompanying assumptions are reasonable. The proposition that stock prices fully reflect the homogeneous expectations of investors is nonsense. It is a notion which a sensible investor can accept only after he has been brainwashed by the complexity of the mathematics used to support it. Probability theory and statistics should be used to support evidence that is not obvious to our common sense, but not evidence that plainly contradicts common sense.

Valuing Common Stock by the Efficient Market Theory

Now that we have examined the efficient market theory, we need to examine its implications for our main concern, the valuation of common stock. These implications are dazzling, especially when viewed from the more traditional perspectives on valuation. If, indeed, prices fully reflect information, one would suspect that the price of a security reflects a judgment about its value. However, the implications of the efficient market theory are actually much more complex. It is not simply the price of a stock which reflects a judgment of value, but the price of that stock in relation to the prices of all other stocks. The value of stock, then, is not a function of security analysis but of portfolio management.

The efficient market theory holds that the prices of stocks—as well as the relation between these prices and disclosed financial information—vary randomly. Therefore, no publicly disclosed information can yield nonrandom results. Even earnings and growth estimates behave randomly. There is little to be gained, most business economists believe, from employing the traditional methods of security valuation. Traditional valuation rests on the determination of "point estimates," that is, the determination of specific expected earnings or price-earnings ratios. We have seen that these estimates are determined by business economists primarily by employing some formula for discounting the present value of future dividends. Security analysts merely make enlightened guesses of future earnings and price earnings estimates. The efficient market theorists believe that the valuation of common stock is mainly concerned with expected values even though they do not think that discounting the present value of future dividends is, in itself, adequate.[29] Indeed, I think it would be fair to say that most efficient market proponents believe that determining value by analyzing the financial statements of a company is a waste of time.[30]

The risk–reward theory of valuation

Value, efficient market theorists believe, must be a function of what they call the "risk–reward" relationship. Since risk is based on a probability distribution and reward on an expected rate of return, the value of a security can be determined only when it is understood as a function of this relationship. The chief problem with this view stems from its belief that value can *only* be determined by the use of probability theory. Efficient market theoreticians do not believe that any meaningful concept of value can ever be arrived at without the use of probability theory.

The reason for this is quite simple. Although everybody believes that reward (expected value or return on investment) is desirable, this reward cannot be precisely calculated. If it could, these theoreticians say, investors would not diversify. They would only own one or two stocks which promise the highest reward. Therefore, reward only makes sense when analyzed together with risk. The expected return on a particular stock can be analyzed only in the context of the likelihood that that return may not be realized. Investors of course regard increased expected return as desirable and increased risk as undesirable.

Investors, the theory holds, must regard increased variability in their anticipated returns unfavorably for two reasons. First, they can lend at a riskless rate of interest; in other words, they can always invest their money in treasury bills or the equivalent. Second, though all investors prefer returns higher than the riskless rate, they will invest in common stock instead of risk-free loans only if they can be reasonably sure of making more money during the same period of time. It would not make sense for them to invest in common stock if the chances of making 10 percent, for example, were too small. They would tend to buy treasury bills yielding a sure 6 percent. How much more return the investor seeks should be a function of how much risk he can accept. Since, according to the theoreticians, investors are risk-averse,[31] their desire to increase returns is limited by the increase in risk (that is, variability in returns) which they take.

In other words, risk is a function of the probability distribution of anticipated returns from each security. This return is not determined by discounting present value or estimating future earnings of the security viewed in isolation, but by analyzing the average return plus the riskiness of the portfolio of stocks in which it is found. The riskiness or variability of return of the complete portfolio is usually assessed using a statistical measure of dispersion, such as the standard deviation. For the present it is only necessary to understand that efficient market theoreticians believe that the value of an individual security cannot be established independently of its existence within an efficient portfolio of stocks. An efficient portfolio is one which varies the same amount as a standard market index like Standard and Poor's index of 500 industrial stocks. An efficient portfolio will be no more or less risky than the market index to which it is related.

A security pricing model

William F. Sharpe developed what theoreticians now consider to be the basic capital asset pricing model for determining the value of an individual security. This model is only valid assuming equilibrium, that is, assuming the efficient market theory. Oversimplifying, this model states that the expected return E on a security is equal to the treasury bill yield or riskless rate of return T, plus the difference between the market rate of return M and the treasury bill rate, multiplied by the beta coefficient β of the security. Thus:

$$E = T + (M - T)\beta$$

The beta coefficient is a statistical correlation coefficient intended to measure the degree to which an individual security follows the fluctuations of a market index. (See previous discussion in this chapter in the section "What Is Risk?" concerning the limitations of fluctuation measure based on *squared* deviations from an average; the beta coefficient suffers from these limitations as much as the standard deviation does.) A beta coefficient of one means that the individual security will gain or lose about as much as a market index. A beta coefficient of two means that it can gain or lose twice as much. Treasury bills have a beta of about zero. The beta coefficient measures the degree of "systematic" risk because it only measures the risk of an individual security relative to that of an efficient portfolio or the market as a whole.

If the *T* bill rate is 6 percent, *M* 10 percent, and the beta coefficient one, the expected return on the market price of an individual security will be 10 percent. If the beta were two, the expected return would be 14 percent. If it were one-half, the expected return would be 8 percent.[32]

We can now better understand what the efficient market theoreticians mean by value; to them it can only be determined by analyzing the behavior of stock prices. Since stock prices are random variables, the value of an individual stock can only be determined through statistical measures of its variation relative to the variation of all other stock prices (or a market index). In other words, value must depend on the judicious use of statistics and not on security analysis. Thus, the valuation of an individual security (for instance, valuation using the capital asset pricing model) is essentially an abstract, impersonal endeavor. According to the theoreticians, the value of an individual security must be valid for all investors—value cannot be defined as a benefit to a specific individual.

The efficient portfolio

In Chapters 3–5 we saw that the valuation of individual securities depended on the benefits expected by the individual shareholders. According to the efficient market theory this is an impossibility—the value of an individual stock must be the same for everybody. This is, as we saw earlier in this chapter, a direct consequence of the inability of the efficient market theory to cope with interpersonal comparisons of utility.

For true believers in the efficient market theory, only the construction of an efficient portfolio can hope to satisfy the personal investment criteria of the individual investor. And this cannot be satisfied effectively by choosing four or five stocks on the basis of the financial analysis and expectations associated with each security. Such a selection could not accurately incorporate the risk–reward function which, according to this theory, is the only thing that explicitly expresses the investment criteria of the individual investor.

The investor's risk–reward criteria can only be incorporated in the security selection process by constructing an efficient portfolio. If the market rate of return on an efficient portfolio is 10 percent, an investor who wants a higher return will leverage the portfolio to achieve his optimum rate of return. An investor who will settle for less than this 10 percent will invest a proportionately larger amount of his money in risk-free investments such as bonds and treasury bills.

We are therefore left with an interpretation of value resting on statistical estimates of marketwide risks and return to the exclusion of all other personal judgments and expectations. However appealing this may sound to some, it involves substituting a belief in the applicability of mathematical abstractions for a practical understanding of business conventions and financial information. Of course, being able to see the tenuous connection between mathematical abstractions and the actual uncertainties of buying and selling is what distinguishes the real businessman. He understands the degree to which information, in order to be useful, must involve individual disagreement and interpretation. For the business economist, information reflects but the "average" opinion of a homogeneous investing public that seems to live only in a universe of probabilistic abstractions.

The concept of an efficient market portfolio is perhaps most useful to fiduciaries managing enormous pools of equity capital. Since these pools or trusts normally consist of a portfolio of at least fifty stocks, and often are restricted to only the five hundred largest corporations, they are in a very real sense the market. The concepts underlying an efficient portfolio can at least guide fiduciaries of large trusts in forming a policy of diversification which will assure them of not having to suffer greater losses than those suffered by the market. But due to their lack of flexibility, it would also be unreasonable to expect them to consistently produce higher profits.

Portfolio limitations

For smaller portfolios, say, of less than $100 million, the concept of an efficient portfolio leaves much to be desired. These portfolios often have the flexibility to be either in the market or out at the discretion of the investment adviser. But if the adviser believes he should be out of the market, he is to a great extent expressing a disbelief in the efficient market theory, even if he believes his portfolio is efficient.

Such advisers are ultimately traders anticipating market trends and cycles. Some are very successful. Many such advisers also use short selling and option techniques, neither of which has yet been accounted for by the efficient market theory.[33]

Ultimately, perhaps the biggest shortcoming of the efficient portfolio concept is that it is totally tied in to the stock market—and thereby fluctuates according to the same whims and vagaries, despair and elation of the public.

The Uncertainty of Negotiation

In 1949, George L. Shackle published *Expectation in Economics,* a work that was destined to become a basic text in the theory of bargaining. One of his main objectives was to express dissatisfaction with the orthodox or, as we put it, statistical treatment of uncertainty, which by "irrelevant discussion of actuarial principles" aims at "*reducing* or *eliminating* uncertainty in circumstances where it cannot be so eliminated, not [at] *digesting, enjoying, and turning to psychic profit* the uncertainty in those many situations where it *cannot* be removed."[34]

These "many situations" in which uncertainty cannot be removed are those in which at least two parties are involved in an exchange of information based upon expectations, objectives, and strategies which are not, at least initially, identical. These are circumstances in which the greed, tactics, deceit, surprise, and irrationality of each party present challenges which one cannot ignore simply because he does not have the actuarial tools to cope with them. Not only is the estimation of probability irrelevant in these situations but, more significantly, the consequent calculation of risk as a measure of dispersion around some assumed mean value is insufficient in providing the kind of self-assurance necessary to make decisions. These are situations in which uncertainty cannot be eliminated because the disclosure of information occurs in a context of *negotiated understanding.*

Marginal analysis—of limited use

The simplest act of negotiation occurs between a buyer and seller when there is one price offered by the former and another asked by the latter. When a transaction is not preceded by an indication of bid and offer—the expression of the expectation of the participants—it is not a negotiation, but a consumer transaction. As G. L. S. Shackle simply put it, "the chief variables in a negotiation intended to settle price are the asked and offered prices themselves."[35] A consumer transaction, at least when it is effected within our network of retail oligopolies, doesn't involve the sort of strategy and bargaining associated with the nonconsumer buyer. We are all aware that a consumer is not born, he is created. There are very few preferences which are a function of need and not induced desire. Thanks to advertising and merchandising, a consumer transaction doesn't need much in the way of expectations.

Although it may make sense to apply the principles of marginal analysis to consumer transactions, it doesn't make much sense to apply them to the bargaining process.

Marginal analysis is an attempt to quantify the subjective desire of the buyer and seller, to determine the minimum price at which the seller will sell and the maximum price which the buyer will pay. This is done by determining the minimal, that is, marginal, measurable change in the price of a commodity over or under which a transaction should not occur. Consequently, marginal analysis can predict a price equilibrium at which a particular commodity can be both bought and sold. At this equilibrium it is advantageous to both the buyer and seller to exchange goods. A price is efficient—that is, it does not benefit one party more than the other—as long as it occurs within this state of equilibrium. The search for optimum and minimum values determining the state of equilibrium in which goods can be efficiently exchanged is the main purpose behind marginal analysis.

Marginal analysis is dependent primarily on the concept of *cardinal utility,* that is, the notion that value is determined primarily by greater or lesser availability of the same good within a certain price range. It has to a large extent been refined and extended by the use of indifference analysis. Indifference analysis is based on the concept of *ordinal utility*—the notion that value can be used to describe preferences among commodities which are not normally comparable if these preferences are numerically ordered according to sets of preferences.

Before the introduction of indifference analysis to economic theory, economists were able to determine only the price range of a particular commodity over or under which a transaction could not occur, but they could not predict when a consumer would stop buying one particular good and switch to another. They were not able to determine under what conditions one would just as well buy oranges as apples or bananas. Due to ordinal utility, comparisons between disparate choices became possible; after all, one could prefer oranges to apples and apples to bananas under certain conditions of price.

A closer look at market equilibrium

Marginal and indifference analysis, two of the basic tools of economics, are of little use to us in understanding the essential uncertainty of any bargaining process. They presuppose knowledge of and the relevance of all available information. They further presuppose that people act not only rationally but consistently. Although marginal and indifference analysis are somewhat useful in examining consumer behavior, they are not necessarily relevant to an analysis of the bargaining inherent in negotiation. There is no reason to believe that a negotiator always acts rationally, that his expectations always have to be consistent, and that his interpretation of information is similar to his adversary's. There is no reason to believe that irrational greed and calculated deceit cannot enter into the negotiation. Nor is there reason to believe that we are above being simply mistaken. Information, when it develops out of a process of communication between people of different interests, is always uncertain.

In order for equilibrium to represent optimum economic behavior, we have to assume complete and relevant knowledge of information. In a real bargaining negotiation, this is hardly ever the case. We rarely begin a negotiation with sufficient relevant information to complete a transaction. What happens is that we either receive new information or reinterpret already available information in redefining our expectations and strategies. We become involved in a constant, though not necessarily consistent or even conscious, effort to arrive at a final, concluding transaction. Thus, our attempt at rational and economically efficient behavior is not necessarily optimum.[36]

Negotiation does not even have to terminate in a transaction in order to be meaningful. All that is required is that it is entered into with an initial bid and offer. In the stock market the last sale may be a convenient symbol for indicating where one could begin to buy or sell, but knowing the last sale price can never entirely remove the necessity to learn the original bid and offer (and size, if possible).

It has sometimes taken me days and even weeks to dispose of a block of stock in a predominantly bullish market. I certainly felt I knew much more after committing myself to negotiate about what price I was going to have to accept, and under what conditions, than I did before. Indeed, sometimes my very desire to sell has been altered, and I have had to revise my expectations both upward and downward as a result of having committed myself to doing business.

The process itself, with its exchange of information and rethinking of expectations, is as meaningful as the final consummation of the transaction. Yet not even after the final transaction have I ever had the feeling that I really dissipated the uncertainty to which I was subject during negotiation. Quite frankly, sometimes I have thought that I was had, as it were. At other times I have felt elated over my prowess. The market still surprises me.

Underneath the Stockholder–Management Relationship

I have suggested that the relation between shareholder and management, as ambiguous and nondescript as it appears, is made legitimate—perhaps we should just say acceptable—by the disclosure of information by management. The shareholder is involved in this exchange through direct contact with management, through research analysts acting on his behalf, through his ability to vote for directors and those corporate matters requiring direct shareholder approval, through derivative shareholder suits, and, lastly, through his ability to affect the market price of the company's stock. Perhaps no other field of corporate study still lacks so much clarity as that of the relationship between shareholder and management.

Where else is there a concept of property bereft of the normal rights of property ownership? Where else is the right of ownership control vested in the dubious, sometimes insignificant, right of voting, conceived according to the political concept of majority control rather than minority rights of property?[37] Where else do we have a title to a claim on which an expectancy for recovery is so uncertain? Where else are we exposed to the concept of participation in income where the claimant has no right to know how much he will receive in dividends or how much will be retained by the corporation? Where else do we find a capital instrument, supposedly negotiable, representing a claim which becomes less enforceable once it has been bought from its original claimant?[38] (A shareholder who buys his stock on the open market has no right to claim recision from management.)

The relationship between a shareholder, his property, and management is complex because it is almost entirely vested in the disclosure, dissemination, and exchange of information, and not on any concept of value which either management or stockholder can hold the other to. This is the nature of the beast which, for the nonce, must be accepted as it is.

For me, accepting this relationship means recognizing that the information which passes between management and stockholder is intrinsically uncertain. And this is because the interests of the two are not identical. Their expectations differ, based as they are on different concepts of value. What is relevant to one is not always relevant to the other. Furthermore, both can be tempered by the greed and deceit to which, as human beings, they are not entirely immune. The managers want to preserve their jobs and their power; they want to continue pursuing their "enlightened self-interest." But shareholders may ignore the grossly undervalued stock of some companies and deny management its just recognition and ability to refinance under favorable conditions. Stockholders—only a few are needed—can also legally inflate the price of a stock by disseminating information concerning their own expectations, which management may not always accept or even appreciate.

This uncertainty, then, arises because each party is looking out for his own best interests. Each is bargaining, and if not necessarily with the other, with the other in mind. It is difficult for management to completely ignore the fact that stockholders exist, although sometimes its actions seem to confirm this ignorance. It is more difficult for shareholders to ignore management.

Whether one believes that the relationship between shareholder and management is confined solely to the contract between the two, as specified in the articles of incorporation and by-laws of the company, or that it is subject to an additional "implied" contract stipulating how earnings will be disposed of, the essence of the relationship rests in the exchange and negotiation of information. It is negotiated occasionally through confrontation, but usually management's need to remain accountable is a much bigger factor.

It is one thing to treat the market as a game, and something else to view it as an abstract theory devoid of human input. Some people, such as Lord Keynes and our own "Adam Smith," treat the market with the same joy and abandon with which they play. The feeling of winning is more important than the desire to make money or conserve capital. This gaming instinct is imbedded in the irrational, if often calculated, propensity to gamble.

On the other side are those who see the market as an exercise in mathematical theory, where stocks are numbers devoid of capital value, where strategy signifies only the computed consequence of known probabilities, and decisions are but attempts to maximize preconceived and unalterable expectations. Of course, reducing information to a system of mathematical expectations is of inestimable value in constructing models aimed at quantifying behavior. This is always useful. The problem is that sometimes in the process of reduction, you can alter your own sense of reality.

8

The Use of Expectations under Uncertainty

When we rely on information in formulating judgments about which stocks to buy and at what price, we confront uncertainty. If we were to rely solely on whim, a feeling for destiny, or the throw of dice or darts, we would not have to concern ourselves with uncertainty because we would have no need for information.

There are as many ways of dealing with uncertainty as there are of coping with reality. We can use words or numbers, science or myth. Basically, we confront uncertainty through our expectations, which we form, revise, and relinquish to the extent that they are satisfied or prove unreasonable. Whatever our expectations may be, it is important that we believe in them to some degree.

An expectation is the expression of an attitude toward or commitment to any situation whose outcome is uncertain. It is by definition subjective. An expectation which minimizes the significance of its subjectivity is misguided, to say the least. It may even be irresponsible. An expectation can only be relevant when an analysis of the information at our disposal can lead us to a belief that a certain outcome is possible. This belief is usually not dependent on the expectation itself, but precedes it or even gives rise to it. No expectation can result in a binding decision if it is not accompanied by the belief that we are indeed subjectively committed to the results of this judgment.

One of the supposed benefits of statistical analysis and game models is the degree of detachment with which a decision can be contemplated. This detachment is a function of knowing that the outcome of the decision will really have no bearing on the decision maker's immediate reality. Mathematicians and economists have always been aware of this rather crucial limitation, yet some modern business economists prefer to ignore its significance.

Expectations Require Commitment

No matter how important it is to have a knowledge of actuarial risk when formulating one's expectations, this knowledge cannot entirely erase the possibility of financial loss. There is no real comfort in purely mathematical safety margins. The construction of an efficient portfolio according to the principles of actuarial risk may become irrelevant, at least momentarily, if the market value of the portfolio falls with a general drop in the market. Even though one of the main ideas behind the construction of an efficient portfolio is to avoid the possibility of losses greater than the market's, obviously loss can still occur, even if only on "paper" and only for a limited period of time. In short, it is not a sufficient measure of fiduciary responsibility to justify value primarily on mathematics that coordinate expectations with market fluctuations. Actually avoiding losses is more important than being able to calculate what losses you should avoid. It is not sufficient to abandon, or redefine, fiduciary responsibility simply because one does not have the actuarial tools to handle it.

By saying our expectations ought to be grounded on belief, I mean that they ought to be taken with that personal commitment usually referred to as responsibility, and not derived from a totally detached view, actuarial or otherwise. It is not necessary that we believe in the product of the company, in the efficiency of its management, or even in an increase in earnings in order to buy stock; but it is necessary that we believe our expectations are relevant to whatever information they are based on. One cannot buy the stock of a semiconductor company solely on the expectation that in ten years every red-blooded American will own a pocket calculator. If this were the case, one should perhaps sell calculators rather than buy stock. Belief ought not to betray the context of the commitment; conversely, it is useless to form an expectation about buying a stock without a belief in the context of this commitment. If the price of the semiconductor stock is too high, according to one's own expectations, its purchase cannot be justified on the basis of the proliferation of calculators.

Some time ago I bought the stock of Taylor Wine because of its outstanding financial record. Yet, I don't care for wine made from slip-skin grapes, nor would I pay more for a New York State wine than for California or French wine, nor did I like Taylor Wine's advertising campaign. In short, there was every reason in the world to believe that Taylor wines should not be bought. However, these were all considerations which had nothing to do with my expectations that I was buying Taylor Wine at a price cheaper than my estimation of its capital value. What I had to believe to make this commitment was that my determination was correct that Taylor Wine had an outstanding financial record, and that this record would persist in the face of continuing adversity confronting the domestic wine industry.

The realization that expectations are the consequence of a commitment and depend on a state of belief is an indication of the extent to which they are utilized as normative and not positive means of analysis. No matter how objective seem the data on which the expectations are based, the latter always reflect a subjective interpretation of those data. However, when the belief exceeds the parameters of the expectation, it becomes irresponsible. The expectation becomes so confused that no reasonable judgment can be derived from it. When, on the other hand, an expectation is entertained without personal commitment, it becomes irrelevant to the information under consideration. One simply cannot form an accurate judgment about the price of stock isolated from the process of information. Such expectations may have value as exhortations to others to buy or sell, but they have no value for judgments about the value of capital. Ultimately, the belief which enables us to make a commitment stems either from a desire to gamble or a desire to act prudently.

The Impulse to Gamble

The desire to gamble in the stock market usually stems from the belief that one can beat the market at its own game. Gambling implies a will to bet on, to commit oneself to, a particular outcome, whatever the probability or expectation. A gambler will favor a particular outcome no matter how it was chosen. Sometimes his commitment will be based on nothing more than a hunch that things will go well for him; sometimes he may gamble on a more reasoned interpretation of reality, such as one based on numerical probability. In the latter case he is playing odds, which he believes are in his favor.

However he plays, the gambler must always believe that he will prevail over the forces he is up against; thus, the greater his optimism, the stronger his commitment can be. It is, of course, possible to gamble without being particularly optimistic; one may simply be aroused by a fascination with the nature of the risks involved. A good example of this would be the purchase of an option, with little or no premium and for a reasonable length of time, on a highly volatile stock.

In general, the desire to gamble hardly ever follows from a formulation of expectations about the intrinsic worth of an investment.

Thus, the wish to make a long-term investment of one's capital is usually not motivated by the gambling instinct, even though risk is involved.

Nobody is free from the gambling instinct and, as Lord Keynes put it, the game of professional investment not only would be intolerably boring without it, but also might not be as profitable.[1] I suspect that this boredom is caused by the fatigue which invariably overtakes us when we try to form a reasonable set of expectations to cope with the market's essential uncertainty. It is a fatigue resulting from a lack of immediate satisfaction. It is the boredom that usually accompanies a highly illiquid investment at a "cheap" price in a company manufacturing a basic commodity like salt, cement, or coal, when no other investor is taking any notice whatsoever.

The Desire to Act Prudently

The motivation to be prudent differs from the impulse to gamble in that the former springs as much from doubt as from belief. Indeed, doubt, coupled with a desire to commit oneself to a judgment, is characteristic of a prudent formulation of expectations. A prudent person will form expectations so that, to the extent that his doubts are valid, so will his judgment be valid. Prudence invariably leads to a situation where the outcome of one's expectations is different than originally anticipated. It involves an allowance for one's own mistakes, as well as for the deceit and machinations of others.

Prudence is not just an expression of timidity, indecision, or lack of commitment. In fact, it always stems from a commitment, and it expresses the desire of the individual to benefit from that commitment in some way. Prudence involves a willingness not only to reduce one's expectations but also to formulate them in such a way that they can be reduced. Expectations can be reduced in this way only if they do not anticipate an all-or-nothing, winner-take-all conclusion.

Expectations that stem from what mathematicians call a "zero-sum game" cannot be reduced and, hence, cannot be a consequence of prudence. For example, expectations that depend heavily on other people paying more than the market price cannot be called prudent. The capacity to reduce expectations, in effect, depends on the ability to derive satisfaction from them even at their reduced state. As I see it, prudence goes hand in hand with being able to derive satisfaction from a broad range of expectations.

The motivation for prudence is a recognition of the essential uncertainty with which information is both disclosed and interpreted.

One simply cannot act prudently if he believes that his expectations could be entirely invalidated by the disclosure of new information. New information may indeed invalidate an expectation, but the prudent formulation of expectations will always make allowances for the adverse impact of new information. For example, if an investor buys an overpriced stock solely on the rumor of a takeover, he has acted imprudently, perhaps driven by a desire to gamble. If the takeover is not realized within the anticipated period of time, there is no reason to hold the stock which was known at the outset to be overpriced. The investor, therefore, has either to produce a new expectation and continue holding on to the stock, or he has to abandon the idea behind the original commitment altogether and sell the stock.

Prudence is a quality of the procedure by which expectations are taken and judgments formed, but it is not properly a description of a judgment itself. Furthermore, in the sense of the word as used here, there is no such thing as a prudent investment but only a prudent commitment. I believe, as did Benjamin Graham before me, that price is crucial in determining the merit of an investment—a "low quality" investment can be just as prudent as a "blue chip" investment if it is bought cheaply enough.[2] Purchase price is the most important single factor in determining the eventual profitability of an investment. But more to the point, it is the procedure with which expectations are formed that ultimately reflects prudence. It is possible to overpay even when one thinks the price paid represents a deep discount from the investment's exchange value. What enables us to make prudent commitments is the analytical procedure used to form expectations so that one can derive some degree of satisfaction from them even if they are altered. This satisfaction is determined primarily by the nature of the expectations themselves, and should not depend entirely on the disclosure of new information, such as market price and earnings reports.

Prudence in Expectations

There are many procedures for prudently forming expectations. Expectancy, since it involves a procedure for analyzing return on equity in consideration of an opportunity cost, is an expectation guided by prudence. An expectancy can give a shareholder some degree of satisfaction despite how the market interprets the value of his shares. This will hold true as long as the company continues to produce earnings close to its historical earnings trend; as long as the original concept of opportunity cost is reasonably maintained; and as long as the price paid provides a reasonable margin of safety from the initial analysis of the company's exchange value.

Hedging and arbitrage are examples of procedures that reflect prudence. No matter how they are used, they attempt to assure the investor or trader that there is some extent to which his commitment will be satisfied.

Benjamin Graham's now famous concept of a "margin of safety" is another example. By a "margin of safety," Graham was essentially concerned with the procedure one should use in forming expectations. When he writes that "a true margin of safety is one that can be demonstrated by figures, by persuasive reasoning, and by reference to a body of actual experience,"[3] he is essentially calling for an approach that, being independent of market timing and fluctuation, will not result in total despair should the price of the stock fall subsequent to its purchase. For Graham the margin of safety rests in a procedure for buying below what one thinks the value of the investment ought to be. It does not consist of buying "cheaply," for no matter how inexpensive a stock may appear to be, it can still become cheaper.

Graham's method is essentially comparison shopping, if I may be permitted the indiscretion. One of the characteristics of comparison shopping is that it usually can provide some measure of satisfaction. This is why Graham was able to say that "to achieve satisfactory investment results is easier than most people realize. . . ."[4] His critics, however, do not by and large believe that superior results can be attained by discovering undervalued securities since the market discounts all available information, and this is reflected in the price of the stock.

Viewed within the perspective of the past few years, much can be said in defense of Graham's concept of prudence. There have been, and still are, hundreds of oligopolies, selling at a discount from book value and not much above working capital per share, which have at the same time generated a historic return on equity in excess of the rate of return on comparable long-term bonds. How can this situation persist if there really exists a market efficient in the allocation of funds? Should Graham's wisdom be rejected simply because it is out of rhythm with the contemporary academic litany?

The satisfaction that prudence demands from an expectation cannot always be measured quantitatively. The response to new information is not necessarily confined to an analysis of the numbers involved. Sometimes a drastically low quarterly earnings report must in fairness be evaluated in the context of other information which minimizes the long-term consequences of the report. At times, this need for satisfaction could perhaps be better described as a recognition of the value of consolation. Suppose we purchase a stock at a steep discount from its capital value. Obviously we will not be entirely happy should it fall in price, but we should at least have the consolation that we were not entirely mistaken in our original judgment. Under optimum conditions we should want to increase our commitment, but these conditions rarely exist. No consolation can exist if the criterion used to measure the prudence of our commitment is market value. The ultimate test of the prudence of our decision is how we continue to interpret information in the face of the market's continuing uncertainty.

I am not saying that a dollar lost in fact is gained in hope—this may be a consolation, but it is not very prudent. I am saying that the expectations used to cope with uncertainty are not invalidated by it as long as they are at least somewhat responsive along the lines anticipated. The degree to which uncertainty can invalidate expectations is often a function of the lack of experience of the investor and his unwillingness to study the actual process of the exchange of information.

Self-Consistent Schemes

Prudence needs the skill born of experience in interpreting information. This skill, as we have seen, ties in with the procedure used in making a commitment. The important thing about this procedure lies in its insistence that some degree of satisfaction remain possible no matter how much the original expectation is reduced. This is only possible when the satisfaction is integrally related to the expectations themselves and not by irrelevant criteria. For example, the expectation of higher market price can only be satisfied by higher price. It would be difficult to characterize such an expectation as prudent. However, an expectation based on a continuing historic rate of return on equity or on an increase in retained earnings or margin on sales can be more readily satisfied. Even if the specific return on equity is not met, it will almost surely fall to some extent within its historic pattern.

This skill, a function of experience, tells one not only which expectations ought to be chosen in forming a judgment, but how they should be ordered so as to form a self-consistent scheme of expectations. If one's objectives are basically oriented toward long-term growth of the exchange value of the firm, only those expectations which affect this growth ought to be considered. Thus, one might form expectations concerning sales, cash flow, dividend policy, return on investment, increase in retained earnings, and all the other expectations describing the financial situation of the firm. One may also analyze the oligopolistic nature of the firm's position to ascertain the strength of the firm's earning capacity. A small firm with sales of less than $100 million, manufacturing three different products sold to three different markets, usually has no oligopolistic strength. It is very difficult for a firm to sell cloth and frozen fish at the same time, and it is usually an indication of a firm's basic weakness in marketing one of these that it has chosen to market the other. Expectations concerning the quality and quantity of management's disclosures of information may also be formed. Any number of expectations may be taken so long as they are manageable.

The nature of this self-consistency revolves around the unity of purpose of the expectations. As long as all expectations bear on expected and retained earnings, for example, they can be described as self-consistent. However, as soon as an expectation also considers market price, or market volatility, or the potential for future product development, it is engaged in the anticipation of an event which, though important in itself, has no direct bearing on the initial judgment.

Prudence would also demand that each expectation within a self-consistent scheme be treated independently of other expectations. No attempt ought to be made to correlate expectations and to arrive at a forecast of expected values. I suggest that expectations of sales be kept independent of expectations concerning earnings, and that expectations concerning retained earnings be kept independent of dividend payout policy. In other words, all financial data should be graphed or tabled and then inspected separately. A simple procedure would be to inspect the figures on a *Value Line* company report and see what they have been independently for at least five years past.

If one were to inspect the *Value Line* report for General Motors, for example, one would see that for the years 1969–1977, the net return on equity was 17%, 6.3%, 18.1%, 18.7%, 19.3%, 7.6%, 9.6%, 20.3%, and 21.4%. For me, independent inspection of these figures reveals more than any one forecast figure ever could. Looking at these figures, I know that whatever expectation I form concerning return on equity, I must acknowledge that GM is as capable of earning 7 percent on equity as it is of earning 18 percent. This means that I will buy GM only if, at the very worst, I can form an expectation which would be satisfied if next year it only earned a 7 percent return on equity, or at any rate, much less than 18 percent; that way I will be able to maintain the expectation, based on past performance, that GM has good years as well as bad years.

Specifically, this means that I shouldn't be averse to paying a bit more than GM's current book value of about $54 per share. How much more, of course, is dependent on my opportunity cost and other expectations I have, such as the dividend payout. It appears to me that the current market price of about $65 is reasonable. However, it would most certainly be imprudent to buy GM stock at, say, $100 in 1979, since at that price the satisfaction of reasonable expectations concerning GM's financial worth would be severely jeopardized; the criterion for the satisfaction of some expectations would be too high. No matter how prosperous GM's future may now appear to be, no matter how much I may feel GM will cut into Ford's share of the automobile market, no matter how much better I feel GM's cars really are, I should not allow these expectations to infringe on my analysis of GM's exchange value.

The task for forming a self-consistent and independent scheme of expectations for a company like IBM is considerably easier than it is for GM. If we inspect IBM's return on equity, we see that it has varied between about 16 percent and 19 percent. Should IBM ever earn less than this—say, a 12 percent return on equity—our expectation would fail very badly, assuming we had based it on the higher range. Yet, for the present, there is little danger of this; I don't see how anybody can form any reasonable expectation concerning IBM's exchange value when its stock is selling at about $270 per share (unless one were to assume an opportunity cost of about 5 percent).

The kinds of schemes people devise differ according to their skill and experience and the investments being analyzed. As dissimilar as they may be, however, the principle of expectancy is relevant to any scheme involving long-term investment policy. It is only by admitting the relevancy of expectancy that one can also admit the relevancy of retained to expected earnings.

One of the best managed and largest of American pension funds has a policy of holding a limited number of what it considers to be very high quality common stock investments. It has held these shares for a very long time. Its policy is to gradually sell them as it thinks they become overpriced and gradually buy more as they become underpriced. A fund of this size really does not have the liquidity to sell its entire holdings in anticipation of a very bad market. Its investment policy is based on the realization that its holdings are worth something irrespective of the market. Though not very daring, this policy requires only prudent expectations and not market performance. In contrast are the large number of investment funds which have held stocks never worth a quarter of what they paid for them because they couldn't find buyers, even at their reduced prices. But upon careful examination it can be seen that these investments were made primarily on the anticipation of a higher market price rather than on increased investment value.

Arbitrariness

Although the procedure for forming expectations is often rational and sometimes prudent, the actual desire to form expectations and to make commitments is always arbitrary. If one believes in the market's essential uncertainty, there can be no rational preordained scheme according to which commitments can be established in advance of actual market conditions and the disclosure of information. Commitments are usually made in response to an interpretation of relevancy; likewise, investment strategies are modified to conform to one's expectations, not vice versa. Because information is always disclosed in a climate of uncertainty, and because this disclosure is always a part of the bargaining process of a negotiated market, expectations are constantly being reaffirmed and revised one way or another. Since one never knows exactly what is going to happen, the decision to form an expectation is arbitrary.

Is it true that an inordinately successful investment is based on perfect foresight and knowledge of future events? Or is it rather that an investment made according to an arbitrary choice, but coupled with prudent procedure, usually turns out to exceed the original nature of the expectations? Were the original investments in IBM and Kodak, in Berkshire Hathaway and Geico (before it soured), really based on perfect foresight? Or was it not that the performance of these companies exceeded original expectations and induced investors to reinterpret available information?

Some of these original investors were prevented from selling by fiduciary or other limitations not entirely connected to an interpretation of investment value. Yet the phenomenal success of these investments, seen from the perspective of the original commitment, was arbitrary. It is the measure of a successful investor that he recognizes this arbitrary potential and reaffirms his commitments according to it. It is the mark of an average investor that he hasn't developed a prudent procedure that can look beneath the arbitrariness of present and future events, and also lacks the flexibility to revise his expectations accordingly.

Arbitrariness is proof that relevancy is subjective. To deny that we assume expectations arbitrarily in response to situations and opportunities, is to assume that they are shared by others according to some prevailing scheme of rationality. Although one may often have good reason to believe that such a scheme exists, it is not an assumption that can be made with impunity. The purpose of others cannot be known without the possibility of error due to deceit or mistaken judgment, for when such information is disclosed, it is almost always by people who have an interest in the process of the disclosure.[5]

The recognition of arbitrariness governing the choice of expectations is a factor which every investor implicitly admits whenever he chooses to own more than one stock, that is, when he decides that he would rather own a portfolio of stocks than concentrate his investment capital in the one common stock he thinks offers him the best investment opportunity. Diversification is the normal investor's reaction to arbitrariness.

Diversification

Economists have long been preoccupied with why investors diversify. Contemporary economists say that investors diversify because it is their way of coping with uncertainty. If one were to invest in a world of perfect certainty, they say, one would not need to diversify because then he would be able to form a perfect judgment about the anticipated rate of return of the investment and the cost of money. If one could know that IBM would always yield a 17 percent rate of return and increase its dividend according to a corresponding rate, and if one could anticipate the cost of money, he would not need to invest in any other common stock.

Business economists believe, then, that diversification is the investor's response to the uncertainty generated by his defective procedures for judging future income. In other words, since investors can't really be said to know what they are doing, they try to spread the risks by diversifying their incompetency. This is like saying that if you don't know for sure which horse is going to win, you can still gamble intelligently by spreading your bets according to some thoughtful scheme. Diversification, for these economists, is spreading one's bets.

The investor's need for "naive" diversification has led business economists to formulate their theories of what they call *real* (or *systematic*) *diversification.* According to these economists, naive diversification simply implies the aggregation of stocks irrespective of their correlative market behavior. Thus, if these stocks all had the same beta coefficient, one might be as well off owning a portfolio comprising only one of them. By contrast, systematic diversification, which is based on the covariance of the returns from different stocks, is supposed to reduce the overall variance of the portfolio's return. Some stocks must be expected to depreciate while others appreciate. How many stocks a portfolio must include for real or systematic diversification is still a matter of scholarly debate.

Having accepted this interpretation of diversification, some business economists have proceeded with great diligence and mathematical foresight to devise procedures by which one can more competently and rationally construct a diversified portfolio. Basically, these increase the parameters by which an investor can choose the stocks he wishes to include in the portfolio. According to Baruch Lev, the investor should consider the "securities' expected rate of return and the uncertainty involved in this expectation; the latter element being measured by the extent to which the actual return may deviate from the predicted one"[6] And in desiring some sort of balance between the various securities, he ought to also consider the degree of volatility of the market price of the individual stocks so that the overall stability of the portfolio will bear some relation to that of the market in general, and in particular to the degree of risk he wants to take.

The diversification theory was articulated in response to what its theoreticians consider market uncertainty. It is also an attempt to dispel some of the arbitrariness with which expectations are normally encountered; but this has been achieved essentially by ignoring arbitrariness, not by removing it. It is assumed that the choice of individual stocks is important only as part of an overall strategy of constructing a balanced, efficient portfolio.

In this scheme one not only admits the irrelevance of choosing one investment opportunity over another, except insofar as the portfolio as a whole is concerned, but he also ignores any attempt at determining the value of any individual investment opportunity. There is no rational and proven method for selecting individual stocks based on expectations affecting their exchange value. This theory holds that traditional security analysis, because it is based on the formulation of arbitrary expectations, cannot produce superior results; and indeed, superior results can never be produced because the market is efficient. Security analysis, it is said, cannot cope with uncertainty; only diversification can. Therefore, one should construct his portfolio according to actuarial definitions of risk and reward and not according to the expectation of profit and real dollar risk of the individual investments.

I am not against submitting a portfolio to the sort of analysis the modern portfolio theory proposes, but I most strongly disagree with a construction that disregards analysis of the exchange value of the individual investments. It is perhaps quite sufficient that a portfolio increase in value as much as any of the predominantly used market averages in a bullish market. It is by no means acceptable that it also lose as much in a predominantly bearish market. No justification can ever be made for losing money, even though we all have to lose sometime or another. But as long as the market is the measure of success, it cannot help but also serve as the measure of failure.

It is not by ignoring the arbitrariness with which expectations are made that we can cope with uncertainty more effectively. (I sometimes feel that for some of these theoreticians victory in love or war would be determined primarily by a probability estimate of past encounters.) It is rather by having a clear understanding of value and the flexibility to use expectations in anticipation of the possibility that they may have to be revised, that one is able to cope with uncertainty. The arbitrariness with which we confront the uncertainty of the negotiation and disclosure of information is not an evil but a description of the marketplace. Arbitrariness is the recognition that opportunities exist even if one does not know where and to what extent. I cannot accept a concept of market efficiency which denies the significance of opportunity because it cannot be anticipated, that is, because it is arbitrary. Indeed, it appears to me that risk, when confined to the actuarial notion of probability estimates, becomes an expression of the cost of forsaking opportunities.

Some Practical Considerations Concerning Portfolio Diversification

I have no intention in this book to offer an exhaustive discussion of portfolio management. However, I would like to suggest that for the private investor, if not for the institutional fund, diversification need not be a response only to market uncertainty; it may also be a response to alternative opportunities that appear equally attractive.

As long as the cost of an investment is low, as long as it has a big enough margin of safety in relation to other investments, why should one diversify? Can one really justify diversification solely on the basis of uncertainty? Not being able to form one's expectations prudently is not the same as being uncertain about what they should be. If the opportunity were to exist whereby the financial risk of the investment is as low as for any comparable alternative, but its cost in relation to its exchange value is considerably lower, how could one justify not committing a larger than usual sum, never mind the market's uncertainty?

If the one-asset portfolio is not an ideal, it is because market uncertainty continuously seems to provide the opportunity for new expectations and judgments. Another reason is that it is difficult to trust one's investment capital entirely to a claim which management can so easily render less legitimate and worthwhile through its own periodic fits of arrogance, silence, and misconduct.

For me, diversification can be explained not only as a consequence of market uncertainty and the need to protect myself from the defective use of expectations, but also as a way of confronting the arbitrary appearance of unexpected opportunities. One can claim that this distinction is purely rhetorical, that opportunity is just the other face of risk, and that in an efficient market opportunity is always a function of risk. But this is not necessarily so. To say that the market is an efficient allocator of information is not identical to saying that it is an efficient allocator of capital.

Furthermore, it is the very existence of alternative investment opportunities which gives rise to the distinction between utility and exchange value. The need to diversify property which is measurable primarily by its utility value is a recognition of the risk of a possibly diminished utility. But the desire to diversify property which is primarily measurable by its exchange value is a recognition of the liberty to seek and invest in other opportunities for capital appreciation. This is what distinguishes the power of management's property from the property without power of the shareholder. What the shareholder loses in power, he gains in the variety of opportunities for capital appreciation. To view this variety of opportunity primarily as a need to diversify risk could lead one to the conclusion that the best way to avoid risk entirely is to avoid investing in common stock. For a normal unhedged portfolio, it is impossible to diversify away the risk of investing in the stock market.

I am not really happy with the view that the purpose of diversification is to accommodate the uncertainty of a fluctuating market. This is a hazard which no diversification can ever really successfully accommodate. One diversifies in order to avoid the prospect of large losses due to factors other than a general market decline. But one also diversifies in order to confront a wealth of opportunity whose timing is arbitrary to the extent it is out of our control. Finally, for me a successful diversification is one which simply does not exceed the number of investment opportunities one can manage attentively and prudently.

Expectations and the Future

We have been concerned so far with how to use expectations in coping with the uncertainty of information. There is another aspect of uncertainty that we have tended to ignore—the uncertainty that is generally associated with the unforeseen future. However well we think we understand information and are able to employ it to our best advantage, we still have to face the mystery of what time will bring, especially since it has been quite generous here in the late seventies. It often appears that the present is more fraught with anxiety and lack of stability than the past, but insofar as management of our capital is concerned, we sometimes have to assume an even higher degree of confidence in the future than justified by our interpretation of the past. Yet, even a small imbalance in an otherwise stable period can be enough to destroy or at least jeopardize our forecasts and our equity capital.

Ducking the future

Coping with the future is a great unsettling problem, especially when money is at stake. We formulate expectations with degrees of belief varying from the most optimistic to the most pessimistic. And whatever our belief may be, we are never really free from the subjective influence of our state of confidence. Sometimes our confidence in our expectations is so low, and the burden of our responsibility so great, that we look for a convenient and accepted way to abdicate responsibility.

One way is through belief in mathematical expectations. It is amusing that Lord Keynes, who was so involved in applying mathematical expectations to neo-classical economics, should have remarked as follows:

> We are merely reminding ourselves that human decisions affecting the future, whether personal or political or economic, cannot depend on strict mathematical expectation, since the basis for making such calculations does not exist; and that it is our innate urge to activity which makes the wheels go round, our rational selves choosing between the alternatives as best we are able, calculating where we can, but often falling back for our motive on whim or sentiment or chance.[7]

Some contemporary business economists have tried to remove the "whim or sentiment or chance" by creating systems of mathematical expectations of such complexity and, not incidentally, expense that our confidence is bolstered by its ingenuity. As important as probability theory is for so many fields of human endeavor, it is not an article of faith that leads to confidence in the future of our investments.

How then are we able to assume that degree of belief which Keynes calls a "state of confidence" in the formulation of expectations about the future of our investments? He suggests that we really have to "fall back on what is in truth, a convention. The essence of this convention—though it does not, of course, work out quite so simply—lies in assuming that the existing state of affairs will continue indefinitely, except insofar as we have specific reasons to expect a change."[8]

Belief in conventions

In explaining why falling back on convention can be so precarious and full of pitfalls and, indeed, so arbitrary, Keynes, in a brilliant exercise in rhetoric, develops his notions on the function of the stock market. The upshot of his argument is that belief in the conventions governing the general state of affairs of a society can produce that state of confidence without which an investment in industrial assets cannot be made only when one also believes that these conventions will persist over the "long term." If one's beliefs are influenced primarily by the fluctations of the stock market and not by the persistence of society's conventions, then the confidence required to make long-term investments will not exist. Conventional valuations based on a desire to judge mass psychology, to beat the gun, to play the game, derive more from a desire to gamble on successful interpretations of short-term market fluctuations than from a commitment to pursue a long-term investment policy.[9]

An investor with long-term expectations Keynes calls an entrepreneur. An entrepreneur is imbued with a high state of confidence because he is willing to accept the conventions underlying the political and economic realities of his time for what they appear to be. Even though his confidence will always be suspect—because that barometer of investor confidence, the stock market, will always fluctuate—an entrepreneur must have the strength and the independence—the enterprise—to act on his interpretation of the validity of society's conventions. His state of confidence is really based on the degree to which he feels he can confidently predict the marginal efficiency of his investment. He will demonstrate enterprise insofar as he will be able to determine that the prospective yield from his investment will exceed the cost of alternative and comparable investment opportunities over the long run. Of course, Keynes is quick to point out that entrepreneurship has many shortcomings. Short-term market fluctuations can make the entrepreneur look very stupid, and the ability to deal with borrowed funds is limited.

Keynes was primarily interested in explaining the role of confidence in determining the marginal efficiency of investment capital rather than in ascertaining the value of long-term commitments of financial capital in the stock market. In spite of the difficulties which the entrepreneur will always confront, not the least of which is his inability to correctly calculate or forecast the prospective return on his financial investment, Keynes prefers the attitude of the entrepreneur to that of the speculator or even the professional investor. He writes: "Speculators may do no harm as bubbles on the steady stream of enterprise. But the position is serious when enterprise becomes the bubble on a whirlpool of speculation!"[10] The preference is influenced by his belief that marginally efficient long-term industrial investment is beneficial to society and the economy. Apart from its social benefit, Keynes believes that an investment policy dictated by long-term expectations can be successful as long as it is possible to maintain confidence in the long-term conventional state of affairs.

Looking at the state of affairs in Great Britain today, perhaps we ought to respond to Keynes's attitude with great caution. In spite of a near collapse of convention and an anticipation that future conventions may bear no resemblance to the present state of affairs, the Briton should still judge for himself whether long-term commitments can be reasonably made, even if he chooses not to make them. As so often happens, one's state of confidence is more affected by the bubbles of inflation, monetary policy, and production than it is by the deep underlying conventions which make all of these possible, and even necessary. But to be successful, an investment policy must not only understand society's conventions, but determine whether they are still valid.

Popular wisdom has it that correct forecasting is the most effective way of coping with the unforeseeability of the future. Business economists have attempted to show that correct forecasting is but a pastime, the success of which has eluded everybody. Yet many of these same economists, rather than refrain from forecasting, pursue it with ingenuity. My own feeling, expressed from beginning to end of this book, is that forecasting is a senseless endeavor. There is no way in which the uncertainty of the future can ever be eliminated even when an attempt is made to correlate, by statistical method, the disparate contingencies on which the future depends.

Prudence as a Means of Looking Forward

There is a way in which an investor can and does cope with the future. It may not be obvious, but it does exist; otherwise, investment policies simply would not be formed in the face of such remote and futile expectations as the future often holds. The inducement to invest is not solely dependent on the gambling spirit. Nor does it entirely depend on the kind of social responsibility which dictates that an investment in plant and labor is socially necessary. As insipid as it is importunate to think of it, prudence is what it takes to cope with uncertainty of the future.

Prudence at once leads us to believe that we can assume meaningful expectations, and it requires that these expectations be put through a procedure which can assure us of their continuing relevance. Prudence demands that these expectations be self-consistent and continuously subject to some measure of satisfaction.

I think it would be useful here to quote at length from an essay by George L. S. Shackle in the formation of expectations:

> *Subjective stability* or *reposefulness* is a quality which, from the very nature of the purpose they serve, the individual is bound to seek for his expectations, though all experience would teach us not to look for objective stability. For though in fact his system of expectations will be continually suffering smaller or greater shocks and dislocations and may sometimes be shattered, yet the making and the execution of a plan takes time, and at its inception is expected to take time, and a plan if it is to make sense must be based on one self-consistent scheme of expectations, that is to say, a system in which, for each of the variables embraced, we have for each hypothesis as to its value at each calendar date one constant degree of belief. To call forth from the individual the mental and nervous energy required to devise and try to execute a plan of any consequence, the incentive arising from the *content* of the outcome he pictures must be insulated from the distractions arising from uncertainty; the picture must be steady and clear while it lasts, not blurred by oscillation between different versions.
>
> To attain this subjective stability, the individual will defer repeatedly the crystallization of any plan, waiting continually for a situation where he can feel the number of unanswered questions is at a minimum, and is likely to increase on balance through the obsolescence of some of the data now in his possession, than to decrease through the acquisition of fresh knowledge. Only at such a time of *freedom from impending fresh knowledge* will he consent in important matters to decide and act. But this desire for stability has a further consequence; not only must the outcome be represented in his mind by a very small number of dominant hypotheses, which alone vividly hold his attention, rather than by a distribution over which his attention is widely dissipated, but these few special levels of success or misfortune must be determinate maxima of some actual mental experience, not mere mathematical abstractions. . . .[11]

In this quotation, as well as throughout his book, Shackle is concerned with how we can form expectations about an uncertain future in such a way that we can retain that certain degree of reposefulness (or satisfaction, as I have called it) which enables us to confront the future without the anxiety and unhappiness which would make most judgments impractical, if not impossible. He suggests that a commitment can be made if it is also accompanied by the belief that the consequence of one's expectations can to some degree be satisfied. He also feels that whatever the procedure, it should be free from the distracting and disconcerting effect of new information. New information should not be ignored, but a judgment cannot be relevant and still be invalidated completely by every newly disclosed bit of information. Shackle suggests that this plan be guided by a limited number of "dominant" or readily satisfiable expectations.

If we were to apply Shackle's scheme to the valuation of common stock, we would be engaging prudence. Remember, prudence means not confusing market value with exchange value. The market will always fluctuate, and these fluctuations cannot be allowed to distract us from our basic analysis. Prudence means buying cheaply, hedging or arbitraging. It requires that, whatever the scheme of expectations we adopt, we also bear in mind the extent to which these expectations are guided by the expectancy of a return on invested capital. Without the calculation of an expectancy, we find ourselves adrift without the ballast of reasonable judgment.

Prudence—Hedging Against Anxiety

A confrontation with the unforeseen future, as awesome as it can appear in our daily lives, is really mitigated by one's will and power to apply prudence to an investment policy. What distinguishes the mystery of how the future will rule our lives from the uncertainty of how it will govern our investments is that the latter, at least, can be offset somewhat by careful interpretation of information. Our inability to know what tomorrow will bring is often an indication of the lack of information available to us, or our incapacity to interpret it with any degree of relevance. Yet capital is not a thing subject to the law of nature. Capital management implies judgment about the value of expectations. Without information by which to judge it, management of capital would be a nightmare.

Knowing how to negotiate, how to form expectations, and how to use information carries one a long way in being able to deal with the future. Although prudence can have no effect on the power of coercion or the truly unknown, it can be quite significant in the formulation of expectations in situations where we have little or no real power to affect our destiny. Ultimately, when doubt about the future is understood as the uncertainty of future disclosures of information, one begins to see that uncertainty can be confronted practically and directly by exercising prudence.

9

The Practice of Valuing

In this chapter we shall be concerned with the actual practice of the investment theory developed in the preceding chapters. There, I was primarily concerned with developing and clarifying those ideas without which I felt an investor could not confront the conceptual realities of his investment policies.

I introduced some terms commonly used by all investors, terms that are nonetheless not always clearly understood: corporation, common stock, earnings, price-earnings ratio, present value, market price, and claim on income. Although it is not absolutely necessary to understand these terms in order to manage capital, a lack of understanding can cause serious error, especially in the actual practice of valuing.

I also introduced some terms that are generally unfamiliar to the contemporary investor—for example, endocracy, exchange value, maximization of wealth, efficient market, expectancy, uncertainty, and opportunity cost. These, I feel, should be clearly understood before the decision is made to ignore them. Another concept, prudence, is of such crucial significance to the process of valuation that I have reserved the next and last chapter to it.

Concepts can be burdensome, especially when they are interrelated and require one to see his customary investment practice from a different perspective. There are two reasons why I feel justified in having described in theoretical terms what ought always to be practical. First, in a democratic and capitalistic economy, ignorance of its terminology can lead to economic paralysis or, at least, malaise. There is little hope for success when a shareholder believes he actually owns a share of the assets of the company rather than a fuzzy, not very well defined claim against its income. If he believes the former, he might be perfectly justified in being suspicious of owning financial property and in preferring to own "real" property like land, art, or commodities. Nor is his belief going to lead him to any appreciation of the process of valuation to which he, as a participant in a market society, is entitled. The opportunity to value is a prerogative only of a society that tolerates private ownership of property; ignorantly confusing market price with market value is equivalent to relinquishing the responsibility of valuing.

The second reason I have so heavily relied on theoretical terms is, in a sense, the obverse of the first. It has to do not with ignorance but with knowledge, especially academic knowledge. Business economists who analyze the valuation of equities have produced a body of knowledge that is, to this perhaps biased observer, irrelevant. There was a time when economics was a branch of philosophy, in particular of moral philosophy. This meant that economics was primarily an analysis of certain concepts and values arising out of the commerce between people. To a certain extent this is the branch of economics now described as political economy. However, today's business economics is not directed toward the study of the values governing man's behavior in the market or in the corporate world; it is engaged in trying to quantify this behavior by use of occasionally complicated mathematical techniques and often expensive mathematical applications. It is not concerned with clarifying or understanding concepts and values but with quantifying them.

Business economists have produced a body of knowledge which is for the most part irrelevant and therefore inapplicable to the practice of valuing. Can any practical investor seriously consider calculating the present value of a share of common stock? Can any prudent investor determine value solely on the basis of forecasted earnings? Finally, would any prudent investor relinquish his right to make a judgment, even if it is fallible, on the grounds that the market is efficient? Rather than bring clarity, the academic literature has brought confusion. It has steadfastly refused to analyze and understand the concepts it is dealing with. Acceptance of an operating premise becomes the very basis for the sought-after conclusion—a most unscientific approach to validation.

A Practical Approach to Investing

Before enumerating various aspects of the investment practice related to my investment theory, I should emphasize that in this chapter I shall not be concerned with the construction or valuation of a portfolio of marketable securities or anything else. I shall be concerned only with the practice of valuing individual stocks. I shall ignore the very important consideration of how much of a specific pool of capital ought to be invested in equities. I shall also ignore the principles of diversification that ought to be applied even to that portion of a portfolio specifically set aside for common-stock investments.

The construction and valuation of a portfolio is a very complicated affair. There are so many variables to consider. Who owns the portfolio? What is its purpose? What must be the relation between current and capital income? What is its life? How will its size be defined? What are the applicable fiduciary laws? How will its performance be measured? What are the tax consequences?

These are all questions that to some extent must be asked by the individual investor as well as the professional. But they are all questions to which, we must assume, the investor already has a satisfactory answer. The only questions we shall be concerned with here deal with the actual choice of common stock. The basic inquiry will be: How do we know when a share is over- or undervalued? What follows is not a "how to" guide but rather an enumeration of the precepts one should bear in mind in the practice of valuation.

1. *Laying the groundwork.* Defining a particular stock's *exchange value* is the main point of valuing for investment. This means that the process of valuation begins with a definition of the claim on the income of a corporation that the stock represents. Since this claim is on the expected earnings as well as the retained earnings and other capital resources of the corporation, we must begin valuing equities by analyzing the financial ratios clarifying the relationship between expected and retained earnings. That is, we must start by analyzing the intrinsic value or financial structure of the company independently of market price. Market price can only tell us for how much others are willing to sell us the stock should we wish to buy it. However, market price and all other related variables, such as volatility, volume of trading, and institutional holdings, do not affect a share's value. If we cannot make the distinction between value and price, there isn't much point to investing because equities, unlike other traded goods, have no utility value.

2. *Computing book value.* The point of departure in the process of valuation is understanding and defining the *book value* of the common stock under consideration. Value can only be understood in relation to book value. We must always ask how much more or how much less than book value we ought to pay. Later in this chapter we shall examine how book value is defined and what can and cannot be included in

it. For the present it is enough that we accept book value as the per-share definition of total assets less liabilities usually provided by the company in its annual report.

The basis for valuing is not the price-earnings ratio, the earnings forecast, or the technical analysis of a share's market price. We understand "overvalued" or "undervalued" in relation to book value and not market price. For example, in valuing McDonald's, which as of this writing has a tangible book value of about $12 per share and a market price of $50, we must first ask how much more than its book value we are willing to pay. If the current market price seems too high, then we must say its price is too dear. On the other hand, if Spring Mills has a book value of $32 and a market price of $19, we would still need to find out the extent to which that price represents undervalued equity. It may very well be that even at $10 per share, or $22 less than its book value, we would think it too dear to buy.

3. *Employing financial ratios.* Earnings must never be analyzed by themselves but only in relation to financial variables of the company, such as sales, depreciation, retained earnings, or book value. Analyzing earnings trends and earnings growth patterns independently of other financial variables is a waste of time. Comparing earnings to market price can be useful only if past rather than future earnings are used, and then only if this ratio is used as an indication of past market behavior, not of intrinsic value.

The principal earnings ratio that must always be considered is the *return on stockholders' equity,* or return on book value. This is the basic ratio at a stockholder's disposal for determining the profitability of the firm and his claim against its income. How this ratio is calculated will depend on the immediate expectations of the individual investor. He may want to examine this ratio for a few or many years in the past. He may try to find an average ratio, or he may decide to buy when the ratio is at its historic low or high, depending on the significance of other financial information available to him. If he is very cautious, for example, he may wish to buy the stock of steel companies only when this ratio is very low, on the grounds that the cyclical nature of the steel industry will bring about higher ratios in the future.

He may wish to concentrate exclusively on the ratio of net earnings to retained earnings, ignoring surplus paid-in capital derived from the sale of stock over book value. If the company has a variable tax pattern, he may wish to use only pretax earnings. The variations are many and depend on the explicit expectations of the individual investor. However, the basic precept—that earnings never be analyzed by and for themselves—remains.

It is absurd to try to forecast earnings from other earnings figures or even to try to discover a meaningful pattern to earnings.[1] The one solid indication of growth a shareholder can rely upon is not larger earnings but the maintenance of a high return-on-equity (ROE) ratio. Thus, if we analyze the ROE of IBM, we will see that it has been at a fairly constant 17 percent to 19 percent. On the other hand, looking at a so-called growth company like Texas Instruments, which has had an ROE ratio of between 10 percent and 17 percent for the past five years, one may conclude that the growth is more in the expectation of the shareholder than in the profitability of the company.

The limitation of using the ROE ratio is illustrated in valuing the shares of a company like National Semiconductor Corp., whose ROE has fluctuated between 13 percent and 34 percent during the past five years. Here it would be much wiser to base one's expectations on some notion of reasonable expected ROE rather than on the explosive cash flows that can be generated by semiconductor industry booms.

Benjamin Graham has made a point that would be helpful to remember here: "Obvious prospects for physical growth in a business do not translate into obvious profits for investors."[2] The best way I know of protecting oneself from being seduced by the prospects for earnings growth is to rely on the ROE ratio.

4. *Determining expectancy value.* Any attempt at valuing equities for the purpose of investment must include an analysis of their expectancy value. One has to be able to form a judgment about the maximum value of a share of stock that would still enable one to benefit from unrealized or expected income. For example, if International Flavors and Fragrances has a book value of $6 per share and an expected return on equity of 21 percent and our minimum opportunity cost is 10 percent, the expectancy value of these shares should not exceed $12 to $13 ($EV = \$6 \times 21\%/10\% = \$12.60$). Even if we were to accept an opportunity cost as low as 8 percent, these shares would not have an expectancy value of over $15.75 per share.

One must bear in mind the expectancy value even if he chooses to pay a price considerably in excess of it. The premium of price above the expectancy value essentially involves a belief that the shares ought to be worth more because other people will pay more for the premium. Paying that premium means that one is willing to at least temporarily forfeit that amount of capital in hopes that the price will rise.

If International Flavors and Fragances is selling at $25 per share and we have an opportunity cost of 10 percent, we are contributing $12.40 to a price premium. Our expectations for increased wealth generated by the future income of the company are penalized by this amount. This means that if the price of the stock were to fall $12.40 to $12.60, one could only suspect mismanagement on the part of the investment adviser, not the firm's management. A minority stockholder's appraisal at a price in excess of $12.60 would be unreasonable. What one has bought at a price of more than $12.60 is not property in the form of equity capital but a kind of market premium on this equity. We have only paid for what we hope somebody else will buy.

There are many fine, well-managed companies like IFF which have historically enjoyed a market premium over expectancy value. But who is not familiar with at least a few of those hundreds of companies that have sold at very high market premiums and yet were led by either dishonest or incompetent management, or at least by a management incapable of measuring up to market expectations?

If we believe that prudence involves a respect for the preservation of property, it is foolish to ignore the property rights inherent in equity ownership by denying the relationship of these rights to their value. Perhaps in no other kind of property is the concept of equity right so inextricable from value as in common stock. Therefore, any practical process of valuation ought to take into account the expectancy value of the shares being valued.

5. *Adding opportunity cost.* No one should attempt to value common stock without being able to specify his opportunity cost. If the investor does not know what his minimum desired rate of return ought to be, he cannot attempt to value equities independently of market price. Whatever it may have been in the past, today the average shareholder's opportunity cost ought not to be less than 8 percent. I suggest that an opportunity cost of between 10 percent and 12 percent be used by most investors.

The same opportunity cost will apply whether a stock is valued in terms of its dividend payout or its retained earnings. Remember, however, that to value an equity solely on the basis of its dividend payout is unwise, for one does not own a claim (that is, one has no guarantee) that this payout can or will continue.

6. *Interpreting disclosed information.* The availability of disclosed information by management provides the only basis for appraising the value of common stock. Therefore, one ought to avoid investing in equities whose management is reluctant to reveal information in a form that is easily understood by shareholders. Likewise, one ought to avoid investing in those conglomerate companies, real estate investment trusts, or bank holding companies where one does not feel that

the complexity of the financial structure is disclosed adequately enough to make a satisfactory appraisal of value. Usually the more management is willing to discuss its operations and provide its shareholders with useful financial ratios, the more accurate and confident an appraisal of value can be made. The annual reports of many of the nation's utilities provide just such disclosures of information. When the annual report of an industrial company avoids breaking down its financial information and neglects preparing a detailed financial history of its operations, one has an indication that management will not contribute much more information when interviewed personally.

Information is disclosed by management, whose interests are basically different from, if not in conflict with, those of shareholders. Thus it takes negotiation between shareholder and management in order to get to the real facts. Without this, any discussion of the firm's history and prospects and financial ratios is useless.

Below are samples of the kinds of questions every investor should weigh when evaluating a company's information:

- Why should a company with huge cash reserves and whose shares are selling at a premium over book value offer to buy back some of its own shares rather than to increase its dividend? (IBM's offer in 1976 is a case in point.)
- Why should a company with huge cash reserves selling at a discount from book value offer to buy for cash the shares of another company at a considerable premium over book value? (Here, Kennecott's purchase of Carborundum in 1977 comes to mind.)
- Why should management suggest to shareholders that it is in the shareholders' interest that they vote for a staggered board of directors?
- Why should management decide to change an unusual expense or write it off against earnings in an otherwise unusually profitable year rather than declare an extraordinary dividend?
- Why should management decide it is in the shareholders' best interests to pay a premium over book value for a business dealing in a field in which it has no experience?
- Are the photographs in annual reports descriptive or are they intended to induce a particular kind of response?

An investor should try to interpret only disclosed information or information which, if it is not available, can be legally disclosed by management. The pursuit of so-called "inside" information is a waste of time. Those who like to pursue inside information think that management always knows something that would automatically make the stock rise or fall upon its disclosure. Except in instances of management malfeasance or an extraordinary discovery of a new product, invention, or natural resource, this is never the case. The reality of the situation is that management does not always know what stockholders think it should, and it is usually no more clairvoyant than anybody else. You can be sure that usually if management has not disclosed something, it isn't worth disclosing. In reality, it is the shareholder's (and analyst's) responsibility to extract pertinent information by personally asking for it.

7. *Weighing oligopolistic strength.* It is often more prudent to invest in companies that are oligopolies or even monopolies than in companies that have no clearly definable market. There are very many "cheap" stocks of companies having sales of less than $200 million that are derived from a number of totally independent and isolated markets. Brennand-Paige, Columbia General, and Kaman Industries are examples of some of the better-managed of these companies. In spite of their superior management, the diversified nature of their operations may be conducive to their operating as a close corporation rather than a public company. One of the consequences of not being an oligopoly is that the firm's management is unable or unwilling to disclose very much information. This is because these companies have only recently become public, and the legacy of the closed corporation still influences management. Of course, diversification does not imply smallness. American Brands, for instance, while catering to many different markets, has an oligopolistic position in each of these markets.

A consequence of this precept is that it is not size but oligopolistic position which is of paramount importance. Companies such as American Filtrona, Florida Cypress Gardens, and Y&S Candies, Inc., while having a relatively small volume of sales, nevertheless have a clearly defined and entrenched oligopolistic position in their respective markets.

8. *Keeping sight of value.* Disregard the significance of, or at least put very little emphasis on, information not directly related to the interpretation of a firm's financial variables. It should not be a resurgence of a building boom or an increase in housing starts which induces you to buy cement or furniture stock, but whether or not they are cheap according to your own criterion of value. Nor should you buy motion picture stocks because a particular motion picture is very successful or airline stocks because you expect a heavy increase in air passenger or freight traffic. All these expectations may indeed be realized, yet the price paid may have been too dear. These expectations should only serve to bolster your conviction that the initial price paid is still relevant or help you to refrain from increasing your commit-

ment in a company whose price, though cheap, may be suffering from a prolonged industrial incertitude.

9. *New issues.* Refrain from purchasing new issues on the original offering. They are usually overpriced.

10. *Weighing market price.* Never use market price as an indication of value but only for what it is: the price of the last sale. Even the bid and asking prices should only be used as an indication of what one may have to pay or sell at once one has already determined the equity's value. In spite of what business economists may say, one would do well to remember that the stock market does not value, it only prices.

11. *Analyzing liquidity.* Liquidity is a function of investors' favorable interpretation of information rather than the size of the daily trading volume. One should not be afraid of buying 5,000 shares of stock of a company whose average daily trading volume appears to be less than 2,000 shares. What usually happens is that the trading volume tends to increase as the price of the stock increases, accompanied by increased response of the investing public to pertinent information about the company. For example, below $14 per share the stock of the Cross Company appeared highly illiquid. It would have been difficult to sell a few thousand shares without unduly depressing the market. Selling 10,000 shares would have been almost impossible. However, at $25 per share the increase in investor response to information about the company also served to increase the daily trading volume. Selling a block of 5,000 or 10,000 shares became much more feasible.

Conversely, a decline in trading volume accompanying a decline in price is usually indicative of investor apathy and discontent. It is not as easy to sell on bad news as it is on good news. And so-called "good" news doesn't always lead to a higher market price and increased liquidity. It usually has to be the kind of good news which, like a takeover bid at a substantially higher price, will induce a similar interpretation from existing as well as new shareholders.

It must be remembered that liquidity is not some sort of absolute quantity which is a direct function of a company's market capitalization. In a pronounced bearish market selling even a small block of a company with a large market capitalization can be a not entirely happy experience. Sometimes, of course, investors' interpretation of information is so dismal that dumping occurs, leading to liquidity. Yet, under these circumstances it is not always possible to liquidate blocks of stock in excess of the average daily trading volume. The possibility of liquidating a block of stock favorably almost always exists during a sharp rise in the price of stock, but it sometimes doesn't exist at all during a pronounced decline.

Analysis of liquidity is not an easy matter. It certainly is not a simple function of the average daily trading volume. Nor is it even a function of the relation of that volume to the total market flow of a company's shares. Under depressed circumstances it may be more difficult to sell 50,000 shares of U.S. Steel than 1,000 shares of Proler International—even though these amounts represent the same proportion of the total number of outstanding shares for each company.

12. *Buying and selling at the right time.* There's not very much that is certain about investing in equities. The very nature of the equity instrument, as well as the nature of the marketplace, virtually guarantees uncertainty. Practical investors sometimes try to cope with this uncertainty with their own analysis of market timing. Accordingly, there is supposed to be a proper time to buy and a proper time to sell. There are some traders and speculators who have a good "sense" of market timing, but more than an intuitive feeling it is not. A practical investor who is interested in the long run cannot take market timing too seriously. Obviously, if he sees that the price of steel or sugar is in a long-term down trend, he may refrain from buying steel or sugar companies. But even then the appearance of an investment opportunity will be primarily reflected in the price of the stock rather than an analysis of prospects for the industry. An investor must judge value and discover opportunities from an analysis of the financial statements of the company and not from market information the timing and relevancy of which is uncertain. It is easier to cope with the uncertainty of the future by trying to understand the significance of a company's financial situation as one sees it, forgetting about whether others will arrive at the same conclusion.

Situations will constantly arise in which a particular investment judgment seems more relevant or appropriate than another. But it is a mistake to put an arbitrary time limit to these judgments. If Pabst was cheap at $22 a share in 1975, it is even cheaper at the same price in 1976 and 1977 as long as this company's financial reports conform to one's basic scheme of expectations. Again, it is buying cheaply—not necessarily at the right time—that is crucial to the process of valuing. One cannot make a formal judgment about time, only intuitive and uncertain judgments.

13. *Accounting for arbitrariness.* Another aspect of uncertainty which every investor must face before and after he has chosen to invest in a particular stock is the realization that, although the process of valuation may itself be rational, the actual opportunity for investing is arbitrary. There is no way to remove the arbitrariness with which the most profitable investment opportunities make themselves known. An investor simply cannot think that because stocks appear to be ex-

tremely undervalued in the steel industry they will provide the best future performance. It may very well be that another stock he already holds in his portfolio will prove to be a better "performer."

In 1975, for example, I bought the shares of Lehigh Portland Cement at an average cost of about $10 per share on the grounds that it was a greatly undervalued situation. I saw no immediate prospects for an increase in market price. There was no way I could have calculated that these shares would come to have a market price of $25 in 1977. According to my scheme of expectations there were other stocks in my portfolio which should have out-performed Lehigh Portland Cement, but which did not.

It is as impossible to foresee where we will derive the most gain as it is to foresee where we will suffer the most losses. Opportunities present themselves arbitrarily. They are not dependent on investor wisdom or foresight. This is one of the reasons why investors diversify. However, arbitrariness only describes the market performance of an investment, not the practice itself of valuing, and however arbitrary the market may prove to be, one can always set up a scheme of rational expectations to determine the exchange value of an investment.

14. *Formulating expectations.* Prudent investment practice requires that the process of valuing be subject to an orderly scheme of expectations. At the heart of this scheme will be the particular share's expectancy value. One will also form expectations concerning certain of the company's financial variables. For example, one ought to consider the significance of the highest and lowest expected return-on-equity ratio, the dividend, the debt-to-equity ratio, inherent expense, depreciation, backlog of orders, and pension-funding liability. If the company manufactures a commodity, one will need to understand how the pricing structure of this commodity affects the company's income.

Each investment will involve its own particular set of essential variables about which one ought to form certain minimum and maximum expectations. In prudent practice these expectations are formed cautiously so that they can almost always be satisfied to some degree. For example, if one were interested in United States Sugar, it would be more advisable to determine the impact on earnings of an entire price range of from 12 cents to 30 cents a pound than to assume that sugar will not fall below 15 cents a pound. Although the price of sugar may fall below 12 cents a pound, not all satisfaction will be lost because the investor has lowered his initial expectations. Of course, this may also mean that the opportunity to buy U.S. Sugar doesn't exist (yet) because the price is too high.

The purpose of forming a scheme of expectations is to ensure that even if one particular expectation has to be reduced more than anticipated, the overall scheme will still be subject to some continuing satisfaction. Thus the scheme ought to be formed so that no one reduction will lead to complete dissatisfaction.

Perhaps an example would further clarify this point. In 1975 I bought the shares of Ohio Ferro-Alloys at $14 per share on these considerations: its book value was $24 per share; its average ROE was about 15 percent; its working capital was $6 per share, and its debt was $8 per share. The investment in new plant and equipment was declared to be about $12 per share by 1977, and the company was constructing one of the most modern silicon plants in the country. The dividend was 72 cents per share. According to my analysis, the management had an excellent reputation in its own industry. I was impressed with the frugality and efficiency with which it ran the company. There were no jets or limousines; the company headquarters were efficient and functional. They had a respectable oligopolistic position in the American market for silicon and manganese ferro-alloys as well as silicon metal, which are indispensable for the production of steel, cast iron, aluminum alloys, and silicone.

The company was, in a word, an essential industry. I established an expectancy value of about $35 per share, or $21 in excess of the price paid. The price of the shares rose to $23 in 1976. But in 1977 it fell to about $9. Apparently, recession abroad had induced foreign producers to dump in the U.S. at prices below production cost. Thus the company, while retaining its share of the American market, had to depress its prices in an extraordinarily unforeseen manner.

In spite of the outcome, I do not think that the original scheme of expectations on which I made a judgment of value was misleading. The company's finances are still strong. From the point of view of a new investor, these shares are, as of this writing, more undervalued than they were before in spite of the severe reduction in income. Thus, although my expectations concerning the current return on equity have had to be reduced more than anticipated, I believe that these shares could still be bought.

Perseverance is, of course, as difficult to practice in valuing equities as it is in any other human endeavor. It is also just as difficult to distinguish it from foolhardiness. Ultimately, however, the satisfaction of increased wealth can only be realized by persevering in the conviction of one's orderly scheme of expectations.

15. *Sell as you buy.* Sell according to the same process of valuation with which you buy. The judgment to sell is just the obverse of the

decision to buy; it is not independent of it. One should not adopt a particular criterion of value to buy and then discard it when the time comes to sell. For example, if we judge that the exchange value of Johns-Manville is about $34 per share and we paid $22 per share, we should not discard the original scheme of expectations which led to the initial valuation and try to sell the stock at a higher price because "the market looks good." It may very well be that our initial valuation was too low, but we cannot substitute another based only on market factors.

A fall in market price is, to the investor, hardly ever a cause to sell. This is why it is often wise to spread one's purchases over a protracted period rather than buy all at once. As Benjamin Graham noted, the true investor is hardly ever forced to sell his shares. The reason is that for the true investor, lower price means better opportunity.

After having considered the tax consequences adequately, an investor can scarcely ever be faulted for having sold too soon and taken too small a profit, as long as the sales are in excess of the original opportunity cost with which he undertook the investment. In summation, we could say that a prudent investor should both buy and sell below his judgment of an equity's exchange value. Selling short is a technique better used by the trader and speculator than the long-term investor.

Capital Value

Throughout this book, we have been concerned with *expectancy value* (EV), which I claimed is the theoretical basis for measuring the worth of common stock. Expectancy value is calculated by the formula $EV = BV\ (ROE/OC)$. In my actual investment practice, I have derived a convenient application of the concept of expectancy value, which I refer to as the *capital value* of a share of common stock. The formula for capital value is

$$CV = BV \frac{AIBV + DYBV}{OC}$$

where CV = capital value, BV = current book value, $AIBV$ = average increase in book value, $DYBV$ = dividend yield on current book value, and OC = opportunity cost.

There are several points to be noted about this formula. First, it is not objective but subjective, as all value judgments must be. It enables me to judge how much more or less I should accept as purchase or selling price of a particular stock. Second, it gives me a per-share dollar value against which I can compare market price. Thus it is more useful than a ratio. Third, it allows me to express my understanding of capital as the value of assets used in the production of income rather than as the value of these assets independent of the income already produced or the value of future income independent of the assets used to produce it.

I call the quantity derived from this formula capital value, because it represents the value of a share held by a minority or average stockholder as an instrument of financial capital. Thus, this is not a formula for either present or future value. It completely ignores the time value of money. To put it more positively, it implies that in valuing equities, it is futile to calculate the time value of money disbursed and received.

The main difference between the capital value formula and the formula for expectancy value is that the former allows me to analyze the return-on-equity ratio in such a way that I can readily distinguish growth in retained earnings from dividend payout. (I personally like to invest in companies that are spending heavily to upgrade plant and equipment or expand markets.) Although expectancy value remains the theoretical basis for the approach to common-stock valuation presented in this book, it must always be interpreted and applied according to the investment criteria of the individual investor. Insofar as the distinction between retained earnings and dividend yield is felt to be important, the capital value formula is the more appropriate valuation tool. In particular, if the investor were to attach a higher value to either dividend yield or growth in retained earnings, it would be an easy matter to give a higher weight to either *AIBV* or *DYBV* in the capital value formula.

It should be noted that if we follow generally accepted accounting practice, the two formulas yield only comparable, not identical, results. Generally, the figures for capital value will be somewhat higher than the corresponding expectancy values—or, to put it another way, *AIBV* + *DYBV* in my capital value formula tends to be greater than *ROE* in the expectancy value formula. This is due primarily to the fact that ROE is commonly determined using earnings and book value of the *same* fiscal year. One could argue that the ROE for a given year should in fact be derived from that year's earnings and the book value for the *previous* year, because clearly the return is on the equity at the beginning, not the end, of the accounting period. However, throughout this book I have adhered to the prevailing accounting practice; thus all ROE figures, including the ones in the examples in this section, are based on earnings and book value of the same year.

Let me add that my formula for capital value is far from being a secret formula for success. Even if somebody used it, the market would still fluctuate and there would still be discrepancies between capital value and market price.

A detailed analysis of each of the variables in the formula follows.

Book value

If one examines the academic literature on valuation formulas for common stock, one becomes aware that almost none includes book value as a variable. Even Myron J. Gordon's *r*, or return on equity, is only a ratio. His actual formula excludes book value as a variable.[3]

In 1964, there appeared in a financial journal an article entitled "The Place of Book Value in Common Stock Evaluation," written by Frank E. Block. Because book value was so out of fashion among professionals and academicians, Block used the introduction to apologize for his interest in the subject. He wrote:

> From the beginning young securities analysts are taught that common stock prices are dependent upon earnings, dividends, future growth rates, and certainty of such growth rates, quality and similar considerations. Only in cases of possible merger or liquidation is the analyst encouraged to consider book value. It is not surprising that book value gathers dust on the back row of the analyst's set of tools, to be used only in cases of utter desperation.[4]

Block then proceeded to describe the merits of using book value, but he cut short its function in valuing equities because he felt constrained by the prevailing academic wisdom. Unfortunately, his formulas for using book value fail for one simple reason: they all include some reference to market price or the price-earnings ratio. As we have shown throughout this book, the relationship between a stock's exchange or intrinsic value and its market price is always coincidental at best.

The purpose of using book value in a valuation is to provide a standard for determining how much more or less than book value a share ought to be worth, given a particular opportunity cost. The book value in a valuation cannot be used to discover why the market should make it worth more or less than it is. (Is there ever any sense to paying ten times book value for a company producing a 25 percent ROE? Of course not, yet people were freely doing so during the sixties and are sometimes still doing it.)

The question will be raised, of course, whether book value can itself be used as a fair description of value.[5] As I have used it throughout this book, book value is identical to shareholder's equity. It represents the amount left after all liabilities representing contractual obligations are deducted from all the assets of the company. It consists of a firm's original paid-in capital, surplus capital derived from the sale of equities to the public over book value, and retained earnings. The capital can consist of one or various classes of common stock and one or various classes of preferred, or preferred convertible stock. Convertible debentures can be figured into book value only by increasing the number of shares by which a firm's net worth should be divided.

Book value is supposed to represent the residual amount which could be paid to common stockholders after all other claimants of the firm have been paid off. In calculating EV or CV, we always use current BV. For practical purposes, it is sufficient to use the BV figure from the firm's most recent quarterly financial statements.

Obviously, book value in itself means very little if one's primary concern is liquidation. I would guess that no more than 10 percent of the companies listed in the NYSE, if liquidated, would bring a dollar amount within 10 percent of their stated book value. After all, with respect to a firm's fixed assets, book value only represents its depreciated cost, not its replacement or salvage value, so the stated liquidation value of most inventories is meaningless. Valuing inventory apart from the rest of a firm's financial variables is impossible for the average shareholder. Even management primarily values inventory not for its liquidation value but as a measure of the relationship of costs to revenue. A firm's goodwill can represent either the nominal amount it attributes to its indispensable marketing position, or the excess over book value that management has paid for a company it has acquired.

Management has many legitimate means at its disposal for reducing book value. The most common, of course, is depreciation. This is an item which, through contributing to a firm's cash flow, reduces a firm's earnings and hence its retained earnings. Research and development is another such item which some managements choose to capitalize rather than deduct from current income. The most conservative managements will usually pick the latter course. Obviously, given comparable circumstances, the firm which expenses research and development is worth more than one which does not.

The pension fund is another item which management may use to increase or decrease book value. Some managements completely fund or expense the current contribution to the pension fund, thereby showing a reduction in current income and, hence, retained earnings. Other firms (for instance, most tire manufacturers) have huge unfunded pension funds. This means that their current income and retained earnings are stated independently of the future liability incurred by the unexpensed pension fund.

The repurchase of common stock, above book value, is another method management has of reducing the company's book value. Sometimes companies with excess cash (like IBM) will exercise this prerogative, since only a reduction in cash flow, not current income, is involved. By repurchasing its shares above book value, management is able to reduce its commitment to produce continually larger overall earnings. It can maintain the same per-share earnings with less current income, for the overall net worth of the company is reduced by the amount used to repurchase its own shares. However, when management repurchases its own shares at below book value, it is actually contributing to a per-share increase in the shareholder's equity. Usually management exercises this prerogative when it has excess cash to gainfully employ. Sometimes it does this in order to "squeeze out" the minority shareholder in an attempt to reduce the number of outstanding shares to the point where the company becomes private, or almost so. Sometimes management just thinks (true or not) that a reduction in the number of publicly owned shares increases the power of its control over the firm.

Obviously book value is anything but an objective standard. It does not really reflect the liquidation value of the firm or any other objective criterion for the measurement of a firm's value. It would not be entirely unreasonable to say that book value is what management wants it to be. Like earnings, book value is stated and defined according to the convenience it affords management. If so, what is the point in using it? Shouldn't we believe, as most business economists do, that it is an undependable and futile measure of value?[6]

The significance of book value, as a measurement of value, rests in its relationship to income. Essentially the same accounting used to calculate book value is also used to calculate income. Both are an expression of how management wants its shareholders to judge the value of their claim. Taken independently of each other, book value and earnings can become an indication of just about any measure of performance. But taken together as a ratio—the return-on-equity ratio—it can be the stockholder's only reliable indication of how management is using the firm's assets and, therefore, how he can value his claim.

However arbitrary it may appear to be, book value does express an indication of how well management is using its net assets in the production of income for its shareholders. A managerial performance which is able to produce a constant 20–30 percent return on equity is obviously better than one that can only produce a return on equity of 5–10 percent. It is true, then, that book value is a reflection of the value management gives to capital in the production of income. To say that book value is useless and undependable because it does not reflect an "objective worth" of a company is to misunderstand its significance.

A minority or average shareholder is not really concerned with the objective value of his company's assets and book value. He owns a claim on income and can only hope this claim will bring him increased wealth. This is only possible if the company is able to maintain its return on equity within the parameters of its historic variations. It must remain in the business of producing income, not losses. Now, it is an obvious, though ignored, phenomenon that as long as a company is able to retain some income, its book value will increase. Earnings and market price will vary year after year; the book value increases annually, no matter how irregular this increase is. And this increase in book value represents an increasing responsibility by management to produce at least enough income to maintain the minimum return on equity which will satisfy its shareholders.

The recent effort by the Securities and Exchange Commission to force the managements of some of our larger corporations to provide a separate evaluation of the replacement or liquidation value of the firms' assets is, I think, completely misguided. I can understand this requirement being made of a company with a long history of sustained losses, but I cannot see why this should be put to United States Steel, Du Pont, or Exxon. The actual value of their assets is far in excess of their stated book value. To oblige them to account for the value of their assets independently of their value in producing income is, essentially, to accept the view that the production of income against which a stockholder has a legitimate, continuing claim is not as important as the measurement of assets against which a shareholder has only a residual or theoretical claim.

For the examples in Tables 1–9 I have used an opportunity cost of 10 percent.

Average increase in book value

AIBV reflects the arithmetic average of the percentage increase in book value taken over a certain period of time. There is really no hard, fast rule for the number of years over which the average should be calculated. If one is confronted with a particularly erratic or cyclical pattern, as for an automotive or machine tool company, one may wish to average for a longer period of time.

I use a simple arithmetic average. A median might do slightly better at "smoothing out" one or two abnormally profitable years, and there are some more complicated averaging techniques, like exponential smoothing, where one can assign heavier weights to more recent years to supposedly account for recent trends. However, we are not concerned here with a high degree of arithmetic precision. The actual averaging is somewhat of an arbitrary affair. In order to gain understanding, there is no substitute for visual inspection of each year's results. Trying to find an "optimal" statistical averaging technique is a waste of time.

It is easiest to average, of course, for those companies whose return on equity doesn't fluctuate much. See, for example, the case for IBM in Table 1. (This calculation and those that follow are based on the *Value Line Investment Survey,*[7] perhaps the best low-cost research tool available to the individual investor. Generally, however, the annual reports of the companies being analyzed should be consulted as well. In some instances there may be appreciable differences due to an increase in the number of shares issued or because of restated past income figures.)

It is fairly easy to find the average increase in book value for IBM because its return on equity is very stable year in and year out. This stability has been perhaps the major cause of investor confidence in its shares. One wouldn't really go far wrong in anticipating a continuing increase in retained earnings of about 13 percent. However, choosing a lower expectation of 12 percent might perhaps be preferable because of the apparent tendency of the company to pay out an increasingly larger percentage of its dividends (as can be seen by dividing Increase in BV by ROE). Thus, although overall profitability seems to be

TABLE 1. Book value, increase in book value, dividend yield, and ROE for IBM.

	BV	Increase in BV	DYBV	ROE
1976	$84.60	11.0%	9.4%	18.8%
1975	76.18	11.7%	8.5%	17.4%
1974	68.19	13.5%	8.2%	18.2%
1973	60.06	15.5%	7.4%	17.9%
1972	52	13.0%	8.3%	16.9%
1971	45.99	—	9.0%	—
Average		12.9%		17.8%

$$CV = \$84.60 \times \frac{12.9\% + 9.4\%}{10\%} = \$84.60 \times 2.23 = \$188\tfrac{5}{8}$$

TABLE 2. Book value, increase in book value, dividend yield, and ROE for General Motors.

	BV	Increase in BV	DYBV	ROE
1976	$48.80	10.3%	11.4%	20.5%
1975	44.23	5.5%	5.4%	9.6%
1974	41.93	1.0%	8.1%	7.6%
1973	41.54	7.0%	12.6%	19.3%
1972	38.81	7.2%	11.5%	18.7%
1971	36.22	—	—	—
Average		6.2%		15.0%

$$CV = \$48.80 \times \frac{6.2\% + 11.4\%}{10\%} = \$48.80 \times 1.76 = \$85\tfrac{7}{8}$$

increasing, the company needs less retained income to sustain its operations. This is a company for which analysis of the dividend payout ratio is crucial.

It is as difficult to find the AIBV for GM as it was easy for IBM. (See Table 2.) Over the five years represented, the return on equity has varied from 7.6 percent to 20.5 percent, and the increase in BV has varied even more, from 1 percent to 10.3 percent. This is another company for which an analysis of the dividend policy is crucial. The fluctuations in the ROE variable are, of course, a testament to the cyclical nature of the automotive industry. Given that, it would be helpful to examine DYBV and ROE for an additional five years prior to those studied in Table 2. GM obviously has needed to retain less than half of its income in order to sustain its oligopolistic strength. However, an analysis of the future of the automotive industry might make us feel that this company may soon need to retain more than it has historically. Personally I would feel fairly comfortable using an AIBV of 6 percent, because it would probably err on the side of caution rather than extravagance.

If one thought it was difficult to determine an average ROE or increase in book value for General Motors, Proler International (see Table 3) presents us with an even more difficult situation. The problem is that we have one year, 1974, in which the company made an extraordinary operating profit. During that year the price of No. 1 scrap iron reached an unprecedented high of $125 per ton, and this extremely well-managed metals recycler reaped a fantastic profit. I don't think it would be really appropriate to refer to 1974 as having been part of the more profitable side of the scrap-iron cycle. It was an

TABLE 3. Book value, increase in book value, dividend yield, and ROE for Proler International.

	BV	Increase in BV	DYBV	ROE
1976	$37.15	5.9%	3.7%	9.3%
1975	35.07	20.5%	4.0%	20.4%
1974	29.20	80.7%	4.8%	50.0%
1973	16.16	23.0%	5.6%	24.2%
1972	13.14	7.0%	7.0%	13.9%
		AIBV[a] = 27.4%		Average[a] = 23.6%
		AIBV[b] = 15.9%		Average[b] = 18.4%

$$CV = \$37.15 \times \frac{15.9\% + 3.7\%}{10\%} = \$37.15 \times 1.96 = \$72\tfrac{7}{8}$$

Note: AIBV[a] includes an extraordinary year (1974); AIBV[b] disallows that year and assumes a 23% increase in BV on the basis of the BV increase for 1973.

extraordinary year which one should not expect to be repeated, and it is a testament to Proler's management that it was able to take full advantage of it by retaining the better part of its income for upgrading and building new plant and equipment. Obviously I don't think that a simple arithmetic average would correctly reflect the AIBV. That's why I used AIBV[b] in Table 3. This assumed 1974's increase in book value to be 23 percent, based on the premise that that increase (as in 1973) would be the maximum possible in any ordinary year. This is, of course, very arbitrary. But even if the maximum expected ROE is 24 percent, it is reasonable to assume that future dividends will be larger than in the past. Not many companies, fortunately, present the analytical complexities of Proler.

I include Combustion Equipment (Table 4), a superbly managed pollution control and waste management company, only to emphasize the need to distinguish between an increase in BV due to the sale of stock on a secondary offering at a premium over book value and an increase in BV due to an increase in retained earnings. In the case of Combustion Equipment, the gain resulting from the capital surplus acquired in 1971 and 1972 must be ignored in compiling the AIBV because it represents the extraordinary gain from the sale of stock to the public and not from earned income.

Sperry & Hutchinson (Table 5) again presents certain analytical difficulties. For example, it shows an ROE on which it is difficult to base any kind of reasonable value judgment. Before 1970 the ROE was consistently over 20 percent. At that time it would have been very

TABLE 4. Book value, increase in book value, dividend yield, and ROE for Combustion Equipment.

	Shares Outstanding (millions)	BV	Increase in BV	DYBV	ROE
1976	7.32	$7.61	20.0%	.01%	16.6%
1975	7.02	6.34	17.4%	.005%	14.1%
1974	6.80	5.40	10.0%	—	12.9%
1973	6.74	4.91	17.5%	—	14.5%
1972	6.68	4.18	53.1%	—	12.7%
1971	5.12	2.73	73.9%	—	10.4%
1970	4.16	1.57	—	—	7.3%
Average			16.2%		14.1%

$$CV = \$7.61 \times \frac{16.2\% + 0.01\%}{10\%} = \$7.61 \times 1.62 = \$12\tfrac{3}{8}$$

difficult indeed to spot the extent of its instability. Through 1973 one might have suspected that a lower ROE was more in keeping with the company's expected future performance, but I doubt anyone could have really foreseen the actual drop in ROE in 1974 and 1975. No matter how much one questioned the future of the trading stamp in-

TABLE 5. Book value, increase in book value, dividend yield, and ROE for Sperry & Hutchinson.

	Shares Outstanding (millions)	BV	Increase in BV	DYBV	ROE
1976	8.90	$17.05	14.5%	5.8%	9.9%
1975	8.89	14.89	—	6.7%	6.2%
1974	8.89	15.42	1.7%	6.4%	5.9%
1973	9.06	15.16	2.9%	6.6%	11.7%
1972	9.99	14.73	7.7%	6.8%	16.8%
1971	10.74	13.68	6.3%	7.3%	16.5%
1970	10.77	12.87	—	7.7%	16.9%
1969	10.70	13.19	—	—	20.0%
1968	10.52	8.52	—	—	20.1%
1967	10.61	8.27	—	—	22.5%
Average			5.4%		10.0%

$$CV = \$17.05 \times \frac{5.4\% + 5.8\%}{10\%} = \$17.05 \times 1.12 = \$19\tfrac{1}{8}$$

or, if intangible assets of $6.72 per share are included:

$$CV = \$19\tfrac{1}{8} + \$6.72 = \$25\tfrac{3}{4}$$

dustry, it was difficult to foresee the extent to which its failure would affect the company.

However, if one were to have paid more attention to the BV and especially to the increase in BV, I think one would have had some indication of the degree to which the company's past profitability imposed a burden on management. In spite of its attempts at diversification, management was not really capable of maintaining the high ROE derived in its glorious trading stamp days. An abnormally high amount of earnings had to be paid out as dividends. Management's inability to use its income in building up and reinforcing its basic trading stamp business can be seen in its repurchase of over two million of its own shares at an average cost of about $25 per share, or about double its then book value. A low AIBV of a company which is not essentially cyclical is an indication to be extremely cautious in pricing its stock.

Today Sperry & Hutchinson is a conglomerate, and as with any other conglomerate, each part must be analyzed separately, although no one is sure whether the sum ought to be greater or less than its component parts. Like Gulf + Western, Teledyne, United Technologies, and all other conglomerates in disparate, unrelated businesses, S & H is an analyst's nightmare—one must be prepared to work hard and sleep little. This company can serve as a reminder that numbers and ratios are of value only when they are based on an understanding of the economic behavior of business.

Publicker Industries (Table 6) is an example of a company that was apparently never, or almost never, run for a profit. Thus it is really impossible to analyze its value as a function of return on equity. However, the value of its real estate holdings is considerably higher

TABLE 6. Book value, increase in book value, dividend yield, and ROE for Publicker Industries.

	BV	Increase in BV	DYBV	ROE
1976	$ 9.79	—	—	—
1975	11.04	—	—	—
1974	11.16	—	—	6.6%
1973	10.27	—	—	2.1%
1972	9.94	—	—	—
1971	10.27	—	—	—
1970	10.22	—	—	—

CV not applicable

TABLE 7. Book value, increase in book value, dividend yield, and ROE for Chrysler Corporation.

	BV	Increase in BV	DYBV	ROE
1976	$46.10	16.8%	0.6%	11.7%
1975	39.45	—	—	—
1974	44.08	—	3.0%	—
1973	49.22	6.5%	2.6%	9.4%
1972	46.23	6.5%	2.0%	8.9%
1971	43.40	4.5%	—	3.7%
1970	41.51	—	—	—
Average		6.0%		6.0%

$$CV = \$46.10 \times \frac{6\% + 0.6\%}{10\%} = \$46.10 \times 0.66 = \$30\tfrac{3}{8}$$

than stated in its balance sheet. Valuing this company may be worthwhile only in determining the value of a controlling position from which one would either liquidate or change and improve management.

Chrysler Corporation presents us with the case of a company with a very high book value and a very low return on equity (see Table 7). The company periodically shows huge losses. Even when it earns money, it isn't as profitable as either Ford or General Motors. In this instance book value is almost meaningless. On the one hand, the company's debt is proportionally much higher than it is for its two competitors. On the other, its capital expenditures show that it is committed to trying to make a profit.

As in most instances in which BV is decreased because of losses, I chose not to add the decrease in BV in my calculation of AIBV but rather count the IBV and ROE as zero. My main reason for this is that management, when faced with a loss, tends to increase the loss as much as possible by writing off as many expenses as possible. In spite of its periodic losses, Chrysler is in the business of making money. Although this method of dealing with losses affecting a negative ROE and decrease in BV is not entirely satisfactory, I think it can be fairly reasonably applied to those cyclical companies subject to periodic losses.

Comparing Polaroid and Eastman Kodak (Tables 8a and 8b), we see that judging by the ROE, Kodak should always be worth at least twice as much in relation to its book value as Polaroid, since it has always been at least twice as profitable. Strictly from the point of view of

TABLE 8a. Book value, increase in book value, dividend yield, and ROE for Polaroid.

	BV	Increase in BV	DYBV	ROE
1976	$22.99	9.6%	1.7%	10.6%
1975	20.97	8.1%	1.5%	9.1%
1974	19.39	2.9%	1.7%	4.5%
1973	18.84	7.2%	1.7%	8.4%
1972	17.57	6.0%	1.8%	7.4%
1971	16.57	—	1.9%	11.2%
Average		6.8%		8.0%

$$CV = \$22.99 \times \frac{6.8\% + 1.7\%}{10\%} = \$22.99 \times 0.85 = \$19\tfrac{1}{2}$$

TABLE 8b. Book value, increase in book value, dividend yield, and ROE for Eastman Kodak.

	BV	Increase in BV	DYBV	ROE
1976	$24.84	8.6%	8.3%	16.2%
1975	22.87	8.3%	9.0%	16.6%
1974	21.12	10.0%	9.4%	18.4%
1973	19.19	13.2%	9.4%	21.0%
1972	16.95	13.2%	8.2%	19.8%
1971	14.97	—	—	17.3%
Average		10.7%		18.4%

$$CV = \$24.84 \times \frac{10.7\% + 8.3\%}{10\%} = \$24.84 \times 1.9 = \$47\tfrac{1}{8}$$

ROE, Kodak has always been a better managed company than Polaroid. This kind of comparison can also be applied to other related companies such as the McGraw-Hill and Macmillan publishing conglomerates.

Retained versus paid-out earnings

Recall my formula for capital value:

$$CV = BV \frac{AIBV + DYBV}{OC}$$

The plus sign in the numerator is an indication that, as a minority or average shareholder, I am indifferent to having my claim on income interpreted as an increase in retained earnings or paid out as dividends. This is to say I do not value money received from dividends more highly than money retained by the corporation in the form of increased inventory, plant, and equipment. This again is a personal preference.

The opinion prevailing among most academicians and security analysts is that income received as dividends is worth more to the shareholder than income retained by the corporation. But to me, since the claim on income received as dividends is not legally binding on the corporation, it is not as important as interest or even preferred dividends. Dividends are constantly diminished periodically due to decreases in income. Because I cannot count on the value of future dividends, the practice of discounting present value of future dividends is useless for me.

I prefer to invest in a company which is committed heavily to investing in new plant and equipment. This more than anything else gives me confidence that management is doing all it can to maintain its oligopolistic strength. Therefore, I tend to prefer companies with a dividend-payout ratio of about 25 percent of their total earnings. Of course, my preferences are not shared by the majority of the investment community, nor should they be. Most pension funds, endowment funds, and trusts require dividend income to help defray current operating expenses and annuities. However, these are considerations that have nothing to do with the valuation of financial capital but rather with the actual erosion of this capital.

One of the few exceptions I take with Graham, Dodd, and Cottle is that I do not think dividends received are worth four times income retained.[8] However, this is a matter of practical preference rather than an ideological difference, and the practical wisdom of these authors is certainly not inferior to my own. As I have mentioned, furthermore, revising my capital value formula to admit a preference for dividend income presents no problem; all that needs to be done is to attach different weights to *AIBV* and *DYBV* in the formula. Thus if we were to value dividend income three times as high as retained earnings, the numerator *AIBV* + *DYBV* in the capital value formula would be replaced by the weighted expression (0.25 *AIBV* + 0.75 *DYBV*).

Dividend yield on book value

The most important aspect of DYBV is that the dividend is taken as a yield on book value rather than on market price. Since exchange

TABLE 9. Examples of capital values for two classes of common stock.*

	1976				1974				1972				1970			
	Low MP	High MP	Av. P/E	CV	Low MP	High MP	Av. P/E	CV	Low MP	High MP	Av. P/E	CV	Low MP	High MP	Av. P/E	CV
STOCKS WITH HIGH P/E RATIO																
IBM	223	288	14.5	189	150	254	16.5	143	265	341	35.5	115	175	309	33	101
Eastman Kodak	81	120	24.6	47	57	117	23.1	43	93	149	37.7	32	57	84	28	36
McDonald's	48	68	21.3	47	21	63	25.1	21	37	77	59	13	9	15	40	6.2
Avon	32	50	15	31	18	65	28	26	94	139	55	24	59	92	44	19
International Flavors & Fragrances	19	28	23	11.6	19	42	36	9.4	25	43	58	6.3	14	21	45	5
STOCKS WITH LOW P/E RATIO																
U.S. Steel	43	59	10.3	62	23	32	3.6	43	18	23	10	19	18	26	12	23
General Motors	57	78	6.9	86	28	55	13.4	63	71	89	10.5	66	59	81	33	47
Exxon	42	57	8.5	65	27	50	5.2	53	34	44	11	28	25	36	10	26
International Harvester	22	33	4.5	43	16	29	5.7	32	26	40	10	19	22	29	13	25
Johns-Manville	23	35	11	27	14	22	6.4	25	27	41	12.7	23	26	40	16	22
AT&T	50	64	9.4	57	39	53	8.8	51	41	53	10.4	42	40	53	11.7	43

* Based on an opportunity cost of 10 percent; AIBV averaged over five years. MP = market price.

value or expectancy must be derived independently of market price, it would be senseless to judge the value of a dividend solely as a function of market price.

As noted earlier, in my capital value formula I am essentially dividing the return-on-equity ratio into two separate ratios. The first, AIBV, gives me an indication of how management is building up the value of my residual claim; the second, DYBV, tells me how much of its income management is prepared to give up to shareholders.

Stock dividends are not really dividends at all, but represent an increase in the number of outstanding shares. That is, they are simply fractional share splits. Practically, stock dividends do benefit shareholders, because a 5 percent or 10 percent stock dividend often does not diminish the market price of their shares. Management will sometimes consider paying a stock dividend when it needs to retain most or all of the company's income for its operations. Nonetheless, it seems clear that stock dividends should not be included in calculating capital value.

Opportunity cost

Although I continually revise the overall yield I require on the purchase of stock, I normally stick to a 10 percent to 12 percent opportunity cost. Thus, if the average return on equity is 12 percent for most industrial equities, and if my opportunity cost is 10 percent, I may choose not to pay more than 60 percent of book value so that the current overall yield on my purchase price is not less than 20 percent. In the calculations of capital value in Table 9, I have used an opportunity cost of 10 percent.

10

Prudence

In Chapter 8, prudence was said to dictate the development of a self-consistent scheme of expectations capable of leaving the shareholder with an enduring state of satisfaction. Prudence implies a discipline for valuing, not a description of the consequence of some valuation; that is, it is the judgment that is prudent, not the investment. In short, prudence describes a way of ordering the various kinds of expectations a shareholder entertains when confronted with the real, not just mathematical, uncertainty of buying and selling his property.

As my discussion in Chapter 8 was theoretical, it was somewhat lacking. However, it did emphasize certain practical considerations without which no valuation could ever be considered prudent.

First, prudence cannot be used to describe any scheme of expectations that is not based on an expectancy. Thus all prudent valuations must consider the value of a shareholder's equity (book value), an analysis of a reasonable rate of return produced on this equity, and the minimum opportunity cost pertaining to the stock purchase.

Second, market price represents the degree of opportunity available rather than a dependable judgment about the value of the shareholder's investment.

Third, prudence demands that the investor strive for an understanding of disclosed information. Information, whether in the form of market price or financial reports, must be interpreted by the shareholder if it is to be relevant to him. Without this conscious effort to participate in the process of the disclosure of information, no judgment can ultimately be prudent.

Fourth, no decision making can be prudent if the shareholder is not aware of what I have called the *endocratic nature* of his relationship with management.

Two topics that were neglected in my earlier discussion of prudent judgments are risk and what business economists now call the *time horizon* of an investment. Risk was defined according to Benjamin Graham's intuitive and now outmoded concept of *margin of safety*. It was seen to be a function of the cheapness or discount of the opportunity presented, defined by market price and the investor's independent appraisal of value.

Risk has a direct bearing not only on how the shareholder perceives a company's finances but on whether he thinks management will give credence to his perception. Although loss of capital is the ultimate judge of an investment's risk, it is of no use until the investment is in fact sold for a loss. To me shareholder risk is more properly a function of exchange value than of market fluctuations.

Time horizon is a concept that stems from the fact that in a real and uncertain world no one can ever judge how long it will take to realize a profit from a prudent judgment. Prudence can never be limited to a specific period of time. The future is uncertain for shareholders and management alike. A shareholder has no contract obliging management to perform as he thinks it should. Any expectation he forms regarding the length of time necessary to realize a profit is arbitrary to the extent that it is subjective. It was because of this arbitrariness that I have insisted that expected value formulas not be used as part of the prudent process for valuing most industrial common stock.

I have repeatedly suggested that, even though the shareholder is relatively powerless in affecting the course of his investment, the ultimate imprudence is for him to ignore the property rights to which he is entitled. In reality, what rights a shareholder has depends on the price he has paid for his shares, for that determines how much he can expect from his property. An investor who has bought stock at five times book value and 30 times earnings is entitled to expect little other than somebody else's concurring folly. The significance of his right to vote at stockholders' meetings is diminished by the fewer shares to which his outlay has entitled him. His appraisal right is diminished to the extent that he cannot insist on a reasonable appraisal commensurate with his purchase price. Finally, being able to exchange one investment for another is a consequence of a shareholder's insistence on using his right or power to act prudently.

Although shareholders are constantly accused of being passive—modern rentiers—I think this accusation is only partly accurate. A shareholder is not, by definition, a coupon clipper, although he may in fact be very little more, especially if somebody else is managing his money for him. In the end the activity and concern demonstrated by the shareholder is commensurate with the degree to which he takes prudence seriously.

Prudence as Practical Wisdom

If the American interpretation of liberty is a consequence of an individual's right to transact business, it would seem that prudence is a major safeguard of this liberty. I say this in the same sense that wisdom (*sophia*) was considered by the Greeks to be essential in theoretical knowledge, and practical wisdom (*phronesis*) desirable in social, political, and commercial intercourse. Indeed, the "pursuit of happiness," within the long and varied tradition of Western philosophical thought, requires prudence. The word has virtually become synonymous with practical wisdom.

It has always been difficult to define prudence, just as it has always been difficult to define practical wisdom. The application of an attitude and discipline to the practical world is always more difficult than characterizing the theoretical or abstract concepts underlying it. Although philosophers have always regarded prudence as a virtue, they have usually had to rely on the reader's intuitive and subjective interpretation of what it really consists of. It was always understood that prudence cannot be defined according to some mechanical and deterministic theory of behavior, precisely because it is a practical concept whose application demands experience and a sense of what is relevant.

Nonetheless, prudence is important not only in guiding the valuing of equities by the individual shareholder but also because it is, legally, the principle which is supposed to govern the behavior of those corporate fiduciaries who manage so much of our country's financial assets.

It follows, then, that one way to measure the importance of prudence is to appraise the amount of money under so-called prudent control. One such calculation was made by Raymond W. Goldsmith.

> [In] 1968 corporate stock having a total value of fully $1,000 billion (excluding intercorporate holdings) represented about one-fourth of the value of all financial assets outstanding in the United States, while the assets of financial institutions, including personal trust departments, came to approximately $1,600 billion, equal to another two-fifths of the total. Eliminating the duplication involved in the corporate holdings of stock by financial institutions of about $250 billion, financial institutions and corporate stock together represented more than one-half of the financial superstructure of the United States.[1]

Since so much of this nation's financial capital is managed by its fiduciaries rather than its beneficiaries, one would expect that the courts and Congress would have defined prudence very precisely. But this is not the case. The courts and Congress have apparently inherited the classical philosophical dilemma of defining prudence as it is actually applied by people of practical wisdom. One would have also thought that contemporary business economists, cognizant of the enormous role of the fiduciary, would have devoted a good share of their discourse to prudence. Instead, business economics appears to have become a branch of mathematics rather than moral philosophy, and has ignored the problem. The business economist has to a certain extent substituted the concepts of optimal financial decision and risk–reward for that of prudence. We shall see that this substitution is not entirely felicitous.

In subsequent sections of this chapter we shall analyze both the legal and economic interpretations of prudence, in keeping with our institutional approach to valuing common stock. Our ultimate concern is not with the legal complexities of the issue but with the process of valuation itself. Some of the questions we shall probe are: Is there an absolute standard of prudence? Can there be one? Is prudence dependent on a concept of value? Does valuation involve more than just pricing? Can prudence apply to situations in which the valuation of equities is thought useless and wasteful?

How Is Prudence Defined?

In the United States there have been two fundamentally different approaches to the characterization and definition of prudence. One is the "legal list" approach, often referred to as the New York rule. The other is the "prudent man" or Massachusetts rule.

The prudent man rule, which we shall discuss in greater detail later in this chapter, characterizes prudence according to a general principle left open to interpretation by the fiduciary and the court. The legal list approach does not attempt to establish the general guidelines counseling the fiduciary, but it does, in effect, define prudence by limiting the fiduciary to those investments appearing on an approved "legal list" of investment possibilities. In New York, until 1970, fiduciaries who wished to act prudently, as it were, were restricted to purchasing only those securities on the legal list.

Even though the New York rule has been repealed and a new standard of prudence—essentially the Massachusetts rule—adopted by the federal government in 1974, I think it would be beneficial for us to examine the attitude underlying the legal list approach in order to clarify our understanding of prudence.

The legal list

The main principle underlying the legal list approach is protection of the trustee from liability arising from the expenses and possible losses of administering a trust in what could be considered an imprudent manner.[2] New York followed the practice of the English courts in realizing that not all fiduciaries are expert and skilled investment advisers. Therefore, the best way of providing security for the fiduciary was to limit the investments he could make to a legal list of acceptable securities.

It is not very difficult to see that preserving the corpus of a trust and producing a reasonable income were not the main concerns of those states which adopted this approach. It has even been suggested that in England, where legal lists at one time could consist only of government securities, a compelling reason for omitting corporate securities was "the desire to create a market for government securities."[3] In New York it was not until 1950 that investment in certain corporate equities was permitted. (One wonders what would have happened had the Massachusetts rule not been adopted by New York in 1970.)

In New York the legal list approach was of a permissive, nonmandatory type. Although the fiduciary could not purchase nonlegal investments, he still had to use his discretion in choosing from among the securities available on the legal list and in deciding whether and for how long he should retain any nonlegal investments which may have formed a part of the initial estate. Thus, even according to the legal list approach, a trustee could still be held liable for imprudence or lack of discretion.[4]

The main impetus behind the repeal of the legal lists in New York came from the New York State Banking Department.[5] With the realization that the vast majority of trust funds were actually administered by corporate fiduciaries—that is, bank trust departments and large investment advisory concerns—the need to protect trustees from fiduciary incompetence became less urgent. Legal lists became just too restricting for the corporate fiduciaries. If corporate fiduciaries could not make use of their investment expertise, skill, and discretion, what were they to be paid for? Furthermore, if they all had to compete for the same legal list securities, they would be forced to bid up the price of these securities, at the ultimate expense of the beneficiaries.

The repeal of the legal list approach to prudence in New York and its subsequent substitution by the prudent man standard was due to several important considerations. The first was that the corporate fiduciaries had finally made it clear to the state legislature that they could not tolerate the legislative definition of prudence any longer. The legal lists, which were supposed to help guide the individual fiduciary, only served as legal straitjackets for the New York based corporate fiduciaries. How could they assure themselves of the burgeoning trust business if the legal list prescribed not only the securities which could be purchased but also the maximum percentage of equity securities allowed for each portfolio? (Between 1950 and 1965, only 35 percent of a portfolio could consist of equities. In 1965, this was increased to 50 percent.)

The second consideration was that since a corporate fiduciary is by definition expert in selecting and valuing equities, he ought to be allowed to exercise this charge without legislative constraints. The theory was that, given adequate leeway to exercise his skill, sagacity, and discretion, the corporate fiduciary would actually be able to increase the income, as well as maintain the safety, of funds under his charge. He would be able to choose from a wider range of securities, but, more significantly, he would have greater discretion in how he chose, the price he paid, and the diversification he adopted.

The New York rule didn't absolve the fiduciary from exercising caution and discretion, even in selecting from the legal list, but did make the definition of prudence a matter of legislation. Since legislation has a tendency to become more complex and restraining with time, the New York corporate fiduciary felt it was ultimately easier and safer to be subject to the general counsel of the Massachusetts rule.

Fiduciaries have usually felt that excessive legislation inevitably restricted not just their ability to select stocks but, perhaps more important, their ability to judge the price at which it would be prudent to include a security in a portfolio. (Most trust agreements probably limit the fiduciary to purchasing only those securities that would have been proscribed by the legal lists anyway.) In part the repeal of the legal lists was an inducement to use discretion in pricing as well as in selecting securities for purchase. The definition of prudence became the prerogative of the fiduciary, not the legislature. Even if the courts might be called in to adjudicate, the main issue would likely be one of negligence and abuse of discretionary power rather than of faulty judgment.

I most certainly regard the repeal of legal lists as beneficial to both the fiduciary and the beneficiary. Since prudence is primarily a matter of discipline, a beneficiary is ultimately better off having a fiduciary of skill and practical wisdom acting on his behalf rather than an unskilled "doorman on duty" whose prudence is measured by the degree to which he conforms strictly to the compliance of the law.

Fortunately, the history of legal lists is one of increasing liberalization. Nevertheless, we must not understate the importance of their repeal in New York in favor of the prudent man standard. The decision in 1970 by the New York legislature was reaffirmed by the Congress of the United States in 1974. Now, not only are virtually all the financial centers of the United States subject to a state-imposed prudent man standard, but, more important, they are subject to essentially the same standard as defined by the federal government. In other words, prudence is no longer the subject of interest by an elected legislature but only by the courts.

This may not seem important, but if we compare it to the corporate revolution described in Chapter 2, its significance can be more easily appreciated. There we described how, as a consequence of the Fourteenth Amendment, the state legislatures were divested of their monopoly power over the creation and control of the corporate vehicle. The modern industrial corporation became a "new American"; it became the creature of the businessman's ability to exercise his economic power. We saw that one of the consequences of this new corporate person was that its functioning tended to become the subject of interpretation by the courts rather than the legislature.

Nobody can predict what the consequences of the new federal prudent man standard will be. It is fairly obvious, however, that it is the corporate fiduciary who is the ultimate beneficiary of the present standard. When we realize that the trust departments of our nation's banks are acting as fiduciaries for half of the corporate equity capital of the United States, we must acknowledge that how prudence is going to be defined will, to a great degree, depend upon how the banks define it.

Viewed from another perspective, the situation appears somewhat disquieting. As Peter Drucker points out in his *Unseen Revolution,* in five to ten years the pension funds alone will have a claim on over 50 percent of our nation's equity capital; and although the worker is the ultimate beneficiary of this claim, it is apparent that the control over this claim is held not by the worker but by the corporate fiduciary. The real "unseen revolution" is that control, whether exercised or not, over the majority of our corporate stock is in the fiduciary charge of our nation's banks.[6]

The prudent man rule

Before discussing the prudent man rule in greater depth, it

would perhaps be helpful if I paused to remind the reader why I am spending so much time discussing prudence and fiduciary responsibility in a book that is mainly concerned with the valuation of equities. I believe that whether the individual is investing as a shareholder for himself or as a fiduciary for somebody else, the process of valuation, if it is to be made for the purpose of long-term investment and not speculation or trading, requires the same skill and discretion. Whether this is referred to as a discipline when it concerns one's personal fortune or as prudence when it affects the fortune of others is of little consequence; the terms reflect more on the degree of liability involved rather than the process itself. Thus, the individual has much to learn from an understanding of the legal concept of fiduciary prudence, even though he has much less at stake.

The standard of prudence now applied by most states and the federal government is the prudent man rule. This is often referred to as simply the Massachusetts rule, because it stems from a decision rendered in 1830 by Judge Putnam of Massachusetts involving Harvard College and Massachusetts General Hospital versus Francis Amory, a trustee in charge of a $50,000 trust fund, which was a small part of a large estate left by his brother-in-law, John McLean. Jonathan Amory (who died soon) and Francis Amory were appointed executors and trustees. They were to pay all the income and profits from this sum to the testator's wife during her lifetime. Afterward, the remainder of this sum was to be divided equally between Harvard College and Massachusetts General Hospital. When Mrs. McLean died and the remaining trustee tendered his resignation to the court, the remainder was only worth $38,000, $12,000 less than what it originally had been. Thinking that Francis Amory had been negligent in his fiduciary duty and hoping to recover the lost $12,000, the college and hospital sued. They lost the case and never bothered to appeal.

There are several aspects of this case which we should remember. First, the testator chose Jonathan and Francis Amory as trustees because he had "full and entire confidence in the[ir] ability, fidelity and diligence." Second, the trustees invested all the $50,000 in the common stock of three companies—a bank, an insurance company, and a manufacturing firm. Judge Putnam agreed that this portfolio complied strictly with the terms of the will. It should be pointed out that these corporations presented a different investment prospect from our modern corporation in one important aspect: they tended to pay out most of their income in dividends. Thus, the main reason for investing in them rather than bonds was the expectation of a higher annual income. As a matter of fact, the income from these three equities yielded an income of $20,493 for a five-year period, considerably above the 5 percent rate of interest commonly available at that time.[7]

Third, in spite of this high dividend income, the testator and trustees, as well as Judge Putnam, were fully aware that all common-stock investments must by their very nature be subject to continued market fluctuations. Amory, in fact, brought proof that his stocks had not fluctuated any more than other stocks which might have been selected. Judge Putnam said, "Do what you will, the capital is at hazard."

Fourth, Judge Putnam expressed his suspicion of the English legal list approach to prudence, which limited the investment of an estate to public funds. "If the public funds are resorted to, what becomes of the capital when the credit of the government shall be so much impaired as it was at the close of the last war?" In other words, any kind of investment involves a risk, and the trustee cannot be held liable as long as he has skillfully and diligently fulfilled the conditions of the will.

Fifth, Judge Putnam expressed the view that successful investing, in spite of the risks and hazard involved, cannot "be ascribed to accidental causes, but to calculation and reflection." In other words, successful investing always depends on prudence, in spite of the uncertainty involved. Finally, as part of the record in defense of Amory's prudence, Judge Putnam allowed that Amory and his cousin were diligent in enforcing all claims against the companies in which the trust owned stock. They followed the course of their investments with the same diligence they applied to the initial selection.

I have spent some time discussing Judge Putnam's decision because the prudent man standard was derived from his complete ruling, not simply from the following famous paragraph, which is conveniently referred to as the prudent man rule. Judge Putnam wrote:

> All that can be required of a trustee to invest is that he shall conduct himself faithfully and exercise sound discretion. He is to observe how men of prudence, discretion, and intelligence manage their own affairs, not in regard to speculation, but in regard to the permanent disposition of their funds, considering the probable income, as well as the probable safety of the capital to be invested.[8]

Taking a closer look at some of the words and phrases used, we arrive at the following observations. "All" refers to a degree of sufficiency rather than exclusion. One may determine the prudence of a fiduciary's behavior based on his good faith and sound judgment as long as these are in conformity with the expressed aim of the trust. "Faithfully" refers to the extent to which the trustee respects the aim of the trust and the expected benefit to the beneficiary. "Sound discretion" refers to the degree to which investments are selected according to some reasonable criterion of value. "Observe" means that the trustee must select his criterion for "sound disretion" on the basis of what other skilled and successful businessmen would do, and that it should not be farfetched and unique.

The phrase "how men of prudence, discretion, and intelligence manage their own affairs" refers to businessmen who have a reputation for having succeeded in their policy of investing for the long term. Judge Putnam was probably referring to men like the testator of this trust. He obviously was not referring to the market as a whole. He was not making the contemporary judgment that since the market is supposed to consist of willing, intelligent, and informed buyers and sellers, any choice made from the largest and most widely traded stocks is inherently prudent. The judge went to great lengths to show that not all men are prudent. Prudence can be applied only to men who have a reputation for "the permanent disposition of their funds." This would refer to businessmen investing their own capital and, I suppose, skilled investment advisers.

"Probable" does not mean the same as "expected" or "possible." By "probable," Judge Putnam meant that the trustee must be capable of supplying some sort of support or evidence governing his expectation of income and analysis of the safety of the capital, on the basis of past performance and of the financial condition of the investments involved. In other words, "probable" expresses the notion that the trustee must be diligent and not negligent in his calculations.[9]

As satisfying as Judge Putnam's decision may have been at the time, it still leaves much to be desired as a source for a standard of prudence. Ultimately the consequence of this standard is that all disputes must be judged by judicial process, and it is only meaningful when applied to the behavior of men of practical wisdom, discretion, and intelligence. It would be meaningless if applied as a mechanical and deterministic standard to men who behave as bureaucrats rather than businessmen. And indeed that is something to watch out for in the future. "Groupthink," as David Dreman, in his book *Psychology and the Stock Market,* called the growing tendency of fiduciaries to act en masse, could lead to some profound, unhealthy changes in the future.[10]

The Impact of ERISA

The Employee Retirement Income Security Act, enacted in September 1974, will almost surely affect the conduct of the securities industry as much as the original Securities and Exchange acts did.

Just as these earlier acts were originally intended to protect the small investor, through the principle of self-regulation of the securities markets, against abuse and manipulation, so does ERISA hope to protect the employee by giving him assurance that industry (not government) will provide the funds necessary for his retirement. Both the securities and retirement acts are concerned with the sanctity of man's savings. The older acts were concerned with protecting savings that the individual himself has control over. The newer act safeguards the individual's funds which are administered by or through his employer.

I would suspect that in great part the success or failure of ERISA will become the success or failure of American capitalism. Here we have a law that proposes legislation for the economic welfare of a nation, with the expressed recognition that this welfare is inextricably tied to the continuing prosperity of business. It is in this context that fiduciary responsibility takes on a new dimension by virtue of the magnitude of its charge.[11] I don't know of any other area of public life where the control of so much financial capital, ultimately contributing to the public welfare, is in the hands of a nongovernmental body. This is why the fiduciary duties described in ERISA take on a very special significance.

ERISA lists four categories of fiduciary responsibilities, the second of which is a restatement of the Massachusetts prudent man rule (the other three will be discussed shortly). The act states that a fiduciary shall discharge his duties "with the care, skill, prudence, and diligence under the circumstances then prevailing that a prudent man acting in like capacity and familiar with such matters would use in the conduct of an enterprise of a like character and with like aims."[12]

This is a restatement of the prudent man standard which originated in Judge Putnam's ruling. Congress expressly intended that the courts interpret this prudent man rule according to the traditional interpretations of the common law, "bearing in mind the special nature and purpose of employee benefit plans."[13] The change in wording is a reflection of the passage of a century and a half. There is no doubt that prudence still requires care, skill, and diligence in the selection of investments. What is disturbing are the phrases "like capacity" and "like character." Here we are concerned with emulating or observing the behavior not of the successful businessman but apparently of the successful fiduciary or successful investment adviser. These phrases can only refer to the management of a trust. Thus use of the prudent man standard, as worded in the act, seems to mean not only that a fiduciary must exercise caution and skill but that the reasonableness and prudence of his selections will be subjected to the test of whether or not other respected investment advisers would act similarly. This is disturbing in that it seems to protect the collective and periodic imbecility of the investment advisory community, as in the mass purchases of "growth" stocks at inflated prices. Polaroid at $100 a share is a classic example.

The only successful investment advisers I know are the ones who avoid the symptoms of "Groupthink" and do not act "like" others in their search for undervalued securities. I would prefer to think that the drafters of this act were overzealous in revising an archaic but otherwise efficiently worded standard. I would hope that they have not created language whereby the standard of professional behavior can only be interpreted by other so-called professionals. Observation would lead me to believe that this hope is not well-founded.

Fiduciary responsibility

Under trust law, a trustee who accepts his charge cannot be relieved of it until the court accepts his resignation. One of his many duties as a trustee is "not to delegate to others the doing of acts which the trustee can reasonably be required personally to perform."[14] Thus, although he may act on the advice of others, he must always bear the responsibility of acting on this advice himself.

This same general principle of nondelegation applies to fiduciary duty under ERISA. However, Congress, in its eagerness to protect the beneficiaries of a retirement plan, has considerably expanded the scope of those people who may not delegate their authority. Under ERISA, not only the named trustees are subject to fiduciary duty, but so are *all* of the fiduciaries involved. In other words, in its efforts to protect pension funds, Congress has extended the concept of fiduciary to include individual and corporate trustees, custodians, paid investment advisers, trust officers, and pension planning committee members.[15]

Much has been made of the liability of fiduciaries under ERISA. However, fiduciaries have always been personally liable for acts of negligence or misappropriation in the discharge of their fiduciary duties under trust law.[16] The real significance of fiduciary liability under this act is the *scope* of who may be held liable as a fiduciary. Today this means not only named trustees but almost any co-fiduciary, even investment advisers. Not only must each fiduciary be responsible for his own acts but also for the acts of his co-fiduciaries if he knows them to be in breach of the act's standards of fiduciary duty. Thus, ERISA extends the concept of liability beyond the common-law sense of fiduciary obligation.

The federal government is actually establishing itself as a testator in the creation of the trust. Thus, the fourth category of fiduciary responsibility (the first and third are yet to be discussed) requires that a fiduciary "conduct himself in accordance with the documents and instruments governing the plan insofar as such documents and instruments are consistent with the provisions of this title."[17] It is obvious that the enactment of ERISA's fiduciary standards will do much to encourage litigation beyond the scope of the common-law standards. Yet this is ultimately as it should be. There is no way to legislate practical wisdom. It must be defined as the case presents itself according to the wisdom of the court.

The first category of fiduciary duty is that a fiduciary shall conduct himself "bearing in mind only the interests of the plan's beneficiaries and participants for the exclusive purpose of (i) providing benefits to participants and their beneficiaries, and (ii) defraying reasonable expenses of administering the plan." This first category is actually Congress's rephrasing of what is known in trust law as the "duty of loyalty"[18] and other common-law fiduciary duties.

The inclusion of both "participants" and "beneficiaries" is a consequence of one of the main purposes of this act, which was to provide for the widest and most equitable participation in pension plan benefits possible for almost any kind of employee. As a result of this act, seasonal, part-time, non-union, and small business employees who were formerly excluded from participation in pension plan benefits may now generally be included. But why this distinction between participant and beneficiary should have been necessary in a discussion of fiduciary duty is not clear. On the face of it, it would seem to imply that a fiduciary is responsible not only to his beneficiaries, but also to those who are eligible to become future beneficiaries. The general significance of this is that a fiduciary must be very much aware of the employer's employment policies and requirements in interpreting benefit plans.

The latter part of this first category of fiduciary duty is also somewhat ambiguous, although its intent is quite evident. The fiduciary must be able to account for his efforts in keeping the expenses reasonable in administering a plan, especially the brokerage, advisory-custodian, and legal fees involved. Some proponents of the market-fund concept understand "reasonable" to mean "minimum" (in fact, one of the principal arguments for market funds is that their "buy and hold" strategy minimizes expenses), but I do not think this is altogether appropriate.[19] I do not think, for example, that Congress could have meant that all expenses involved in the research and continued monitoring of individual stocks are superfluous, otherwise it would have entirely abandoned the prudent man standard. All Congress meant was that expenses should not be excessive. In good part this excessiveness can, and is, avoided by the competition between trust departments and investment advisers.

Reasonableness will, to a large extent, be governed by a standard of comparison between reasonable fiduciaries. Yet it is not quite clear whether reasonableness should also be defined in relation to income. If, for example, the total return on a defined contribution pension plan does not exceed the prevailing rate of return from AAA bonds, could the expense of administering such a plan then be considered unreasonable? If part of a pension plan were invested in small but solidly capitalized companies with the prospects of producing above average equity returns, would the additional expenses needed to administer such a portfolio be reasonable if the returns were higher than those generated by a market index? Will the requirement to maintain reasonable expenses mean that the courts will make it virtually impossible to file a successful suit against a fiduciary on the grounds that such action would involve unreasonable legal expenses?

Historically, I think the expenses involved in administering trusts by responsible corporate fiduciaries have generally been quite low. Certainly they have not increased with the level of inflation. Yet, in light of the income produced by the fiduciaries, the costs have been unreasonably high.[20]

The fourth category of fiduciary duty is diversification "so as to minimize the risk of large losses unless under the circumstances it is clearly not prudent to do so."[21]

I see no reason why the duty to diversify should be interpreted any differently under ERISA than it has always been interpreted according to trust laws. That Congress sought to include it as a separate fiduciary duty is interesting, since the prudent man standard does not in itself require diversification. (We will return to the relation between diversification and prudence later in this chapter.)

Prudence under ERISA

We have traced the development of the legal aspect of prudence from the abandonment of the legal list approach to the adoption of the prudent man rule, which is now the standard for at least 40 states and the federal government through its inclusion in ERISA.[22] However, it has been alleged by various authors that there is "substantial reason to believe that Congress did not intend to compel the courts to rely exclusively on the common law when drawing the contours of ERISA's fiduciary standards."[23] And this is because Congress expects that "the courts will interpret this prudent man rule (and other fiduciary standards) bearing in mind the special nature and purpose of employee benefit plans."[24]

Under ERISA there are basically two types of pension plans, defined benefit and defined contribution. The first is a kind of annuity plan where the employer has to provide a certain level of benefit independently of the plan's actual performance. In the defined contribution plan, the employer only has to make certain periodic contributions to the corpus of the fund and is not liable for any benefits accrued to its participants and beneficiaries. It is obvious that the courts will have to consider which type of plan is involved in any litigation. It is also obvious that they will have to consider the special critical role that this act has given the prudent man rule within the context of fiduciary duties.

Finally, however, one hopes that the courts will not adopt some novel approach in the interpretation of the prudent man rule based on the availability of a government insurance program protecting pension plans. It would be a particularly unhappy situation if this rule were no longer to be interpreted as a standard for fiduciary responsibility. As we shall soon see, some proponents of the modern efficient portfolio would have us believe that the Massachusetts rule is obsolete. The one major defect of the prudent man rule is that when it is not enforced by men of wisdom directing fiduciaries of practical wisdom, it can become a license for a standard of behavior which only the fiduciary, and not the courts, can ultimately determine. Should this ever occur, the consequences will extend beyond economics into the political arena.

Special Powers of the Beneficiary under ERISA

One of the most startling and innovative paragraphs in ERISA's section on fiduciary duties is the last paragraph (Paragraph C):

> In the case of a pension plan which provides for individual accounts and permits a participant or beneficiary to exercise control over assets in his account, if a participant or beneficiary exercises control over the assets in his account (as determined under regulations of the Secretary)—
>
> 1. such participant for beneficiary shall not be deemed to be a fiduciary by reason of such exercise, and
> 2. no person who is otherwise a fiduciary shall be liable under this part for any loss, or by reason of any breach, which results from such participant's or beneficiary's exercise of control.[25]

This paragraph is innovative because it is not really based on any of the accepted principles of trust law. It is startling because Congress actually created a special rule allowing a participant or beneficiary, where authorized by a particular pension plan, to "exercise independent control over the assets in his individual account."[26] Where the defined contribution plan permits, a qualified employee is actually authorized to direct the full balance of his account even so far as investing in the common stock of a single company, as long as the investment does not contradict the terms of the plan or the act.

What is interesting is not so much that under Paragraph C the fiduciary is absolved of all liability for any possible loss, but that Congress has created a situation where under special circumstances a beneficiary is entitled to all the benefits of stock ownership other than the right to dispose of the proceeds without being burdened by the inconvenience of annual taxation. Under this paragraph on fiduciary duties, it is hard to understand what the function of the fiduciary really is, other than to remind the beneficiary of the significance of prudence, diversification, and the legal issues involved. It appears that here the fiduciary would actually be acting as an agent of the beneficiary, although I do not think Congress had in mind substituting the concept of agency for the concept of trust.

Results of Paragraph C

It is still too early to tell what the consequences of this paragraph will be. Presumably the main reason for its inclusion was to allow beneficiaries to choose the investment plan and, perhaps, investment adviser they wish their pension monies to be invested in and with. Presumably Congress did not assume that each beneficiary is capable of acting as his own investment adviser. Thus, where permitted, a beneficiary might decide on the degree and extent of the diversification of his pension interest. If he is afraid of the ravages of inflation, he may feel that all of his funds should be in equities. He may even want his trust invested in the equities of the smaller "lower tier" companies rather than in those 500 companies comprising the Standard and Poor's index. If he is really greedy he might want some of his pension to be invested in "new ventures," presumably at inflated prices.[27] However, a beneficiary will not be allowed to direct a portion of his pension to be invested in the securities of his own employer because of the difficulties in ascertaining the independence of this investment decision.[28]

One of the reasons for the inclusion of this paragraph in the act was to allow a "broad range of investments" to be made available to participants and beneficiaries.[29] I suspect that Congress was trying to create a situation which would avoid the drastic consequences of the two-tier investment market created by corporate fiduciaries in the fifties and sixties. The huge losses in trust funds suffered then were in large part due to the overconcentration and, hence, overpricing of those securities in the favored "upper tier" of investment possibilities.

Although Paragraph C creates the possibility for a beneficiary's control over the assets in his account, Congress was perfectly aware "that there may be difficulties in determining whether the participant in fact exercises independent control over his account."[30] This difficulty, which is ultimately to be resolved by the Secretary of Labor, is due in part to the confusion between the fiduciary responsibility in the selection and monitoring of investments and the intervention of the beneficiary. It is not that the fiduciary role is at stake. On the contrary, this section virtually assures the corporate fiduciary of at least some role in the management of funds even over which he has little control. It is rather that the congressional conferees were unable to foresee the degree to which control, as measured by the selection, voting, and valuation of stock, would be subject to pressure.

It is my feeling that the subsequent development and interpretation of this section of the act bears very close watching because, at the very least, it can create new investor interest in the stock market. It could lead to a whole new attitude toward long-term investing and the process of valuation. It may even cause investment advisers to redefine their values and perspectives in such a way that they can be intelligently expressed and presented to a new, concerned class of beneficiaries.

A Prudent Definition of Real Income

One of the most important questions that must be raised in any discussion of prudence is whether or not it is dependent on a concept of value. An examination of the common law and the prudent man rule would seem to indicate that it is not.[31] When a fiduciary has purchased shares of common stock of a particular company traded on the New York Stock Exchange, for example, the question is never raised whether the fiduciary paid too high a price. Yet this is a very important issue because it is the basis for much disillusionment by beneficiaries as well as litigation claiming negligence on the part of the fiduciary.

It is fairly easy to understand why the courts disassociate prudence from value. First of all, a fiduciary is usually chosen because of his superior knowledge, experience, and skill in forming value judgments. Mistakes in judgment are a normal occupational disease from which there is no immunity. But as long as these mistakes were made with knowledge of the facts of the investment and executed with care and discipline, they are honest, not negligent, mistakes. Second, mistakes in judgment, it is claimed, can only be determined by hindsight. No court will take upon itself the notion that hindsight is superior to foresight. The court is not about to make a trustee liable for a precipitate market drop caused by, say, the assassination of a president. Third, "wrongful" investments are only those investments which involve some form of negligence, with respect either to the selection of investments or conformity to the trust instrument.

Some people may argue that a charge of negligence can never be brought solely on the basis of the price paid because of the prudent man rule: it applies to those who are assumed legally to have enough sense and experience to know when prices are too high. Yet the fact remains that fiduciaries often pay too much, not as a consequence of mistaken judgments, but because they have no criteria of what constitutes over- or underpricing. Obviously the investment advisers and bank trust departments who went through the high-technology-growth phase in their selection of certain stocks at inflated prices and with a negligible dividend yield showed very little care, skill, and expertise, but, according to the law, not mistaken judgment, per se.

In a recent appeals case, the Bank of New York had been charged with negligence in its management of an $11 million trust fund, the plaintiff being a guardian for the remainder of the trust.[32] Although the bank had managed to increase the value of this trust by $1,700,000 between September 30, 1964 and September 30, 1968, the guardian claimed it had been negligent on four common-stock investments on which it had realized losses of $238,000. The appeal only involved two of these four companies, Parke Davis and Boeing, on which the losses realized were $45,000. The New York Court of Appeals ruled in favor of the Bank of New York. Judge Nunez, who wrote the majority opinion, spoke of the "vast aggrandizement of the estate" and held that the error in judgment with respect to these two investments could not be considered negligence. Judge Markewich, who wrote the minority opinion, thought that Judge Nunez's claim of "vast aggrandizement" was a gross exaggeration. Such an increase in the value of the estate could just as well have been attributed to general market conditions. "One shudders to think what could have happened in a period of decline," he wrote. The bank, in his opinion, did not really exercise skill, discretion, and prudence, for the "doorman on duty" possibly could have managed the estate as well as the bank's skilled investment advisers. Both the majority and minority opinions agreed that the proper selection of securities was indisputably necessary for the carrying out of fiduciary responsibility. Judge Markewich seems to have implied that the judgment of value by which the selection is made is a necessary ingredient of responsible and prudent behavior, but his opinion offered no criteria by which such a responsible value judgment can be made.

In my opinion, future litigation will not be able to avoid the issue of the relation between the price paid and the prudence of the judgment involved. And I think the courts can take a reasonable stand on this issue, even though the underlying nature of reasonableness is not yet apparent.

First of all, the issue of "probable income" should be reexamined. Any determination of probable income must of necessity involve consideration of the price paid. Even if an industrial equity is yielding a dividend of but 5 or 6 percent per annum, that may be sufficient, depending on the actual price paid and the defined objective for capital appreciation, to indicate a fiduciary's intention to produce income for the trust. But if there are no dividends or only very low dividends, then it becomes much harder for a fiduciary to prove his earnestness in providing probable income.

The issue here is what exactly constitutes income from shares of common stock. Trust law has it that only cash dividends, whether regular or extraordinary, are considered income. Neither stock splits nor retained earnings are considered income.[33] However, to say that only cash dividends are income is slightly misleading for it is a definition of income which is generally useful only in distinguishing between the increase in value of the principal of the trust and the income received from the trust. It can be applied in designating the income which is payable to one beneficiary and the remainder of the principal which may be payable to another. (The *Harvard College* v. *Amory* case discussed earlier in this chapter is an example.) However, this distinction is not as relevant where the beneficiary is entitled to the income as well as, ultimately, the principal of the trust. (A defined contribution pension plan would be an instance of this in that the beneficiary in the end benefits from both the dividends received and the increase in principal amount. Another example would be a mutual fund with emphasis on capital appreciation rather than income.)

Historically, where a fiduciary has not had an obligation to produce a regular income for his beneficiary he has understood his fiduciary responsibility not according to the prudent man rule but only insofar as he maximized income from dividends. But this has changed. Today "income" is taken to mean not only dividends but appreciation in the price of equities. Were this not generally accepted, there would have been no way in which a fiduciary could have invested in industrial equities during the past 30 years. The dividend yields on industrial stocks during this period were almost always lower than the interest which could have been earned from comparably rated bonds. Thus the general concept of income has come to include capital appreciation as well as cash dividends.

It is within this context that the relation between prudence in the selection of a stock and the price paid for it becomes particularly murky. If the fiduciary is not bound to consider income only as dividends received, what discipline and criteria will be used in anticipating capital appreciation? Will it be the expected value of future dividends? Will it be the price-earnings ratio? The dismal record of recent history shows either that fiduciaries have exhibited no criteria and discipline in their anticipation of capital appreciation or that whatever criteria they have used have proven both imprudent and ineffective.

I believe that my concepts of expectancy and capital value may be of some use in remedying this situation. One of the advantages in using an expectancy in providing a sound basis for prudent valuation is that expectancy is flexible enough to provide different interpretations but not so flexible that a fiduciary can use it to justify paying any price for a stock. My prescription for capital value distinguishes between income derived from dividends and income retained by the corporation. Retained earnings, though they are not income according to trust law, at least provide a basis for establishing reasonable expectations concerning dividend income. It is my view that the courts may sooner or later have to avail themselves of the return-on-equity ratio in their determination of reasonable, and hence prudent, value. At any rate, the current situation, where a fiduciary is absolved of all responsibility for judging the price paid for a security, cannot continue indefinitely, unless, of course, a fiduciary is to be considered a special kind of bureaucrat.

Probable Income versus Probable Safety

In addition to the concept of probable income, that of *probable safety* also bears examining for our understanding of the relation between prudence and value. A fiduciary's main obligation is to preserve the trust capital. This is normally understood as an obligation to preserve the trust capital at the value it had when it was entrusted to him. Thus, strictly speaking, if a fiduciary were entrusted with a $1 million trust fund to be invested solely in equities, his fiduciary obligation would be fulfilled even if he produced only a minimum dividend income with no capital gains over a ten-year period. Trust law makes no provision for the preservation of capital as measured against the cost of money. Given a constant 6 percent annual cost of money, this trust fund really ought to be worth at least $1,790,000 in ten years' time. So, from a businessman's point of view, the preservation of $1 million means that it must amount to at least $1,790,000 ten years hence. Trust law makes no allowance for inflation even when the government itself is anticipating a certain minimum inflation rate. Some courts have declared that "attention to inflation risk is praiseworthy,"[34] but no court has considered a preoccupation with inflation as part of a fiduciary's duty to preserve the capital of his trust. Thus the duty to preserve the trust corpus is actually much less than one might have thought.

Furthermore, trust law recognizes that investing in common stock is "hazardous" because it is subject to market fluctuations. These fluctuations are, often as not, consequences of general market conditions. No fiduciary can really be held negligent for not being able to anticipate market psychology. Yet if a common stock can be expected to fluctuate in price, and if it is a fiduciary duty to preserve capital, why should a fiduciary be at all permitted to invest in equities? The answer is simply that the rewards from investing in equities are supposed to outweigh the risks. In other words, the "probable safety" is a direct function of the anticipated benefits to the trust capital. There must be some relation between the probable income and the probable safety of investing in common stocks. The pricing of equities must be considered as part of fiduciary prudence. Otherwise probable safety would be meaningless.

If probable safety were to be considered solely a function of market risk a fiduciary would be in a situation where he couldn't buy any volatile equity, such as that of the cyclical industrials. Indeed, I don't see how he could provide any strong evidence supporting his analysis of an equity's safety. Any choice he would make would be subject to a claim of negligence because the market virtually guarantees that every stock will fluctuate.

Regarding risk, trust law states the following:

> In making investments . . . a loss is always possible, since in any investment there is always some risk. The . . . amount of risk, however, is a question of degree. No man of intelligence would make a disposition of property where in view of the price the risk of loss is out of proportion

> to the opportunity for gain. Where, however, the risk is not out of proportion, a man of intelligence may make a disposition which is speculative in character with a view to increasing his property instead of merely preserving it. Such a disposition is not a proper trust investment, because it is not a disposition which makes the preservation of the fund a primary consideration.[35]

In other words, evidence for the safety of an investment must depend on two considerations: the price paid and the gain anticipated. The two are inseparable from each other. Since the opportunity for gain cannot depend exclusively on the expectation of what others will pay—it is not a restatement of the "greater fool theory"—it must depend on how a fiduciary is able to measure the expected income from dividends and capital appreciation. But this, of course, has to be a function of the price paid. In other words, a fiduciary is not doing his job if he cannot justify why he thinks the price he has paid is reasonable. Proof of reasonableness requires more than saying that a price is valid because it was determined in an active market with full disclosure of information. It must have something to do with what I have defined as exchange value.

Some writers have claimed that the "present regulation considers solely the risk of an investment and does not balance risk against expected return."[36] Perhaps in a strictly mathematical sense, where risk is defined as the width of a probability distribution, this is true. But I do not think that this is a valid judgment according to my preceding analysis. The fact that the courts have been reluctant to take a stand on what constitutes reasonable price in determining fiduciary responsibility is not an argument, per se, that they could or should not do so.

It seems to me inescapable that the preservation of capital is in large measure determined by the price paid for individual investments, just as it seems unavoidable that price paid has a bearing on the gain produced. Therefore, the decision of the courts to avoid the issue of the valuation of securities in the definition of prudent behavior would appear to be more a matter of convenience than of legal considerations. In view of some of the arguments presented in this book, I think this issue should be reexamined. Clearly, both fiduciaries and beneficiaries would benefit if a clearer perspective on the meaning of fiduciary responsibility could be gained.

I believe that one of the consequences of adopting a view of fiduciary responsibility that includes valuation in the definition of prudence would be that the possibilities for investment of trust property could be extended to all listed and unlisted equities satisfying certain financial requirements. The prevailing attitude of many investment advisers is that they feel "safer" if they invest in only the largest and best-known industrial equities. They are often willing to pay a higher price than they should, because they feel the risk (and their liability) is greater if they invest in smaller, less well-known companies. Yet one of the purposes of ERISA is to create the possibility of a stronger and more widely diffused securities market. Ultimately a concern for reasonable price on the part of prudent investors and fiduciaries can contribute toward this goal.

The Business Economist's View of Fiduciary Responsibility

The theory of an efficient market and, in particular, of the efficient portfolio, has produced a peculiar attitude toward prudence that has so little to do with its traditional interpretation by the investor and by the law that we are obliged to analyze it.[37] The business economist views fiduciary responsibility solely as a consequence of mathematical probability. For him prudence is not a function of the empirical care, skill, and discretion necessary for the selection of investments. It is not a function of experience as an analyst in the interpretation of information disclosed by management. It has nothing to do with the discovery of under- or overvalued securities. It doesn't even have anything to do with the probable income and safety involved in a choice of an individual equity.

So much trust money is now managed according to efficient portfolio theory in what is commonly referred to as index or market funds, that we are all in some way affected by it.[38] Either part of our pension plan is invested in index funds or we are minority shareholders in companies whose shares are owned by these funds. We cannot, therefore, expect these shares to be intelligently voted by informed fiduciaries because they cannot, virtually by definition, be informed. What happens when we, as informed shareholders, vote against management and they, as uninformed fiduciaries, vote with it?

Index funds as a way to avoid responsibility

Proponents of index funds believe that such funds fulfill a fiduciary's obligation to his trust two ways: by defraying expenses and diversifying the trust's assets.[39] Both of these are, of course, important aspects of a fiduciary's duties, especially as defined by ERISA.

The first consideration, the defraying of expenses, involves those costs typically associated with research analysis and with trading commissions. Since efficient portfolio theory believes that security analysis and all other attempts to interpret information are wasteful and useless, it proposes to eliminate them and thus avoid all associated expenses. Apparently all such costs are unreasonable. Thus, a reasonable expense would come to mean no costs at all for the interpretation of information necessary in the continual monitoring of individual equities. This interest in avoiding "unreasonable" expenses also applies to brokerage commissions. The index funds pursue a buy-and-hold investment policy which involves paying almost no brokerage fees after the portfolio of stocks has been purchased.

The second consideration is diversification. Today, especially after the enactment of ERISA, diversification of a trust portfolio with a view toward minimizing the risk of large losses is a generally accepted category of fiduciary responsibility. According to trust law, "the trustee is under a duty to the beneficiary to distribute the risk of loss by a reasonable diversification of investments, unless under the circumstances it is prudent not to do so."[40] If the trust is not very small and if it consists of proper and marketable investments, the fiduciary has an obligation to avoid large and, perhaps, unreasonable losses by distributing his investments. This diversification should be reasonable in the sense that it should take into account the amount of money involved, the beneficiary, and the goals defined by the trust. Even if a trustee thinks a particular equity is very cheaply priced, he must exercise caution in deciding how much of it should be owned by the trust. This is a fairly simple and straightforward policy which any fiduciary of practical wisdom can understand.

However, the proponents of an efficient portfolio understand diversification quite differently. For them the purpose of diversification is not to avoid the risk of large losses by a reasonable diversification; it is, rather, to create a portfolio of stocks which will behave no better or worse than the market index against which it is to be judged. Ironically, although the risk of large losses in any one individual equity is avoided, no attempt is made to avoid the risk of a large loss of the portfolio as a whole.

Since the expected return of both an individual stock and an entire portfolio is a function of its beta coefficient, there is good reason to believe that investing in an index fund is more similar to investing in the stock of a new company than to investing in shares of a tried and proven mutual fund. It has long been a principle of fiduciary responsibility that an investment should not be made in shares of new, untried companies. This principle has never been applied to the shares of new, traditionally managed, mutual funds, on the grounds that, even if they are new, they are at least managed by experienced fiduciaries relying upon the traditional concepts of care, discretion, and diversification. Yet index funds, even if they are managed by well-known corporate fiduciaries, are clearly not guided by the traditional interpretation of fiduciary responsibilities.

The most a fiduciary of an index fund can do if he anticipates a declining market is to increase the proportion of bonds and treasury bills in his portfolio. He can't do much if he anticipates a market rise, because under most circumstances he cannot borrow to increase his fund's equity assets. Even if a fiduciary attempts to anticipate market movements, he may be acting negligently, especially if his anticipations prove inaccurate. On what reasonable and calculated grounds could these anticipations be based? How could he prove he is managing an efficient portfolio?

The Efficient Portfolio—An Excuse for Imprudence

The efficient portfolio theory is based on a notion of risk that is entirely dependent on probability theory. It recognizes that there are two kinds of risk applicable to the management of a portfolio—diversifiable and undiversifiable risk. Diversifiable risk is risk that can be reduced or even entirely removed by proper diversification. An arbitrage in which one is short against the box would be an example in which the risk of owning the stock has been reduced by having sold the stock short. Buying put options against a long position in the same stock is another. Selling calls against a portfolio is still another case where, depending on how it is done, one attempts to cut at least part of the risk in owning stock through diversification.

Undiversified risk is one that cannot be reduced by diversification. An index fund has this sort of risk. It will fluctuate because the market does. The proponents of this theory believe that undiversified, or systematic, risk is justifiable because nothing can be done to reduce it; worse, they think it is reasonable and prudent. They believe that accepting this systematic risk is all the more justifiable because the expected return from a portfolio is determined by the risk. (This would be calculated either by increasing the beta coefficient or by leveraging the portfolio.)

To me this concept of systematic risk implies a flagrant rejection of fiduciary responsibility. If the purpose of the fiduciary duty to diversify is to avoid large losses, this cannot be accomplished by following the theory of systematic risk. All that is accomplished is that the losses will not be greater than those produced by the market. It is the fiduciary's duty to try to avoid any hazards associated with investing in equities, even if he does not always succeed. Isn't it a fiduciary's task to try to provide diversifiable risk and not just undiversifiable risk? Isn't this the whole point of the traditional approach, which insists on diversifying according to geography, industry, and type of vehicle?[41] The fact that the majority of corporate fiduciaries have demonstrated an incapacity to do this should not become a justification for a new attitude toward fiduciary responsibility. If an investment adviser cannot outperform the market in the long run he is, in fact, no more than a "doorman on duty." Sooner or later every testator and beneficiary is going to wonder whether his funds are being managed by a businessman, a bureaucrat, or a statistician.

The question must also be raised whether overdiversification constitutes a breach of fiduciary duty. If it is true that an efficient portfolio must consist of at least 200 different stocks, chosen primarily for their affect on the riskiness of the total portfolio, what sense can be made of the prudent man standard? Can it be that mathematically "calculated ignorance is really the most prudent approach to investment"?[42] Or will prudence consist only of familiarity with probability theory?

The proponents of the efficient portfolio theory persist in discussing prudence in terms which are sensible only if one accepts their premises. For example, John Langbein and Richard Posner, two professors of law who have accepted these premises, state, "If the risk/return characteristics of the portfolio are at least as attractive as those of an individual security that would be considered a prudent investment for the trustee, there is no basis in logic—and we believe there is none in the law—for inquiring into the prudence of the individual securities constituting the portfolio."[43]

The above is a terribly misleading statement. An inquiry into the prudence of a selection is illogical only as long as one accepts the efficient portfolio theory of risk and expected return. If one does not, is it illogical and contrary to common law to believe that it is prudent to exercise care, skill, and discretion in the selection of investments?

Langbein and Posner go on to say that a trustee "should not be required to exclude the stocks of companies that are bankrupt or in danger of becoming bankrupt, because there is no basis for believing that such stocks are characteristically overvalued."[44] Now, if there were no basis for believing any stock was either over- or undervalued, all buyers and sellers would be imbeciles. And if the only basis for valuing is the imbecility of all buyers and sellers, then we are all in trouble, to say the least. Such is their acceptance of the efficient market theory that Langbein and Posner suggest that a trustee who does believe in exercising traditional care, skill, and discretion "may in the future find his conduct difficult to justify."[45]

Incensed at the logic of these two law professors, John Humbach and Stephen Dresh have issued a rebuttal focusing on the social and economic implications of the efficient portfolio theory.[46] They argue not only that our securities markets will suffer by refusing to acknowledge the significance of information in the formulation of judgments of value, but also that the individual investor and pension plan beneficiary may end up paying for this folly in the form of lower than acceptable returns. The efficient portfolio theory is an excuse for those who have had no experience to draw on. Prudence can never be applied by people who have no market experience and no experience in interpreting information disclosed by management. It is sad that because of so much mathematical skullduggery this is no longer self-evident.

Prudent Fulfillment of Fiduciary Responsibilities

Until now we have examined the relationship between prudence and value as a consequence of the price paid. There is good, though perhaps not sufficient, reason to believe that the price a fiduciary pays for the securities in his portfolio is a function of his skill, care, and discretion in discharging his fiduciary duties. The wisdom underlying the price paid by the individual investors is, of course, the very foundation for the self-imposed discipline of prudence. Yet there is still another aspect of this relationship which merits consideration. This is the connection between prudence and the property rights associated with a trust's common-stock holdings. What is a fiduciary's duty concerning voting, responding to proxies, and enforcing the rights to which his trust entitles him? These are questions which are as pertinent to the fiduciary as they are to the individual investor.

One of the fiduciary's duties is to enforce claims. "The trustee is under a duty to the beneficiary to take reasonable steps to realize claims which he holds in trust."[47] Although a share of common stock does represent a claim against income, the section of trust law referred to here applies not to common stock but to the enforcement of contractual claims like those accompanying bonds or mortgages. Where a company is in default on an interest payment, for example, a trustee has the obligation to try to enforce his claim unless the action would involve unreasonably high expenses and the probability of collecting is remote. Fiduciaries who hold stock in corporations which are involved in a takeover or merger at what could be considered unfair or manipulated prices would not normally demand an enforcement of their appraisal rights. However, where other minority stockholders have initiated this right to an appraisal on behalf of all shareholders, a fiduciary may be delinquent if he abstains from getting involved.

A fiduciary's "powers with respect to shares of stock" is normally derived from the section of trust law authorizing him to "properly vote and exercise the other powers" of common stock.[48] Most trust instruments specifically authorize the trustee to vote and exercise any other relevant powers at his discretion. A fiduciary's obligation to vote is very serious, especially if the trust owns a large or controlling interest in a corporation. So serious is this obligation that it may even constitute a breach of his trust if he votes by proxy rather than in person. He must "use reasonable care in deciding how to vote the stock and in voting it."[49] Voting is especially important where the issue materially affects the reorganization, financial structure, or amendment to the charter of the corporation. Even though a fiduciary is permitted to buy nonvoting shares, this permission is of no practical consequence since listing requirements on the New York Stock Exchange, for example, prohibit nonvoting common stock.

In spite of the seriousness with which trust law considers the trustee's right and duty to vote, in practice this duty is only perfunctorily exercised. It is questionable, for example, how an amendment to a corporate charter creating a staggered board of directors actually benefits minority shareholders. The solicitation of proxies has become a large and highly specialized business in its own right. The firms engaged in soliciting proxies are normally retained and paid by the solicitor to induce or "advise" the shareholder to vote as desired. Obviously most proxies are solicited by management. When the shares solicited on behalf of management are held in trust, they are often voted in favor of management even when a particularly active, although comparatively small, group of minority shareholders vote against it.

I am not saying that trustees should always vote with minority shareholders. But I am suggesting that trustees have not always handled their voting rights with great care and deliberation; at any rate, they did not produce the kind of results that would emphasize that a corporation is run for the benefit of the stockholders rather than management. It has been said that "if stockholders cannot act together, they cannot act effectively."[50] Very often the disinterest of the corporate fiduciary in analyzing proxies and voting presents a serious encumbrance to minority shareholders interested in protecting the value of their property. Indeed, historically the corporate fiduciary has been reluctant to take the steps necessary to protect the shares held in his trust against oppression by management or controlling stockholders, even though the expenses involved might often have been justified by the results of his intervention.

Fiduciaries will increasingly find it necessary to respond more seriously to federal proxy rules as set forth by Section 14 of the Securities Exchange Act of 1934. For example, they may find that their responsibilities do not end with simply reading a proxy statement that outlines a merger and rejecting it. If they find a material misstatement or an omission of facts that would be required for casting a reasonably informed vote, they may be obligated to present their case and seek redress for their beneficiaries, especially if their proxy vote was solicited by management. If they do not seek to actively protect the interests of their beneficiaries by initiating suits against management, they may find themselves acting as agents of "favored stockholders" collaborating with management in opposition to minority stockholders.[51]

Until now it has usually been the individual stockholder, not the corporate fiduciary, who has tried to obtain redress by initiating some type of class action against management. In the future it may well be that the corporate fiduciary will have to respond to any proposal made by minority shareholders for the protection of their rights and enforcement of their claims, with the same diligence he is supposed to give to information disclosed by management.[52] Indeed, the stability of the stock market in the 1980s may well depend on how actively corporate fiduciaries enforce the rights of their beneficiaries.

There may also be times when it would be imprudent for a fiduciary not to take action under SEC Rule 10b-5, which protects the minority shareholder against a "manipulative or deceptive device or contrivance."[53] Beset with such difficulties, the average shareholder may prefer to sell his shares and put his money, even if a loss is involved, to better use elsewhere. Yet this facile, though unhappy, resort may not be readily available to the trustee holding a sizable number of shares in trust. In these situations, not to seek relief, especially where it is provided for by law, may in itself involve a breach of fiduciary duty.

Today, since most fiduciaries are corporate fiduciaries, there is an understandable reluctance to apply legal pressure on corporate management. It may be impolitic for a trust department of a bank to advise a corporation that its policy of keeping dividends to a minimum may not be in the best interest of its stockholders, especially if the bank maintains a commercial relation with the company.[54] Although the law insists on some separation between trust and commercial banking, one corporate entity still accounts for both.

It can be said that silence and inaction have long been the principles guiding a fiduciary's relationship with the management of the companies in which he holds shares in trust. It is as if the trustee refuses to pass judgment on the conduct of another member of the fiduciary fraternity, the corporate manager. Concerning the stockholder himself, David Bayne has written:

> Insofar as the shareholder has contributed an asset of value to the corporate venture, insofar as he has handed over his goods and property and money for use and increase, he has not only the clear right, but, more to the point perhaps, . . . the stringent duty to exercise control over that asset for which he must keep, care, guard, guide, and in general be held seriously responsible. . . . As much as one may surrender the immediate disposition of [his] goods, he can never shirk a supervisory and secondary duty (not just a right) to make sure these goods are used justly, morally, and beneficially.[55]

The degree to which an investor, or even a fiduciary, should question the morality and social impact of his investment is not a subject that we have discussed in this book. (The interested reader is referred to the much discussed *The Ethical Investor,* by John G. Simon, Charles W. Powers, and Jon P. Gunnemann.) However, no investor, or even fiduciary, can ever take the process of valuation lightly if he is to maintain an interest in preserving his equity and full rights of ownership. And without prudence to guide him, the investor or fiduciary risks paying too high a price for the maintenance of that equity.

The shareholder's power

In Chapter 2 we discussed some of the inadequacies of the voting process available to shareholders. A shareholder may have no power to affect the future course of his investment, but, as we have seen, he does have some power to protect its value. This power ultimately is a function of his preoccupation with prudence. And perhaps the best expression of this is a total concern for the process of valuation, of which voting constitutes only one aspect.

It should be remembered, however, that shareholder power brings with it responsibility. As Simon, Powers, and Gunnemann put it:

> It is the power to act which gives the corporate shareholder a responsibility that, for example, the corporate bondholder or noteholder does

> not have. If this power to intervene is what thrusts obligation upon the holder of a voting security, it can logically make no difference that the power was received casually, that it was not the reason for purchasing the security, that it was the by-product (perhaps an undesirable one) of a total return decision made for reasons like those which motivate the bondholder or noteholder.[56]

Simon, Powers, and Gunnemann offer a list of a dozen devices a shareholder may use in exercising his power.[57] Although not all of them may be necessary or even advisable for prudent shareholder and fiduciary conduct, their scope is well worth considering. They are:

1. Declining to invest.
2. Divestment.
3. Posing questions to management or urging management to change its policies in certain respects.
4. Withholding proxies from management or abstaining on certain socially related resolutions proposed by other shareholders.
5. Voting in opposition to management on such resolutions.
6. Voting to unseat management in favor of opposition slates proposed by other shareholders.
7. Undertaking to propose resolutions or slates referred to in Items 5 and 6 on the shareholder's own initiative.
8. Soliciting proxies from other shareholders in order to carry out Item 7.
9. Joining other shareholders who are bringing litigation (derivative or individual) to enjoin certain corporate conduct.
10. Bringing the litigation referred to in Item 9 on the shareholder's own initiative.
11. Taking any of the actions listed above pursuant to an agreement for concerted action with other shareholders.
12. Making public announcements in connection with any of the actions listed above.

The Future of Valuing

This has been a somewhat disquieting chapter. On the one hand, we have examined the practical as well as the legal definitions of prudence, and we have seen that prudence is the investor's only means to protect the value of his capital. On the other hand, we have been concerned throughout with the increasing importance of the corporate fiduciary—or institutional investor, as he is better known—and his interpretation of prudence.

In today's market, corporate fiduciaries are charged with an enormous responsibility to the public. In view of this, it is disturbing to observe their apparent complacency and arrogance and their tendency to sympathize with the needs of corporate management at the expense of the public interest in their trust. They have tended to view prudence exclusively as a legal issue requiring only formal compliance rather than as a broad social and economic issue calling for full use of their practical wisdom and expertise. And instead of pursuing a clear and relevant concept of value designed to protect the public interest, they have conveniently turned to the index fund as a ready escape from their true responsibilities.

In the past, many of the corporate fiduciary's problems were resolved by courts essentially sympathetic to him. However, this sympathy may be very short-lived, especially as the public becomes more concerned with the preservation of its money and its rights.

Since today's stock market is essentially an institutional market, the behavior of the institutional investor will become increasingly visible. By the sheer magnitude of his involvement, the corporate fiduciary will have the power to preserve or destroy the stock market as a free marketplace. If he does not respond in full measure to the need for valuing and prudence, the future stock market may bear little resemblance to what it is today, and there may indeed be very little point to valuing common stock.

Notes

Chapter 2

1. Joseph de la Vega, *Confusion de Confusiones,* selected and translated by Herman Kellenbenz (New York: Kelley, Kress Library of Business and Economics, No. 13, 1957), pp. 23ff. and xviii.
2. Adolf A. Berle, Jr., *Power Without Property,* New York: Harcourt Brace Jovanovich, 1959; see also Carl Kaysen, "The Corporation: How Much Power? What Scope?" in *The Corporation in Modern Society,* ed. by Edward S. Mason (New York: Atheneum, 1966), pp. 85–105.
3. Quoted by James Willard Hurst in *The Legitimacy of the Business Corporation* (Charlottesville, Va.: The University Press of Virginia, 1970), p. 9.
4. *The Trustees of Dartmouth College* v. *Woodward Wheaton,* 518, 636 (U.S. 1819), quoted by Hurst, op. cit., p. 9; see also Robert L. Raymond, "The Genesis of the Corporation," in *Corporations* (Cambridge, Mass.: Harvard Law Review Association, 1966), p. 1.
5. Hurst, op. cit., p. 65.
6. Ibid., p. 14.
7. Ibid., p. 70.
8. Charles A. Reich, "The New Property," *Yale Law Journal,* April 1964, pp. 733–787.
9. George Wheeler, *Pierpont Morgan and Friends* (Englewood Cliffs, N.J.: Prentice-Hall, 1973), pp. 210–211; see also John R. Commons, *Institutional Economics* (republished by the University of Wisconsin Press, Madison, 1961), p. 650.
10. Hurst, op. cit., pp. 155ff.
11. Abram Chayes, "The Modern Corporation and the Rule of Law," in *The Corporation in Modern Society,* loc. cit., p. 40.
12. Berle, *Power Without Property,* p. 107.
13. Bayless Manning, review of J. Livingston, "The American Stockholder," *Yale Law Journal,* Vol. 67, 1958, p. 1494.

14. *Social Responsibilities of Business Corporations,* Committee for Economic Development, New York, June 1971, pp. 25–34.
15. Hurst, op. cit., p. 99; see also Eugene V. Rostow, "To Whom and for What Ends Is Corporate Management Responsible?" in *The Corporation in Modern Society,* loc. cit., pp. 48–49.
16. de la Vega, *Confusion de Confusiones,* p. 4.
17. John R. Commons, *Legal Foundations of Capitalism* (republished by the University of Wisconsin Press, Madison, 1968), pp. 162–163.

Chapter 3

1. James C. Bonbright, *The Valuation of Property* (New York: McGraw-Hill, 1937), p. 16.
2. Ibid., p. 41.
3. Ibid., p. 63.
4. Ibid., p. 61.
5. Benjamin Graham, David L. Dodd, and Sidney Cottle, *Security Analysis* (New York: McGraw-Hill, fourth edition, 1962), pp. 27–28.
6. James H. Lorie and Mary T. Hamilton, *The Stock Market* (Homewood, Ill.: Dow Jones-Irwin, 1973), p. 271.
7. F. Hodge O'Neal, *Oppression of Minority Shareholders* (Chicago: Callaghan, 1975), Sect. 3:08; see also Supplement, 1977.
8. Richard Brignolli, "Options to Buy: Risks and Rewards," *Pensions and Investments,* March 25, 1974; Fisher Black and Myron Scholes, "Valuation of Option Contracts and a Test of Market Efficiency," *Journal of Finance,* May 1972.
9. Commons, *Legal Foundations,* pp. 4 and 374ff.
10. Edwin J. Elton and Martin J. Gruber, "Improved Forecasting Through the Design of Homogeneous Groups," in Elton and Gruber, *Security Evaluation and Portfolio Analysis* (Englewood Cliffs, N.J.: Prentice-Hall, 1972), pp. 75–93.
11. Adolf A. Berle and Gardiner C. Means, *The Modern Corporation and Private Property* (New York: Harvest, revised edition, 1967), pp. 253–263.
12. Ibid., p. 259.
13. Ibid., p. 269.
14. Ibid., p. 262.
15. Ibid., pp. 149–157.
16. Ibid., p. 274.
17. Ibid., p. 277.
18. Sidney Robbins, *The Securities Markets* (New York: The Free Press, 1966), p. 121; see also p. 85.

19. Ibid., p. 155.
20. Ibid., p. 137; see also Ezra Solomon, "Economic Growth and Common Stock Value," *Journal of Business,* July 1955, pp. 213–221.
21. Robbins, op. cit., p. 139.
22. Ibid., p. 149.
23. Ibid., p. 153.
24. Ibid., pp. 152 and 164.
25. Quoted by Robbins, op. cit., pp. 163–164 and fn. 39.
26. Ibid., p. 164.
27. Quoted by Robbins, op. cit., p. 161 and fn. 35.
28. Ibid., pp. 161ff.

Chapter 4

1. John E. Smith, *Themes in American Philosophy* (New York: Harper & Row, 1970), p. 3.
2. Commons, *Legal Foundations,* p. 13.
3. Ibid., pp. 15–16.
4. Ibid., p. 17 and fn. 2.
5. Commons, *Institutional Economics,* p. 652.
6. Quoted by Commons, *Institutional Economics,* p. 653.
7. Rostow, "To Whom Is Corporate Management Responsible?" loc. cit., p. 51.
8. "Corporate Opportunity," *Harvard Law Review,* Vol. 74, 1961, pp. 765ff.
9. Quoted by Victor Brudney and Marvin A. Chirelstein, *Corporate Finance* (Mineola, N.Y.: Foundation Press, 1972), p. 408.
10. Rostow, op. cit., pp. 61ff. and fn. 32 for bibliography.
11. William D. Andrews, "The Stockholder's Right to Equal Opportunity in the Sale of Shares," *Harvard Law Review,* January 1965, p. 507.
12. Ibid.; see also O'Neal, *Oppression of Minority Shareholders,* Sect. 4:05.
13. Bonbright, *Valuation of Property,* p. 231.
14. Ibid.
15. Brudney and Chirelstein, op. cit., p. 4.
16. John Burr Williams, *The Theory of Investment Value* (Cambridge, Mass.: Harvard University Press, 1938), p. 57; see also W. Scott Bauman, "Investment Returns and Present Values," in *C.F.A. Readings in Financial Analysis,* ed. by Chartered Financial Analysts (Homewood, Ill.: Irwin, third edition, 1975), pp. 320–331.

17. Merton H. Miller and Franco Modigliani, "Dividend Policy, Growth, and the Valuation of Shares," *Journal of Business,* October 1961, pp. 411–433.
18. Brudney and Chirelstein, op. cit., pp. 381ff. See also Erich A. Helfert, "Evaluation of Financial Statements," in *Financial Analyst's Handbook,* ed. by Summer N. Levine (Homewood, Ill.: Dow Jones-Irwin, 1975), pp. 619–636.
19. Dean Manning, "The Shareholder's Appraisal Remedy: An Essay for Frank Coker," *Yale Law Journal,* Vol. 32, 1962, p. 261.
20. "Freezing Out Minority Shareholders," *Harvard Law Review,* Vol. 74, 1961, p. 1634.
21. Quoted in Brudney and Chirelstein, op. cit., p. 569, from Melvin A. Eisenberg, "The Legal Roles of Shareholders and Management in Modern Corporate Decision Making," *California Law Review,* Vol. 57:1, 1969.
22. Berle and Means, *The Modern Corporation,* p. 243.
23. Robbins, *The Securities Market,* p. 140.

Chapter 5

1. Alexander A. Robichek and Stewart C. Myers, *Optimal Financing Decisions* (Englewood Cliffs, N.J.: Prentice-Hall, 1965), pp. 79 and 185ff.
2. James T. S. Porterfield, *Investment Decisions and Capital Costs* (Englewood Cliffs, N.J.: Prentice-Hall, 1965), p. 75.
3. Ibid., pp. 44ff. and 59ff.
4. Myron J. Gordon, *The Investment, Financing and Valuation of the Corporation* (Homewood, Ill.: Irwin, 1962), p. 1.
5. Ibid., p. 28.
6. Robichek and Myers, op. cit., p. 57.
7. Ibid., p. 2.
8. Gordon, op. cit., pp. 36–38; see also Porterfield, op. cit., p. 13.
9. Harvey Leibenstein, *Beyond Economic Man,* Cambridge, Mass.: Harvard University Press, 1976.
10. Herbert Simon, *Models of Man* (New York: Wiley & Sons, 1957), pp. 204–205; see also Edwin M. Epstein, *The Corporation in American Politics* (Englewood Cliffs, N.J.: Prentice-Hall, 1969), pp. 119ff., and Gordon, op. cit., pp. 34–36.
11. Porterfield, op. cit., p. 12.
12. Gordon, op. cit., p. 45.
13. Ibid., p. 50; see also Robichek and Myers, op. cit., pp. 62–64.
14. Gordon, op. cit., pp. 39–40 and 219; see also Van Horne, "Finan-

cial Management and Policy," quoted in Brudney and Chirelstein, *Corporate Finance,* pp. 387–393.
15. David N. Dreman, *Psychology and the Stock Market* (New York: AMACOM, 1977), pp. 161–167 and 291–292.
16. Ibid., Chapter 8.
17. Warren E. Buffett, "How Inflation Swindles the Equity Investor," *Fortune,* May 1977, pp. 256ff.

Chapter 6

1. Berle and Means, *The Modern Corporation,* p. 263.
2. John Kenneth Galbraith, *American Capitalism,* Boston, Mass.: Houghton Mifflin, 1956.
3. Hurst, *Legitimacy of the Corporation,* pp. 63 and 65.
4. Commons, *Legal Foundations,* p. 180.
5. Jean-Jacques Servan-Schreiber, *Le Défi Américain* (Paris: Denoël, 1967), p. 55; see also Raymond Vernon, "Foreign Operations," in *Social Responsibility and the Business Predicament,* Brookings Institution, Washington, D.C., 1974, pp. 282ff.
6. Hurst, *Legitimacy of the Corporation,* p. 91.
7. Ibid., pp. 155ff.
8. Ibid., p. 95.
9. See, for instance, Peter F. Drucker, *The Unseen Revolution* (New York: Harper & Row, 1976), p. 1.
10. "Challenge to the Brokers," *Fortune,* April 1969.
11. William J. Baumol, *The Stock Market and Efficiency* (New York: Fordham University Press, 1965), pp. 19ff.
12. Baruch Lev, *Financial Statement Analysis: A New Approach* (Englewood Cliffs, N.J.: Prentice-Hall, 1974), pp. 11ff.
13. Oskar Morgenstern, *On the Accuracy of Economic Observations* (Princeton, N.J.: Princeton University Press, 1963), pp. 8–12.
14. Ezra Solomon, *The Anxious Economy* (San Francisco: Freeman, 1975), p. 108.
15. Baruch Lev, op. cit., p. 222; see also Samuel S. Stewart, Jr., "Corporate Forecasting," in *Financial Analyst's Handbook,* loc. cit., p. 924.
16. John Magee, *The General Semantics of Wall Street,* Springfield, Mass.: Magee, 1959.
17. Lorie and Hamilton, *The Stock Market,* pp. 157–167.
18. Baruch Lev, op. cit., pp. 241ff.
19. Ibid., p. 242.
20. Cf. Milton Friedman's "The Methodology of Positive Economics,"

in *Essays in Positive Economics* (Chicago: University of Chicago Press, 1953), pp. 3–46; see also the rebuttal by E. Nagel, "Assumptions in Economic Theory," *American Economic Review,* May 1953, pp. 211ff. Also compare Konrad Lorenz, *On Aggression* (New York: Bantam, 1967), pp. 68–69.

21. Quoted by Baruch Lev, op. cit., p. 110 and fn. 1.
22. *Wall Street Journal,* January 17, 1977, p. 10.
23. Leonard Spacek, "Business Success Requires an Understanding of Unsolved Problems of Accounting and Financial Reporting," in *Modern Developments in Investment Management,* ed. by James Lorie and Richard Brealey (New York: Praeger, 1972), p. 643.
24. Abraham J. Briloff, *Unaccountable Accounting,* New York: Harper & Row, 1972.
25. R. J. Charles, "Financial Information and the Securities Market," *Abacus,* September 1965; cited by Lorie and Hamilton, *The Stock Market,* p. 145.
26. R. Ball and R. Watts, "Some Time Series Properties of Accounting Income," *Journal of Finance,* June 1972, p. 664.
27. Richard D. Gritta, "The Impact of the Capitalization of Leases on Financial Analysis," in *C.F.A. Readings in Financial Analysis,* loc. cit.
28. Lorie and Hamilton, *The Stock Market,* p. 162.
29. John Lintner and Robert Glauber, "Higgledy-Piddledy Growth in America," in *Modern Developments in Investment Management,* loc. cit., pp. 645–662; see also Baruch Lev, *Financial Statement Analysis,* pp. 109–132.
30. Lorie and Hamilton, op. cit., p. 141.
31. Baruch Lev, op. cit., p. 125 and pp. 109–132 passim.
32. Jack L. Treynor, "The Trouble with Earnings," in *Modern Developments in Investment Management,* pp. 664–667.
33. Samuel S. Stewart, Jr., "Corporate Forecasting," in *Financial Analyst's Handbook,* loc. cit., pp. 913–914; also see his bibliography in fn. 4.
34. William Breen, "Low Price-Earnings Ratios and Industry Relations," *Financial Analysts Journal,* July–August 1968, pp. 125–127; Paul F. Miller, Jr., *Institutional Service Report,* Drexel and Co., Inc., Philadelphia, November 1965.
35. For the years 1947–1961 see *Capital Goods Review,* Machinery and Allied Products Institute, July 1962, pp. 2–3; for the years 1952–1968, see John J. McGowan, "The Supply of Equity Securities, 1952–1968," in *Institutional Investors and Corporate Stock,* ed. by Raymond W. Goldsmith (New York: National Bureau of Economic Research, 1973), pp. 165–202.

36. Amdahl Corporation, initial offering prospectus, August 12, 1976.
37. Ibid.
38. Ibid.

Chapter 7

1. See for example Johannes de Graaff, *Theoretical Welfare Economics* (New York: Cambridge University Press, 1957), pp. 116–121.
2. R. Duncan Luce and Howard Raiffa, *Games and Decisions* (New York: Wiley & Sons, 1957), pp. 36 and 373; see also Porterfield, *Investment Decisions,* p. 111.
3. Luce and Raiffa, op. cit., pp. 324–326; see also Robichek and Myers, *Optimal Financing Decisions,* pp. 1–6.
4. Robichek and Myers, op. cit., pp. 71–79.
5. Lorie and Brealey, eds., *Modern Developments in Investment Management,* p. 597.
6. Lorie and Hamilton, *The Stock Market,* pp. 157–167.
7. A. G. Rayner and I. M. D. Little, *Higgledy-Piggledy Growth Again,* New York: Oxford University Press, 1967; and John Lintner and Robert Glauber, "Higgledy-Piggledy Growth in America," in *Modern Developments in Investment Management,* pp. 645–662.
8. Robichek and Myers, op. cit., pp. 17–18.
9. Baruch Lev, *Financial Statement Analysis,* pp. 191ff.; and William F. Sharpe, "Capital Asset Prices: A Theory of Market Equilibrium under Conditions of Risk," *Journal of Finance,* September 1964, pp. 425–442.
10. Baruch Lev, op. cit., pp. 178–179.
11. Robichek and Myers, op. cit., pp. 67–93 passim; Baruch Lev, op. cit., p. 82.
12. Eugene F. Fama, "Efficient Capital Markets: A Review of Theory and Empirical Work," in *Modern Developments in Investment Management,* pp. 109–161.
13. Ibid., p. 115.
14. Lorie and Hamilton, *The Stock Market,* p. 98.
15. Ibid.
16. Arthur M. Okun, *Equality and Efficiency: The Big Tradeoff* (Washington, D.C.: Brookings Institution, 1975), pp. 2–3.
17. Vilfredo Pareto, *Manuel D'Économie Politique,* excerpts on "Ophelimite," reprinted in *Utility Theory: A Book of Readings,* ed. by Alfred N. Page (New York: Wiley & Sons, 1968), pp. 382–383.
18. de Graaff, *Theoretical Welfare Economics,* p. 8.

19. E. J. Mishan, *Economics for Social Decisions* (New York: Praeger, 1972), p. 14.
20. Robert Dorfman, *Prices and Markets* (Englewood Cliffs, N.J.: Prentice-Hall, 1972), p. 223.
21. Luce and Raiffa, *Games and Decisions,* p. 127; see also Morton D. Davis, *Game Theory* (New York: Basic Books, 1970), pp. 118–119.
22. Alan Coddington, *Theories of the Bargaining Process* (London: Allen and Unwin, 1968), p. 9.
23. Eduard Heimann, *History of Economic Doctrines* (New York: Oxford University Press, 1945), p. 213.
24. Robbins, *The Securities Markets,* p. 33.
25. Baumol, *The Stock Market and Economic Efficiency,* pp. 52–53.
26. Ibid., pp. 70–76.
27. Ibid., p. 83.
28. Baruch Lev, *Financial Statement Analysis,* p. 218.
29. Harry M. Markowitz, "Portfolio Selection," in *Modern Developments in Investment Management,* loc. cit., p. 320.
30. Baruch Lev, op. cit., pp. 226–245.
31. William F. Sharpe, *Portfolio Theory and Capital Markets* (New York: McGraw-Hill, 1970), pp. 91–96; and "Capital Asset Prices: A Theory of Market Equilibrium under Conditions of Risk," in *Modern Developments in Investment Management,* pp. 395–412.
32. Baruch Lev, op. cit., p. 191.
33. Edward M. Miller, "Risk, Uncertainty, and Divergence of Opinion," *Journal of Finance,* Sept. 1977, pp. 1160–1162.
34. George L. Shackle, *Expectations in Economics* (New York: Cambridge University Press, 1949), p. 2.
35. Ibid., p. 103.
36. Coddington, op. cit., p. 77; see also p. vii.
37. Henry G. Manne, "Some Theoretical Aspects of Share Voting," in *The Economics of Legal Relationships,* ed. by H. G. Manne (St. Paul, Minn.: West, 1975), pp. 534–554.
38. O. J. Anderson, *Business Law* (Totowa, N.J.: Littlefield, Adams & Co., 1975), pp. 166–167 and 177.

Chapter 8

1. John Maynard Keynes, *The General Theory of Employment, Interest and Money* (New York: Harcourt Brace Jovanovich, Harbinger Book edition, 1964), p. 157.
2. Benjamin Graham, *The Intelligent Investor* (New York: Harper & Row, fourth revised edition, 1973), p. 284.

3. Ibid., p. 283.
4. Ibid., p. 287.
5. Morgenstern, *Accuracy of Economic Observations,* pp. 17–26.
6. Baruch Lev, *Financial Statement Analysis,* p. 181.
7. Keynes, op. cit., pp. 162–163.
8. Ibid., p. 152.
9. Ibid., pp. 155–156.
10. Ibid., p. 159.
11. Shackle, *Expectations in Economics,* pp. 111–112.

Chapter 9

1. Rayner and Little, *Higgledy-Piggledy Growth Again;* see also Joseph E. Murphy, Jr., "Relative Growth of Earnings per Share—Past and Future," *Financial Analysts Journal,* November–December 1966, pp. 73–75.
2. Graham, *The Intelligent Investor,* p. xiv.
3. Gordon, *Investment, Financing, and Valuation,* pp. 43–54; see also Robichek and Myers, *Optimal Financing Decisions,* pp. 130–135.
4. Frank E. Block, "The Place of Book Value in Common Stock Valuation," *Financial Analysts Journal,* March–April 1964 (reprinted in *C.F.A. Readings in Financial Analysis,* loc. cit., p. 472).
5. Cf. Robichek and Myers, op. cit., p. 131.
6. Ibid.
7. *Value Line Investment Survey,* published by Bernhard Arnold & Co., Inc., New York.
8. Graham, Dodd, and Cottle, *Security Analysis,* pp. 486–487, fns. 5–9.

Chapter 10

1. Raymond W. Goldsmith, ed., *Institutional Investors and Corporate Stock* (New York: National Bureau of Economic Research, 1973), p. 3.
2. "Legal Lists in Trust Investment," *Yale Law Journal,* Vol. 49, 1940, p. 891.
3. Ibid., p. 892, fn. 8.
4. Ibid., pp. 902–903.
5. New York Estates, Powers and Trust Law, Sect. 11:2.2, p. 33, note 17.
6. Drucker, *The Unseen Revolution,* pp. 1–46; see also Willard F. Mueller, *A Primer on Monopoly and Competition* (New York: Random House, 1970), p. 185.

7. *Harvard College* v. *Amory,* 26 Mass. (9 Pick.), 1830, at 452.
8. Ibid., at 461; see also Restatement of Trusts, Sect. 227.
9. Restatement of Trusts, Sect. 227:6, comment on clause (a); see also definitions of "probable" and "negligence" in *Black's Law Dictionary,* St. Paul, Minn.: West, fourth edition, 1968.
10. Dreman, *Psychology and the Stock Market.*
11. Employee Retirement Income Security Act of 1974 (P.L. 93-406), Sect. 2.
12. ERISA, Sect. 404(a), A–D.
13. Joint Explanatory Statement of the Committee of Conference (93-1090), at 302.
14. Restatement of Trusts, Sect. 171.
15. Robert A. Bildersee, *Pension Regulation Manual* (New York: Warren, Gorham & Lamont, 1975), pp. 134–135.
16. Restatement of Trusts, Sects. 261–265.
17. ERISA, Sect. 404(a), D.
18. Restatement of Trusts, Sect. 170.
19. John H. Langbein and Richard A. Posner, "Market Funds and Trust Investment Law," *American Bar Foundation Research Journal,* January 1976, p. 30; see also their "The Revolution in Trust Investment Law," *American Bar Association Journal,* July 1976, p. 888.
20. "Fiduciary Standards and the Prudent Man Rule under the Employee Retirement Income Security Act of 1974," *Harvard Law Review,* Vol. 88, 1975, p. 960, fn. 1.
21. ERISA, Sect. 404(a), C.
22. "Fiduciary Standards," p. 966, fn. 38.
23. Ibid., p. 967.
24. Joint Explanatory Statement of the Committee of Conference, at 302.
25. ERISA, Sect. 404(c).
26. Joint Explanatory Statement of the Committee of Conference, at 305.
27. "Fiduciary Standards," p. 977, fn. 96.
28. Joint Explanatory Statement of the Committee of Conference, at 305.
29. Ibid., at 306.
30. Ibid., at 305.
31. Restatement of Trusts, Chapter 9, Title C, "Value."
32. *In re Bank of New York,* 43 App. Div. 2nd (1975), 105–108.
33. Restatement of Trusts, Sect. 236.
34. "The Regulation of Risky Investments," *Harvard Law Review,* Vol. 83, 1970, p. 623, fns. 114 and 115.

35. Restatement of Trusts, Sect. 227, comment on clause (a), paragraph E.
36. "Regulation of Risky Investments," pp. 604 and 618.
37. Cf. Langbein and Posner, "Market Funds" and "Revolution in Trust Investment Law," with John P. Humbach and Stephen P. Dresch, "Prudence, Information and Trust Investment Law," *American Bar Association Journal,* October 1976.
38. Langbein and Posner, "Market Funds," p. 1.
39. Langbein and Posner, "Revolution in Trust Investment Law," p. 888.
40. Restatement of Trusts, Sect. 228.
41. Jack L. Treynor, Patrick J. Regan, and William W. Priest, Jr., *The Financial Reality of Pension Funding under ERISA* (Homewood, Ill.: Dow Jones-Irwin, 1976), p. 100.
42. Humbach and Dresch, "Prudence, Information," p. 1309.
43. Langbein and Posner, "Market Funds," p. 26.
44. Ibid., p. 27.
45. Ibid., p. 30.
46. Humbach and Dresch, "Prudence, Information."
47. Restatement of Trusts, Sect. 177.
48. Ibid., Sect. 193.
49. Uniform Trust Act, Sect. 8, in Restatement of Trusts, Sect. 193, Comment G.
50. William L. Cary, *Corporations* (Mineola, N.Y.: Foundation Press, fourth abridged edition, 1970), p. 285.
51. O'Neal, *Oppression of Minority Shareholders,* Section 5:31.
52. Cary, op. cit., p. 282; see also O'Neal, op. cit., Sect. 7:09, at 470, 471.
53. O'Neal, op. cit., Sect. 7:09.
54. Ibid., at 467.
55. Quoted by John G. Simon, Charles W. Powers, and Jon P. Gunnemann, *The Ethical Investor* (New Haven, Conn.: Yale University Press, 1972), p. 58; see also p. 59, fn. 90.
56. Ibid., p. 57.
57. Ibid., p. 52.

Index